The Philippics

Marcus Tullius Cicero

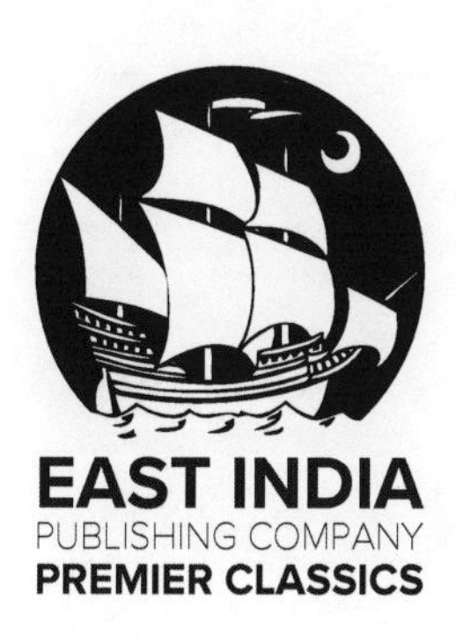
EAST INDIA
PUBLISHING COMPANY
PREMIER CLASSICS

Translation by Charles Duke Yonge

Published by the East India Publishing Company
Ottawa, Ontario.

9781774260814

CONTENTS

THE FIRST PHILIPPIC

THE ARGUMENT

When Julius, or, as he is usually called by Cicero Caius Caesar was slain on the 15th of March, A.U.C. 710, B.C. 44 Marcus Antonius was his colleague in the consulship, and he, being afraid that the conspirators might murder him too, (and it is said that they had debated among themselves whether they would or no) concealed himself on that day and fortified his house, till perceiving that nothing was intended against him, he ventured to appear in public the day following. Lepidus was in the suburbs of Rome with a regular army, ready to depart for the government of Spain, which had been assigned to him with a part of Gaul. In the night, after Caesar's death he occupied the forum with his troops and thought of making himself master of the city, but Antonius dissuaded him from that idea and won him over to his views by giving his daughter in marriage to Lepidus's son, and by assisting him to seize on the office of Pontifex Maximus, which was vacant by Caesar's death.

To the conspirators he professed friendship, sent his son among them as a hostage of his sincerity, and so deluded them, that Brutus supped with Lepidus, and Cassius with Antonius. By these means he got them to consent to his passing a decree for the confirmation of all Caesar's acts, without describing or naming them more precisely. At last, on the occasion of Caesar's public funeral, he contrived so to inflame the populace against the conspirators, that Brutus and Cassius had some difficulty in defending their houses and their lives and he gradually alarmed them so much, and worked so cunningly on their fears that they all quitted Rome. Cicero also left Rome, disapproving greatly of the vacillation and want of purpose in the conspirators. On the first of June Antonius assembled the senate to deliberate on the affairs of the republic, and in the interval visited all parts of Italy. In the meantime young Octavius appeared on the stage; he had been left by Caesar, who was his uncle, the heir to his name and estate. He returned from Apollonia, in Macedonia, to Italy as soon as he heard of his uncle's death, and arrived at Naples on the eighteenth of April, where he was introduced by Hirtius and Pansa to Cicero, whom he promised to be guided in all respects by his directions. He was now between eighteen and nineteen years of age.

He began by the representation of public spectacles and games in honour of Caesar's victories. In the meantime Antonius, in his progress through Italy, was making great use of the decree confirming all Caesar's acts, which he interpolated and forged in the most shameless manner. Among other things he restored Deiotarus to all his dominions, having been bribed to do so by a hundred millions of sesterces by the king's agents, but Deiotarus himself, as soon as he heard of Caesar's death, seized all his dominions by force. He also seized the public treasure which Caesar had deposited in the temple of Ops, amounting to above four millions and a half of our money, and with this he won over Dolabella, who had seized the consulship on the death of Caesar, and the greater part of the army.

At the end of May Cicero began to return towards Rome, in order to arrive there in time for the meeting of the senate on the first of June, but many of his friends dissuaded him from entering the city, and at last he determined not to appear in the senate on that day, but to make a tour in Greece, to assist him in which, Dolabella named him one of his lieutenants. Antonius also gave Brutus and Cassius commissions to buy corn in Asia and Sicily for the use of the republic, in order to keep them out of the city.

Meantime Sextus Pompeius, who was at the head of a considerable army in Spain, addressed letters to the consuls proposing terms of accommodation, which after some debate, and some important modifications, were agreed to, and he quitted Spain, and came as far as Marseilles on his road towards Rome.

Cicero having started for Greece was forced to put back by contrary winds, and returned to Velia on the seventeenth of August, where he had a long conference with Brutus, who soon after left Italy for his province of Macedonia, which Caesar had assigned him before his death, though Antonius now wished to compel him to exchange it for Crete. After this conference Cicero returned to Rome, where he was received with unexampled joy, immense multitudes thronging out to meet him, and to escort him into the city. He arrived in Rome on the last day of August. The next day the senate met, to which he was particularly summoned by Antonius, but he excused himself as not having recovered from the fatigue of his journey.

Antonius was greatly offended, and in his speech in the senate threatened openly to order his house to be pulled down, the real reason of Cicero's absenting himself from the senate being, that the business of the day was to decree some new and extraordinary honours to Caesar, and to order supplications to him as a divinity, which Cicero was determined not to concur in, though he knew it would be useless to oppose them.

The next day also the senate met, and Antonius absented himself, but Cicero came down and delivered the following speech, which is the first of that celebrated series of fourteen speeches made in opposition to Antonius and his measures, and called Philippics from the orations of Demosthenes against Philip, to which the Romans were in the habit of comparing them.

I. Before, O conscript fathers, I say those things concerning the republic which I think myself bound to say at the present time, I will explain to you briefly the cause of my departure from, and of my return to the city. When I hoped that the republic was at last recalled to a proper respect for your wisdom and for your authority, I thought that it became me to remain in a sort of sentinelship, which was imposed upon me by my position as a senator and a man of consular rank. Nor did I depart anywhere, nor did I ever take my eyes off from the republic, from the day on which we were summoned to meet in the temple of Tellus, in which temple, I, as far as was in my power, laid the foundations of peace, and renewed the ancient precedent set by the Athenians, I even used the Greek word, which that city employed in those times in allaying discords, and gave my vote that all recollection of the existing dissensions ought to be effaced by everlasting oblivion.

The oration then made by Marcus Antonius was an admirable one, his disposition, too, appeared excellent, and lastly, by his means and by his sons', peace was ratified with the most illustrious of the citizens, and everything else was consistent with this beginning. He invited the chief men of the state to those deliberations which he held at his own house concerning the state of the republic, he referred all the most important matters to this order. Nothing was at that time found among the papers of Caius Caesar except what was already well known to everybody, and he gave answers to every question that was asked of him with the greatest consistency. Were any exiles restored? He said that one was, and only one. Were any immunities granted? He answered, None. He wished us even to adopt the proposition of Servius Sulpicius, that most illustrious man, that no tablet purporting to contain any decree or grant of Caesar's should be published after the Ides of March were expired. I pass over many other things, all excellent—for I am hastening to come to a very extraordinary act of virtue of Marcus Antonius. He utterly abolished from the constitution of the republic the Dictatorship, which had by this time attained to the authority of regal power. And that measure was not even offered to us for discussion. He brought with him a decree of the senate, ready drawn up, ordering what he chose to have done: and when it had been read, we all submitted to his authority in the matter with the greatest eagerness; and, by another resolution of the senate, we returned him thanks in the most honourable and complimentary language.

II. A new light, as it were, seemed to be brought over us, now that not only the kingly power which we had endured, but all fear of such power for the future, was taken away from us; and a great pledge appeared to have been given by him to the republic that he did wish the city to be free, when he utterly abolished out of the republic the name of dictator, which had often been a legitimate title, on account of our late recollection of a perpetual dictatorship. A few days afterwards the senate was delivered from the danger of bloodshed, and a hook was fixed into that runaway slave who had usurped the name of Caius Marius. And all these things he did in concert with his colleague. Some other things that were done were the acts of Dolabella alone; but, if his colleague had not been absent, would, I believe, have been done by both of them in concert.

For when enormous evil was insinuating itself into the republic, and was gaining more strength day by day; and when the same men were erecting a tomb in the forum, who had performed that irregular funeral; and when abandoned men, with slaves like themselves, were every day threatening with more and more vehemence all the houses and temples of the city; so severe was the rigour of Dolabella, not only towards the audacious and wicked slaves, but also towards the profligate and unprincipled freemen, and so prompt was his overthrow of that accursed pillar, that it seems marvellous to me that the subsequent time has been so different from that one day.

For behold, on the first of June, on which day they had given notice that we were all to attend the senate, everything was changed. Nothing was done by the senate, but many and important measures were transacted by the agency of the people, though that people was both absent and disapproving. The consuls elect said, that they did not dare to come into the senate. The liberators of their country were absent from that city from the neck of which they had removed the yoke of slavery; though the very consuls themselves professed to praise them in their public harangues and in all their conversation. Those who were called Veterans, men of whose safety this order had been most particularly careful, were instigated not to the preservation of those things which they had, but to cherish hopes of new booty. And as I preferred hearing of those things to seeing them, and as I had an honorary commission as lieutenant, I went away, intending to be present on the first of January, which appeared likely to be the first day of assembling the senate.

III. I have now explained to you, O conscript fathers, my design in leaving the city. Now I will briefly set before you, also, my intention in returning, which may perhaps appear more unaccountable. As I had avoided Brundusium, and the ordinary route into Greece, not without good reason, on the first of August I arrived at Syracuse, because the passage from that city into Greece was said to be a good one. And that city, with which I had so intimate a connexion, could not, though it was very eager to do so, detain me more than one night. I was afraid that my sudden arrival among my friends might cause some suspicion if I remained there at all. But after the winds had driven me, on my departure from Sicily, to Leucopetra, which is a promontory of the Rhegian district, I went up the gulf from that point, with the view of crossing over. And I had not advanced far before I was driven back by a foul wind to the very place which I had just quitted. And as the night was stormy, and as I had lodged that night in the villa of Publius Valerius, my companion and intimate friend, and as I remained all the nest day at his house waiting for a fair wind, many of the citizens of the municipality of Rhegium came to me. And of them there were some who had lately arrived from Rome; from them I first heard of the harangue of Marcus Antonius, with which I was so much pleased that, after I had read it, I began for the first time to think of returning. And not long afterwards the edict of Brutus and Cassius is brought to me; which (perhaps because I love those men, even more for the sake of the republic than of my own friendship for them) appeared to me, indeed, to be full of equity. They added besides, (for it is a very common thing for those who are desirous of bringing good news to invent something to make the news which they bring seem more joyful,) that parties were coming to an agreement; that the senate was to meet on the first of August; that Antonius having discarded all evil counsellors, and having given up the provinces of Gaul, was about to return to submission to the authority of the senate.

IV. But on this I was inflamed with such eagerness to return, that no oars or winds could be fast enough for me; not that I thought that I should not arrive in time, but lest I should be later than I wished in congratulating the republic; and I quickly arrived at Velia, where I saw Brutus; how grieved I was, I cannot express. For it seemed to be a discreditable thing for me myself, that I should venture to return into that city from which Brutus was departing, and that I should be willing to live safely in a place where he could not. But he himself was not agitated in the same manner that I was; for, being elevated with the consciousness of his great and glorious exploit, he had no complaints to make of what had befallen him, though he lamented your fate exceedingly. And it was from him that I first heard what had been the language of Lucius Piso, in the senate of August; who, although he was but little assisted (for that I heard from Brutus himself) by those who ought to have seconded him, still according to the testimony of Brutus, (and what evidence can be more trustworthy?) and to the avowal of every one whom I saw afterwards, appeared to me to have gained great credit. I hastened hither, therefore, in order that as those who were present had not seconded him, I might do so; not with the hope of doing any good, for I neither hoped for that, nor did I well see how it was possible; but in order that if anything happened to me, (and many things appeared to be threatening me out of the regular course of nature, and even of destiny,) I might still leave my speech on this day as a witness to the republic of my everlasting attachment to its interests.

Since, then, O conscript fathers, I trust that the reason of my adopting each determination appears praiseworthy to you, before I begin to speak of the republic, I will make a brief complaint of the injury which Marcus Antonius did me yesterday, to whom I am friendly, and I have at all times admitted having received some services from him which make it my duty to be so.

V. What reason had he then for endeavouring, with such bitter hostility, to force me into the senate yesterday? Was I the only person who was absent? Have you not repeatedly had thinner houses than yesterday? Or was a matter of such importance under discussion, that it was desirable for even sick men to be brought down? Hannibal, I suppose, was at the gates, or there was to be a debate about peace with Pyrrhus, on which occasion it is related that even the great Appius, old and blind as he was, was brought down to the senate-house. There was a motion being made about some supplications, a kind of measure when senators are not usually wanting, for they are under the compulsion, not of pledges, but of the influence of those men whose honour is being complimented, and the case is the same when the motion has reference to a triumph. The consuls are so free from anxiety at these times, that it is almost entirely free for a senator to absent himself if he pleases. And as the general custom of our body was well known to me, and as I was hardly recovered from the fatigue of my journey, and was vexed with myself, I sent a man to him, out of regard for my friendship to him, to tell him that I should not be there. But he, in the hearing of you all, declared that he would come with masons to my house; this was said with too much passion and very intemperately. For, for what crime is there such a heavy punishment appointed as that, that any one should venture to say in this assembly that he, with the assistance of a lot of common operatives, would pull down a house which had been built at the public expense in accordance with a vote of the senate? And who ever employed such compulsion as the threat of such an injury as to a senator? or what severer punishment has ever been he himself was unable to perform? As, in fact, he has failed to perform many promises made to many people. And a great many more of those promises have been found since his death, than the number of all the services which he conferred on and did to people during all the years that he was alive would amount to.

But all those things I do not change, I do not meddle with. Nay, I defend all his good acts with the greatest earnestness. Would that the money remained in the temple of Opis! Bloodstained, indeed, it may be, but still needful at these times, since it is not restored to those to whom it really belongs. Let that, however, be squandered too, if it is so written in his acts. Is there anything whatever that can be called so peculiarly the act of that man who, while clad in the robe of peace, was yet invested with both civil and military command in the republic, as a law of his? Ask for the acts of Gracchus, the Sempronian laws will be brought forward; ask for those of Sylla, you will have the Cornelian laws. What more? In what acts did the third consulship of Cnaeus Pompeius consist? Why, in his laws. And if you could ask Caesar himself what he had done in the city and in the garb of peace, he would reply that he had passed many excellent laws; but his memoranda he would either alter or not produce at all; or, if he did produce them, he would not class them among his acts. But, however, I allow even these things to pass for acts; at some things I am content to wink; but I think it intolerable that the acts of Caesar in the most important instances, that is to say, in his laws, are to be annulled for their sake.

VIII. What law was ever better, more advantageous, more frequently demanded in the best ages of the republic, than the one which forbade the praetorian provinces to be retained more than a year, and the consular provinces more than two? If this law be abrogated, do you think that the acts of Caesar are maintained? What? are not all the laws of Caesar respecting judicial proceedings abrogated by the law which has been proposed concerning the third decury? And are you the defenders of the acts of Caesar who overturn his laws? Unless, indeed, anything which, for the purpose of recollecting it, he entered in a note-book, is to be counted among his acts, and defended, however unjust or useless it may be; and that which he proposed to the people in the comitia centuriata and carried, is not to be accounted one of the acts of Caesar. But what is that third decury? The decury of centurions, says he. What? was not the judicature open to that order by the Julian law, and even before that by the Pompeian and Aurelian laws? The income of the men, says he, was exactly defined. Certainly, not only in the case of a centurion, but in the case, too, of a Roman knight. Therefore, men of the highest honour and of the greatest bravery, who have acted as centurions, are and have been judges. I am not asking about those men, says he. Whoever has acted as centurion, let him be a judge. But if you were to propose a law, that whoever had served in the cavalry, which is a higher post, should be a judge, you would not be able to induce any one to approve of that; for a man's fortune and worth ought to be regarded in a judge. I am not asking about those points, says he; I am going to add as judges, common soldiers of the legion of Alaudae; for our friends say, that that is the only measure by which they can be saved. Oh what an insulting compliment it is to those men whom you summon to act as judges though they never expected it! For the effect of the law is, to make those men judges in the third decury who do not dare to judge with freedom. And in that how great, O ye immortal gods! is the error of those men who have desired that law. For the meaner the condition of each judge is, the greater will be the severity of judgment with which he will seek to efface the idea of his meanness; and he will strive rather to appear worthy of being classed in the honourable decuries, than to have deservedly ranked in a disreputable one.

IX. Another law was proposed, that men who had been condemned of violence and treason may appeal to the public if they please. Is this now a law, or rather an abrogation of all laws? For who is there at this day to whom it is an object that that law should stand? No one is accused under those laws; there is no one whom we think likely to be so accused. For measures which have been carried by force of arms will certainly never be impeached in a court of justice. But the measure is a popular one. I wish, indeed, that you were willing to promote any popular measure; for, at present, all the citizens agree with one mind and one voice in their view of its bearing on the safety of the republic.

What is the meaning, then, of the eagerness to pass the law which brings with it the greatest possible infamy, and no popularity at all? For what can be more discreditable than for a man who has committed treason against the Roman people by acts of violence, after he has been condemned by a legal decision, to be able to return to that very course of violence, on account of which he has been condemned? But why do I argue any more about this law? as if the object aimed at were to enable any one to appeal? The object is, the inevitable consequence must be, that no one can ever be prosecuted under those laws. For what prosecutor will be found insane enough to be willing, after the defendant has been condemned, to expose himself to the fury of a hired mob? or what judge will be bold enough to venture to condemn a criminal, knowing that he will immediately be dragged before a gang of hireling operatives? It is not, therefore, a right of appeal that is given by that law, but two most salutary laws and modes of judicial investigation that are abolished. And what is this but exhorting young men to be turbulent, seditious, mischievous citizens?

To what extent of mischief will it not be possible to instigate the frenzy of the tribunes now that these two rights of impeachment for violence and for treason are annulled? What more? Is not this a substitution of a new law for the laws of Caesar, which enact that every man who has been convicted of violence, and also every man who has been convicted of treason, shall be interdicted from fire and water? And, when those men have a right of appeal given them, are not the acts of Caesar rescinded? And those acts, O conscript fathers, I, who never approved of them, have still thought it advisable to maintain for the sake of concord, so that I not only did not think that the laws which Caesar had passed in his lifetime ought to be repealed, but I did not approve of meddling with those even which since the death of Caesar you have seen produced and published.

X. Men have been recalled from banishment by a dead man; the freedom of the city has been conferred, not only on individuals, but on entire nations and provinces by a dead man; our revenues have been diminished by the granting of countless exemptions by a dead man. Therefore, do we defend these measures which have been brought from his house on the authority of a single, but, I admit, a very excellent individual, and as for the laws which he, in your presence, read, and declared, and passed,—in the passing of which he gloried, and on which he believed that the safety of the republic depended, especially those concerning provinces and concerning judicial proceedings,—can we, I say, we who defend the acts of Caesar, think that those laws deserve to be upset?

And yet, concerning those laws which were proposed, we have, at all events, the power of complaining, but concerning those which are actually passed we have not even had that privilege. For they, without any proposal of them to the people, were passed before they were framed. Men ask, what is the reason why I, or why any one of you, O conscript fathers, should be afraid of bad laws while we have virtuous tribunes of the people? We have men ready to interpose their veto, ready to defend the republic with the sanctions of religion. We ought to be strangers to fear. What do you mean by interposing the veto? says he, what are all these sanctions of religion which you are talking about? Those, forsooth, on which the safety of the republic depends. We are neglecting those things, and thinking them too old-fashioned and foolish. The forum will be surrounded, every entrance of it will be blocked up, armed men will be placed in garrison, as it were, at many points. What then?—whatever is accomplished by those means will be law. And you will order, I suppose, all those regularly passed decrees to be engraved on brazen tablets "The consuls consulted the people in regular form," (Is this the way of consulting the people that we have received from our ancestors?) "and the people voted it with due regularity" What people? that which was excluded from the forum? Under what law did they do so? under that which has been wholly abrogated by violence and arms? But I am saying all this with reference to the future, because it is the part of a friend to point out evils which may be avoided and if they never ensue, that will be the best refutation of my speech. I am speaking of laws which have been proposed, concerning which you have still full power to decide either way. I am pointing out the defects, away with them! I am denouncing violence and arms, away with them too!

XI. You and your colleague, O Dolabella, ought not, indeed, to be angry with me for speaking in defence of the republic. Although I do not think that you yourself will be; I know your willingness to listen to reason. They say that your colleague, in this fortune of his, which he himself thinks so good, but which would seem to me more favourable if (not to use any harsh language) he were to imitate the example set him by the consulship of his grandfathers and of his uncle,—they say that he has been exceedingly offended. And I see what a formidable thing it is to have the same man angry with me and also armed; especially at a time when men can use their swords with such impunity. But I will propose a condition which I myself think reasonable, and which I do not imagine Marcus Antonius will reject. If I have said anything insulting against his way of life or against his morals, I will not object to his being my bitterest enemy. But if I have maintained the same habits that I have already adopted in the republic,—that is, if I have spoken my opinions concerning the affairs of the republic with freedom,—in the first place,

I beg that he will not be angry with me for that; but, in the next place, if I cannot obtain my first request, I beg at least that he will show his anger only as he legitimately may show it to a fellow-citizen.

Let him employ arms, if it is necessary, as he says it is, for his own defence: only let not those arms injure those men who have declared their honest sentiments in the affairs of the republic. Now, what can be more reasonable than this demand? But if, as has been said to me by some of his intimate friends, every speech which is at all contrary to his inclination is violently offensive to him, even if there be no insult in it whatever; then we will bear with the natural disposition of our friend. But those men, at the same time, say to me, "You will not have the same licence granted to you who are the adversary of Caesar as might be claimed by Piso his father-in-law." And then they warn me of something which I must guard against; and certainly, the excuse which sickness supplies me with, for not coming to the senate, will not be a more valid one than that which is furnished by death.

XII. But, in the name of the immortal gods! for while I look upon you, O Dolabella, who are most dear to me, it is impossible for me to keep silence respecting the error into which you are both falling; for I believe that you, being both men of high birth, entertaining lofty views, have been eager to acquire, not money, as some too credulous people suspect, a thing which has at all times been scorned by every honourable and illustrious man, nor power procured by violence and authority such as never ought to be endured by the Roman people, but the affection of your fellow-citizens, and glory. But glory is praise for deeds which have been done, and the fame earned by great services to the republic; which is approved of by the testimony borne in its favour, not only by every virtuous man, but also by the multitude. I would tell you, O Dolabella, what the fruit of good actions is, if I did not see that you have already learnt it by experience beyond all other men.

What day can you recollect in your whole life, as ever having beamed on you with a more joyful light than the one on which, having purified the forum, having routed the throng of wicked men, having inflicted due punishment on the ringleaders in wickedness, and having delivered the city from conflagration and from fear of massacre, you returned to your house? What order of society, what class of people, what rank of nobles even was there who did not then show their zeal in praising and congratulating you? Even I, too, because men thought that you had been acting by my advice in those transactions, received the thanks and congratulations of good men in your name. Remember, I pray you, O

Dolabella, the unanimity displayed on that day in the theatre, when every one, forgetful of the causes on account of which they had been previously offended with you, showed that in consequence of your recent service they had banished all recollection of their former indignation. Could you, O Dolabella, (it is with great concern that I speak,)—could you, I say, forfeit this dignity with equanimity?

XIII. And you, O Marcus Antonius, (I address myself to you, though in your absence,) do you not prefer that day on which the senate was assembled in the temple of Tellus, to all those months during which some who differ greatly in opinion from me think that you have been happy? What a noble speech was that of yours about unanimity! From what apprehensions were the veterans, and from what anxiety was the whole state relieved by you on that occasion! when, having laid aside your enmity against him, you on that day first consented that your present colleague should be your colleague, forgetting that the auspices had been announced by yourself as augur of the Roman people; and when your little son was sent by you to the Capitol to be a hostage for peace. On what day was the senate ever more joyful than on that day? or when was the Roman people more delighted? which had never met in greater numbers in any assembly whatever. Then, at last, we did appear to have been really delivered by brave men, because, as they had willed it to be, peace was following liberty On the next day, on the day after that, on the third day, and on all the following days, you went on without intermission giving every day, as it were, some fresh present to the republic, but the greatest of all presents was that, when you abolished the name of the dictatorship. This was in effect branding the name of the dead Caesar with everlasting ignominy, and it was your doing,—yours, I say. For as, on account of the wickedness of one Marcus Manlius, by a resolution of the Manlian family it is unlawful that any patrician should be called Manlius, so you, on account of the hatred excited by one dictator, have utterly abolished the name of dictator.

When you had done these mighty exploits for the safety of the republic, did you repent of your fortune, or of the dignity and renown and glory which you had acquired? Whence then is this sudden change? I cannot be induced to suspect that you have been caught by the desire of acquiring money; every one may say what he pleases, but we are not bound to believe such a thing; for I never saw anything sordid or anything mean in you. Although a man's intimate friends do sometimes corrupt his natural disposition, still I know your firmness; and I only wish that, as you avoid that fault, you had been able also to escape all suspicion of it.

XIV. What I am more afraid of is lest, being ignorant of the true path to glory, you should think it glorious for you to have more power by yourself than all the rest of the people put together, and lest you should prefer being feared by your fellow-citizens to being loved by them. And if you do think so, you are ignorant of the road to glory. For a citizen to be dear to his fellow-citizens, to deserve well of the republic, to be praised, to be respected, to be loved, is glorious; but to be feared, and to be an object of hatred, is odious, detestable; and moreover, pregnant with weakness and decay. And we see that, even in the play, the very man who said,

"What care I though all men should hate my name,
So long as fear accompanies their hate?"

found that it was a mischievous principle to act upon.

I wish, O Antonius, that you could recollect your grand father of whom, however, you have repeatedly heard me speak. Do you think that he would have been willing to deserve even immortality, at the price of being feared in consequence of his licentious use of arms? What he considered life, what he considered prosperity, was the being equal to the rest of the citizens in freedom, and chief of them all in worth. Therefore, to say no more of the prosperity of your grandfather, I should prefer that most bitter day of his death to the domination of Lucius Cinna, by whom he was most barbarously slain.

But why should I seek to make an impression on you by my speech? For, if the end of Caius Caesar cannot influence you to prefer being loved to being feared, no speech of any one will do any good or have any influence with you; and those who think him happy are themselves miserable. No one is happy who lives on such terms that he may be put to death not merely with impunity, but even to the great glory of his slayer. Wherefore, change your mind, I entreat you, and look back upon your ancestors, and govern the republic in such a way that your fellow-citizens may rejoice that you were born; without which no one can be happy nor illustrious.

XV. And, indeed, you have both of you had many judgments delivered respecting you by the Roman people, by which I am greatly concerned that you are not sufficiently influenced. For what was the meaning of the shouts of the innumerable crowd of citizens collected at the gladiatorial games? or of the verses made by the people? or of the extraordinary applause at the sight of the statue of Pompeius? and at that sight of the two tribunes of the people who are opposed to you? Are these things a feeble indication of the incredible unanimity of the entire Roman people? What more? Did the applause at the games of Apollo, or, I should rather say, testimony and judgment there given by the Roman people, appear to you of small importance? Oh! happy are those men who, though they themselves were unable to be present on account of the violence of arms, still were present in spirit, and had a place in the breasts and hearts of the Roman people. Unless, perhaps, you think that it was Accius who was applauded on that occasion, and who bore off the palm sixty years after his first appearance, and not Brutus, who was absent from the games which he himself was exhibiting, while at that most splendid spectacle the Roman people showed their zeal in his favour though he was absent, and soothed their own regret for their deliverer by uninterrupted applause and clamour.

I myself, indeed, am a man who have at all times despised that applause which is bestowed by the vulgar crowd, but at the same time, when it is bestowed by those of the highest, and of the middle, and of the lowest rank, and, in short, by all ranks together, and when those men who were previously accustomed to aim at nothing but the favour of the people keep aloof, I then think that, not mere applause, but a deliberate verdict. If this appears to you unimportant, which is in reality most significant, do you also despise the fact of which you have had experience,—namely, that the life of Aulus Hirtius is so dear to the Roman people? For it was sufficient for him to be esteemed by the Roman people as he is; to be popular among his friends, in which respect he surpasses everybody; to be beloved by his own kinsmen, who do love him beyond measure; but in whose case before do we ever recollect such anxiety and such fear being manifested? Certainly in no one's.

What, then, are we to do? In the name of the immortal gods, can you interpret these facts, and see what is their purport? What do you think that those men think of your lives, to whom the lives of those men who they hope will consult the welfare of the republic are so dear? I have reaped, O conscript fathers, the reward of my return, since I have said enough to bear testimony of my consistency whatever event may befall me, and since I have been kindly and attentively listened to by you. And if I have such opportunities frequently without exposing both myself and you to danger, I shall avail myself of them. If not, as far as I can I shall reserve myself not for myself, but rather for the republic. I have lived long enough for the course of human life, or for my own glory. If any additional life is granted to me, it shall be bestowed not so much on myself as on you and on the republic.

THE SECOND PHILIPPIC

THE ARGUMENT.

This second speech was not actually spoken at all. Antonius was greatly enraged at the first speech, and summoned another meeting of the senate for the nineteenth day of the month, giving Cicero especial notice to be present, and he employed the interval in preparing an invective against Cicero, and a reply to the first Philippic. The senate met in the temple of Concord, but Cicero himself was persuaded not to attend by his friends, who were afraid of Antonius proceeding to actual violence against him, (and indeed he brought a strong guard of armed men with him to the senate) He spoke with the greatest fury against Cicero, charging him with having been the principal author and contriver of Caesar's murder, hoping by this to inflame the soldiers, whom he had posted within hearing of his harangue.

Soon after this, Cicero removed to a villa near Naples for greater safety, and here he composed this second Philippic, which he did not publish immediately, but contented himself at first with sending a copy to Brutus and Cassius, who were much pleased with it.

I. To what destiny of mine, O conscript fathers, shall I say that it is owing, that none for the last twenty years has been an enemy to the republic without at the same time declaring war against me? Nor is there any necessity for naming any particular person; you yourselves recollect instances in proof of my statement. They have all hitherto suffered severer punishments than I could have wished for them; but I marvel that you, O Antonius, do not fear the end of those men whose conduct you are imitating. And in others I was less surprised at this. None of those men of former times was a voluntary enemy to me; all of them were attacked by me for the sake of the republic. But you, who have never been injured by me, not even by a word, in order to appear more audacious than Catiline, more frantic than Clodius, have of your own accord attacked me with abuse, and have considered that your alienation from me would be a recommendation of you to impious citizens.

What am I to think? that I have been despised? I see nothing either in my life, or in my influence in the city, or in my exploits, or even in the moderate abilities with which I am endowed, which Antonius can despise. Did he think that it was easiest to disparage me in the senate? a body which has borne its testimony in favour of many most illustrious citizens that they governed the republic well, but in favour of me alone, of all men, that I preserved it. Or did he wish to contend with me in a rivalry of eloquence? This, indeed, is an act of generosity; for what could be a more fertile or richer subject for me, than to have to speak in defence of myself, and against Antonius? This, in fact, is the truth. He thought it impossible to prove to the satisfaction of those men who resembled himself, that he was an enemy to his country, if he was not also an enemy to me. And before I make him any reply on the other topics of his speech, I will say a few words; respecting the friendship formerly subsisting between us, which he has accused me of violating,—for that I consider a most serious charge.

II. He has complained that I pleaded once against his interest. Was I not to plead against one with whom I was quite I unconnected, in behalf of an intimate acquaintance, of a dear friend? Was I not to plead against interest acquired not by hopes of virtue, but by the disgrace of youth? Was I not to plead against an injustice which that man procured to be done by the obsequiousness of a most iniquitous interposer of his veto, not by any law regulating the privileges of the praetor? But I imagine that this was mentioned by you, in order that you might recommend yourself to the citizens, if they all recollected that you were the son-in-law of a freedman, and that your children were the grandsons of Quintus Fadius a freedman.

But you had entirely devoted yourself to my principles; (for this is what you said;) you had been in the habit of coming to my house. In truth, if you had done so, you would more have consulted your own character and your reputation for chastity. But you did not do so, nor, if you had wished it, would Caius Curio have ever suffered you to do so. You have said, that you retired in my favour from the contest for the augurship. Oh the incredible audacity! oh the monstrous impudence of such an assertion! For, at the time when Cnaeus Pompeius and Quintus Hortensius named me as augur, after I had been wished for as such by the whole college, (for it was not lawful for me to be put in nomination by more than two members of the college,) you were notoriously insolvent, nor did you think it possible for your safety to be secured by any other means than by the destruction of the republic. But was it possible for you to stand for the augurship at a time when Curio was not in Italy? or even at the time when you were elected, could you have got the votes of one single tribe without the aid of Curio? whose intimate friends even were convicted of violence for having been too zealous in your favour.

III. But I availed myself of your friendly assistance. Of what assistance? Although the instance which you cite I have myself at all times openly admitted. I preferred confessing that I was under obligations to you, to letting myself appear to any foolish person not sufficiently grateful. However, what was the kindness that you did me? not killing me at Brundusium? Would you then have slain the man whom the conqueror himself, who conferred on you, as you used to boast, the chief rank among all his robbers, had desired to be safe, and had enjoined to go to Italy? Grant that you could have slain him, is not this, O conscript fathers, such a kindness as is done by banditti, who are contented with being able to boast that they have granted their lives to all those men whose lives they have not taken? and if that were really a kindness, then these who slew that man by whom they themselves had been saved, and whom you yourself are in the habit of styling most illustrious men, would never have acquired such immortal glory. But what sort of kindness is it, to have abstained from committing nefarious wickedness? It is a case in which it ought not to appear so delightful to me not to have been killed by you, as miserable, that it should have been in your power to do such a thing with impunity. However, grant that it was a kindness, since no greater kindness could be received from a robber, still in what point can you call me ungrateful? Ought I not to complain of the ruin of the republic, lest I should appear ungrateful towards you? But in that complaint, mournful indeed and miserable, but still unavoidable for a man of that rank in which the senate and people of Rome have placed me, what did I say that was insulting? that was otherwise than moderate? that was otherwise than friendly? and what instance was it not of moderation to complain of the conduct of Marcus Antonius, and yet to abstain from any abusive expressions? especially when you had scattered abroad all relics of the republic; when everything was on sale at your house by the most infamous traffic; when you confessed that those laws which had never been promulgated, had been passed with reference to you, and by you; when you, being augur, had abolished the auspices; being consul, had taken away the power of interposing the veto; when you were escorted in the most shameful manner by armed guards; when, worn out with drunkenness and debauchery, you were every day performing all sorts of obscenities in that chaste house of yours. But I, as if I had to contend against Marcus Crassus, with whom I have had many severe struggles, and not with a most worthless gladiator, while complaining in dignified language of the state of the republic, did not say one word which could be called personal. Therefore, to-day I will make him understand with what great kindness he was then treated by me.

IV. But he also read letters which he said that I had sent to him, like a man devoid of humanity and ignorant of the common usages of life. For who ever, who was even but slightly acquainted with the habits of polite men, produced in an assembly and openly read letters which had been sent to him by a friend, just because some quarrel had arisen between them? Is not this destroying all companionship in life, destroying the means by which absent friends converse together? How many jests are frequently put in letters, which, if they were produced in public, would appear stupid! How many serious opinions, which, for all that, ought not to be published! Let this be a proof of your utter ignorance of courtesy. Now mark, also, his incredible folly. What have you to oppose to me, O you eloquent man, as you seem at least to Mustela Tamisius, and to Tiro Numisius? And while these men are standing at this very time in the sight of the senate with drawn swords, I too will think you an eloquent man if you will show how you would defend them if they were charged with being assassins. However what answer would you make if I were to deny that I ever sent those letters to you? By what evidence could you convict me? by my handwriting? Of handwriting indeed you have a lucrative knowledge. How can you prove it in that manner? for the letters are written by an amanuensis. By this time I envy your teacher, who for all that payment, which I shall mention presently, has taught you to know nothing.

For what can be less like, I do not say an orator, but a man, than to reproach an adversary with a thing which if he denies by one single word, he who has reproached him cannot advance one step further? But I do not deny it; and in this very point I convict you not only of inhumanity but also of madness. For what expression is there in those letters which is not full of humanity and service and benevolence? and the whole of your charge amounts to this, that I do not express a bad opinion of you in those letters; that in them I wrote as to a citizen, and as to a virtuous man, not as to a wicked man and a robber. But your letters I will not produce, although I fairly might, now that I am thus challenged by you; letters in which you beg of me that you may be enabled by my consent to procure the recall of some one from exile; and you will not attempt it if I have any objection, and you prevail on me by your entreaties. For why should I put myself in the way of your audacity? when neither the authority of this body, nor the opinion of the Roman people, nor any laws are able to restrain you. However, what was the object of your addressing these entreaties to me, if the man for whom you were entreating was already restored by a law of Caesar's? I suppose the truth was, that he wished it to be done by me as a favour; in which matter there could not be any favour done even by himself, if a law was already passed for the purpose.

V. But as, O conscript fathers, I have many things which I must say both in my own defence and against Marcus Antonius, one thing I ask you, that you will listen to me with kindness while I am speaking for myself; the other I will ensure myself, namely, that you shall listen to me with attention while speaking against him. At the same time also, I beg this of you; that if you have been acquainted with my moderation and modesty throughout my whole life, and especially as a speaker, you will not, when to-day I answer this man in the spirit in which he has attacked me, think that I have forgotten my usual character. I will not treat him as a consul, for he did not treat me as a man of consular rank; and although he in no respect deserves to be considered a consul, whether we regard his way of life, or his principle of governing the republic, or the manner in which he was elected, I am beyond all dispute a man of consular rank.

That, therefore, you might understand what sort of a consul he professed to be himself, he reproached me with my consulship;—a consulship which, O conscript fathers, was in name, indeed, mine, but in reality yours. For what did I determine, what did I contrive, what did I do, that was not determined, contrived, or done, by the counsel and authority and in accordance with the sentiments of this order? And have you, O wise man, O man not merely eloquent, dared to find fault with these actions before the very men by whose counsel and wisdom they were performed? But who was ever found before, except Publius Clodius, to find fault with my consulship? And his fate indeed awaits you, as it also awaited Caius Curio; since that is now in your house which was fatal to each of them.

Marcus Antonius disapproves of my consulship; but it was approved of by Publius Servilius—to name that man first of the men of consular rank who had died most recently. It was approved of by Quintus Catulus, whose authority will always carry weight in this republic; it was approved of by the two Luculli, by Marcus Crassus, by Quintus Hortensius, by Caius Curio, by Caius Piso, by Marcus Glabrio, by Marcus Lepidus, by Lucius Volcatius, by Caius Figulus, by Decimus Silanus and Lucius Murena, who at that time were the consuls elect; the same consulship also which was approved of by those men of consular rank, was approved of by Marcus Cato; who escaped many evils by departing from this life, and especially the evil of seeing you consul. But, above all, my consulship was approved of by Cnaeus Pompeius, who, when he first saw me, as he was leaving Syria, embracing me and congratulating me, said, that it was owing to my services that he was about to see his country again. But why should I mention individuals? It was approved of by the senate, in a very full house, so completely, that there was no one who did not thank me as if I had been his parent, who did not attribute to me the salvation of his life, of his fortunes, of his children, and of the republic.

VI. But, since the republic has been now deprived of those men whom I have named, many and illustrious as they were, let us come to the living, since two of the men of consular rank are still left to us: Lucius Cotta, a man of the greatest genius and the most consummate prudence, proposed a supplication in my honour for those very actions with which you find fault, in the most complimentary language, and those very men of consular rank whom I have named, and the whole senate, adopted his proposal; an honour which has never been paid to any one else in the garb of peace from the foundation of the city to my time. With what eloquence, with what firm wisdom, with what a weight of authority did Lucius Caesar your uncle, pronounce his opinion against the husband of his own sister, your stepfather. But you, when you ought to have taken him as your adviser and tutor in all your designs, and in the whole conduct of your life, preferred being like your stepfather to resembling your uncle. I, who had no connexion with him, acted by his counsels while I was consul. Did you, who were his sister's son, ever once consult him on the affairs of the republic?

But who are they whom Antonius does consult? O ye immortal gods, they are men whose birthdays we have still to learn. To-day Antonius is not coming down. Why? He is celebrating the birthday feast at his villa. In whose honour? I will name no one. Suppose it is in honour of some Phormio, or Gnatho, or even Ballio. Oh the abominable profligacy of the man! Oh how intolerable is his impudence, his debauchery, and his lust! Can you, when you have one of the chiefs of the senate, a citizen of singular virtue, so nearly related to you, abstain from ever consulting him on the affairs of the republic, and consult men who have no property whatever of their own, and are draining yours?

VII. Yes, your consulship, forsooth, is a salutary one for the state, mine a mischievous one. Have you so entirely lost all shame as well as all chastity, that you could venture to say this in that temple in which I was consulting that senate which formerly in the full enjoyment of its honours presided over the world? And did you place around it abandoned men armed with swords? But you have dared besides (what is there which you would not dare?) to say that the Capitoline Hill, when I was consul, was full of armed slaves. I was offering violence to the senate, I suppose, in order to compel the adoption of those infamous decrees of the senate. O wretched man, whether those things are not known to you, (for you know nothing that is good,) or whether they are, when you dare to speak so shamelessly before such men! For what Roman knight was there, what youth of noble birth except you, what man of any rank or class who recollected that he was a citizen, who was not on the Capitoline Hill while the senate was assembled in this temple? who was there, who did not give in his name? Although there could not be provided checks enough, nor were the books able to contain their names.

In truth, when wicked men, being compelled by the revelations of the accomplices, by their own handwriting, and by what I may almost call the voices of their letters, were confessing that they had planned the parricidal destruction of their country, and that they had agreed to burn the city, to massacre the citizens, to devastate Italy, to destroy the republic; who could have existed without being roused to defend the common safety? especially when the senate and people of Rome had a leader then; and if they had one now like he was then, the same fate would befall you which did overtake them.

He asserts that the body of his stepfather was not allowed burial by me. But this is an assertion that was never made by Publius Clodius, a man whom, as I was deservedly an enemy of his, I grieve now to see surpassed by you in every sort of vice. But how could it occur to you to recal to our recollection that you had been educated in the house of Publius Lentulus? Were you afraid that we might think that you could have turned out as infamous as you are by the mere force of nature, if your natural qualities had not been strengthened by education?

VIII. But you are so senseless that throughout the whole of your speech you were at variance with yourself; so that you said things which had not only no coherence with each other but which were most inconsistent with and contradictory to one another; so that there was not so much opposition between you and me as there was between you and yourself. You confessed that your stepfather had been duplicated in that enormous wickedness, yet you complained that he had had punishment inflicted on him. And by doing so you praised what was peculiarly my achievement, and blamed that which was wholly the act of the senate. For the detection and arrest of the guilty parties was my work, their punishment was the work of the senate. But that eloquent man does not perceive that the man against whom he is speaking is being praised by him, and that those before whom he is speaking are being attacked by him. But now what an act, I will not say of audacity, (for he is anxious to be audacious,) but (and that is what he is not desirous of) what an act of folly, in which he surpasses all men, is it to make mention of the Capitoline Hill, at a time when armed men are actually between our benches—when men, armed with swords, are now stationed in this same temple of Concord, O ye immortal gods, in which, while I was consul, opinions most salutary to the state were delivered, owing to which it is that we are all alive at this day.

Accuse the senate; accuse the equestrian body, which at that time was united with the senate; accuse every order of society, and all the citizens, as long as you confess that this assembly at this very moment is besieged by Ityrean soldiers. It is not so much a proof of audacity to advance these statements so impudently, as of utter want of sense to be unable to see their contradictory nature. For what is more insane than, after you yourself have taken up arms to do mischief to the republic, to reproach another with having taken them up to secure its safety? On one occasion you attempted even to be witty. O ye good gods, how little did that attempt suit you! And yet you are a little to be blamed for your failure in that instance, too. For you might have got some wit from your wife, who was an actress. "Arms to the gown must yield." Well, have they not yielded? But afterwards the gown yielded to your arms. Let us inquire then whether it was better for the arms of wicked men to yield to the freedom of the Roman people, or that our liberty should yield to your arms. Nor will I make any further reply to you about the verses. I will only say briefly that you do not understand them, nor any other literature whatever. That I have never at any time been wanting to the claims that either the republic or my friends had upon me; but nevertheless that in all the different sorts of composition on which I have employed myself, during my leisure hours, I have always endeavoured to make my labours and my writings such as to be some advantage to our youth, and some credit to the Roman name. But, however, all this has nothing to do with the present occasion. Let us consider more important matters.

IX. You have said that Publius Clodius was slain by my contrivance. What would men have thought if he had been slain at the time when you pursued him in the forum with a drawn sword, in the sight of all the Roman people; and when you would have settled his business if he had not thrown himself up the stairs of a bookseller's shop, and, shutting them against you, checked your attack by that means? And I confess that at that time I favoured you, but even you yourself do not say that I had advised your attempt. But as for Milo, it was not possible even for me to favour his action. For he had finished the business before any one could suspect that he was going to do it. Oh, but I advised it. I suppose Milo was a man of such a disposition that he was not able to do a service to the republic if he had not some one to advise him to do it. But I rejoiced at it. Well, suppose I did; was I to be the only sorrowful person in the city, when every one else was in such delight? Although that inquiry into the death of Publius Clodius was not instituted with any great wisdom. For what was the reason for having a new law to inquire into the conduct of the man who had slain him, when there was a form of inquiry already established by the laws? However, an inquiry was instituted. And have you now been found, so many years afterwards, to say a thing which, at the time that the affair was under discussion, no one ventured to say against me? But as to the assertion that you have dared to make, and that at great length too, that it was by my means that Pompeius was alienated from his friendship with Caesar, and that on that account it was my fault that the civil war was originated; in that you have not erred so much in the main facts, as (and that is of the greatest importance) in the times.

X. When Marcus Bibulus, a most illustrious citizen, was consul, I omitted nothing which I could possibly do or attempt to draw off Pompeius from his union with Caesar. In which, however, Caesar was more fortunate than I, for he himself drew off Pompeius from his intimacy with me. But afterwards, when Pompeius joined Caesar with all his heart, what could have been my object in attempting to separate them then? It would have been the part of a fool to hope to do so, and of an impudent man to advise it. However, two occasions did arise, on which I gave Pompeius advice against Caesar. You are at liberty to find fault with my conduct on those occasions if you can. One was when I advised him not to continue Caesar's government for five years more. The other, when I advised him not to permit him to be considered as a candidate for the consulship when he was absent. And if I had been able to prevail on him in either of these particulars, we should never have fallen into our present miseries.

Moreover, I also, when Pompeius had now devoted to the service of Caesar all his own power, and all the power of the Roman people, and had begun when it was too late to perceive all those things which I had foreseen long before, and when I saw that a nefarious war was about to be waged against our country, I never ceased to be the adviser of peace, and concord, and some arrangement. And that language of mine was well known to many people,—"I wish, O Cnaeus Pompeius, that you had either never joined in a confederacy with Caius Caesar, or else that you had never broken it off. The one conduct would have become your dignity, and the other would have been suited to your prudence." This, O Marcus Antonius, was at all times my advice both respecting Pompeius and concerning the republic. And if it had prevailed, the republic would still be standing, and you would have perished through your own crimes, and indigence, and infamy.

XI. But these are all old stories now. This charge, however, is quite a modern one, that Caesar was slain by my contrivance. I am afraid, O conscript fathers, lest I should appear to you to have brought up a sham accuser against myself (which is a most disgraceful thing to do); a man not only to distinguish me by the praises which are my due, but to load me also with those which do not belong to me. For who ever heard my name mentioned as an accomplice in that most glorious action? and whose name has been concealed who was in the number of that gallant band? Concealed, do I say? Whose name was there which was not at once made public? I should sooner say that some men had boasted in order to appear to have been concerned in that conspiracy, though they had in reality known nothing of it, than that any one who had been an accomplice in it could have wished to be concealed. Moreover, how likely it is, that among such a number of men, some obscure, some young men who had not the wit to conceal any one, my name could possibly have escaped notice! Indeed, if leaders were wanted for the purpose of delivering the country, what need was there of my instigating the Bruti, one of whom saw every day in his house the image of Lucius Brutus, and the other saw also the image of Ahala? Were these the men to seek counsel from the ancestors of others rather than from their own? and out of doors rather than at home? What? Caius Cassius, a man of that family which could not endure, I will not say the domination, but even the power of any individual,—he, I suppose, was in need of me to instigate him? a man who, even without the assistance of these other most illustrious men, would have accomplished this same deed in Cilicia, at the mouth of the river Cydnus, if Caesar had brought his ships to that bank of the river which he had intended, and not to the opposite one. Was Cnaeus Domitius spurred on to seek to recover his dignity, not by the death of his father, a most illustrious man, nor by the death of his uncle, nor by the deprivation of his own dignity, but by my advice and authority? Did I persuade Caius Trebonius? a man whom I should not have ventured even to advise. On which account the republic owes him even a larger debt of gratitude, because he preferred the liberty of the

Roman people to the friendship of one man, and because he preferred overthrowing arbitrary power to sharing it. Was I the instigator whom Lucius Tillius Cimber followed? a man whom I admired for having performed that action, rather than ever expected that he would perform it; and I admired him on this account, that he was unmindful of the personal kindnesses which he had received, but mindful of his country. What shall I say of the two Servilii? Shall I call them Cascas, or Ahalas? and do you think that those men were instigated by my authority rather than by their affection for the republic? It would take a long time to go through all the rest; and it is a glorious thing for the republic that they were so numerous, and a most honourable thing also for themselves.

XII. But recollect, I pray you, how that clever man convicted me of being an accomplice in the business. When Caesar was slain, says he, Marcus Brutus immediately lifted up on high his bloody dagger, and called on Cicero by name; and congratulated him on liberty being recovered. Why on me above all men? Because I knew of it beforehand? Consider rather whether this was not his reason for calling on me, that, when he had performed an action very like those which I myself had done, he called me above all men to witness that he had been an imitator of my exploits. But you, O stupidest of all men, do not you perceive, that if it is a crime to have wished that Caesar should be slain—which you accuse me of having wished—it is a crime also to have rejoiced at his death? For what is the difference between a man who has advised an action, and one who has approved of it? or what does it signify whether I wished it to be done, or rejoice that it has been done? Is there any one then, except you yourself and those men who wished him to become a king, who was unwilling that that deed should be done, or who disapproved of it after it was done? All men, therefore, are guilty as far as this goes. In truth, all good men, as far as it depended on them, bore a part in the slaying of Caesar. Some did not know how to contrive it, some had not courage for it, some had no opportunity,—every one had the inclination.

However, remark the stupidity of this fellow,—I should rather say, of this brute beast. For thus he spoke:—"Marcus Brutus, whom I name to do him honour, holding aloft his bloody dagger, called upon Cicero, from which it must be understood that he was privy to the action." Am I then called wicked by you because you suspect that I suspected something; and is he who openly displayed his reeking dagger, named by you that you may do him honour? Be it so. Let this stupidity exist in your language: how much greater is it in your actions and opinions! Arrange matters in this way at last, O consul; pronounce the cause of the Bruti, of Caius Cassius, of Cnaeus Domitius, of Caius Trebonius and the rest to be whatever you please to call it: sleep off that intoxication of yours, sleep it off and take breath. Must one apply a torch to you to waken you while you are sleeping over such an important affair? Will you never understand that you have to decide whether those men who performed that action are homicides or assertors of freedom?

XIII. For just consider a little; and for a moment think of the business like a sober man. I who, as I myself confess, am an intimate friend of those men, and, as you accuse me, an accomplice of theirs, deny that there is any medium between these alternatives. I confess that they, if they be not deliverers of the Roman people and saviours of the republic, are worse than assassins, worse than homicides, worse even than parricides: since it is a more atrocious thing to murder the father of one's country, than one's own father. You wise and considerate man, what do you say to this? If they are parricides, why are they always named by you, both in this assembly and before the Roman people, with a view to do them honour? Why has Marcus Brutus been, on your motion, excused from obedience to the laws, and allowed to be absent. Why were the games of Apollo celebrated with incredible honour to Marcus Brutus? why were provinces given to Brutus and Cassius? why were quaestors assigned to them? why was the number of their lieutenants augmented? And all these measures were owing to you. They are not homicides then. It follows that in your opinion they are deliverers of their country, since there can be no other alternative. What is the matter? Am I embarrassing you? For perhaps you do not quite understand propositions which are stated disjunctively. Still this is the sum total of my conclusion; that since they are acquitted by you of wickedness, they are at the same time pronounced most worthy of the very most honourable rewards.

Therefore, I will now proceed again with my oration. I will write to them, if any one by chance should ask whether what you have imputed to me be true, not to deny it to any one. In truth, I am afraid that it must be considered either a not very creditable thing to them, that they should have concealed the fact of my being an accomplice; or else a most discreditable one to me that I was invited to be one, and that I shirked it. For what greater exploit (I call you to witness, O august Jupiter!) was ever achieved not only in this city, but in all the earth? What more glorious action was ever done? What deed was ever more deservedly recommended to the everlasting recollection of men? Do you, then, shut me up with the other leaders in the partnership in this design, as in the Trojan horse? I have no objection; I even thank you for doing so, with whatever intent you do it. For the deed is so great an one, that I cannot compare the unpopularity which you wish to excite against me on account of it, with its real glory.

For who can be happier than those men whom you boast of having now expelled and driven from the city? What place is there either so deserted or so uncivilized, as not to seem to greet and to covet the presence of those men wherever they have arrived? What men are so clownish as not, when they have once beheld them, to think that they have reaped the greatest enjoyment that life can give? And what posterity will be ever so forgetful, what literature will ever be found so ungrateful, as not to cherish their glory with undying recollection? Enrol me then, I beg, in the number of those men.

XIV. But one thing I am afraid you may not approve of. For if I had really been one of their number, I should have not only got rid of the king, but of the kingly power also out of the republic; and if I had been the author of the piece, as it is said, believe me, I should not have been contented with one act, but should have finished the whole play. Although, if it be a crime to have wished that Caesar might be put to death, beware, I pray you, O Antonius, of what must be your own case, as it is notorious that you, when at Narbo, formed a plan of the same sort with Caius Trebonius; and it was on account of your participation in that design that, when Caesar was being killed, we saw you called aside by Trebonius. But I (see how far I am from any horrible inclination towards,) praise you for having once in your life had a righteous intention; I return you thanks for not having revealed the matter; and I excuse you for not having accomplished your purpose. That exploit required a man.

And if any one should institute a prosecution against you, and employ that test of old Cassius, "who reaped any advantage from it?" take care, I advise you, lest you suit that description. Although, in truth, that action was, as you used to say, an advantage to every one who was not willing to be a slave, still it was so to you above all men, who are not merely not a slave, but are actually a king; who delivered yourself from an enormous burden of debt at the temple of Ops; who, by your dealings with the account books, there squandered a countless sum of money; who have had such vast treasures brought to you from Caesar's house; at whose own house there is set up a most lucrative manufactory of false memoranda and autographs, and a most iniquitous market of lands, and towns, and exemptions, and revenues. In truth, what measure except the death of Caesar could possibly have been any relief to your indigent and insolvent condition? You appear to be somewhat agitated. Have you any secret fear that you yourself may appear to have had some connexion with that crime? I will release you from all apprehension; no one will ever believe it; it is not like you to deserve well of the republic; the most illustrious men in the republic are the authors of that exploit; I only say that you are glad it was done; I do not accuse you of having done it. I have replied to your heaviest accusations, I must now also reply to the rest of them.

XV. You have thrown in my teeth the camp of Pompeius and all my conduct at that time. At which time, indeed, if, as I have said before, my counsels and my authority had prevailed, you would this day be in indigence, we should be free, and the republic would not have lost so many generals and so many armies. For I confess that, when I saw that these things certainly would happen, which now have happened, I was as greatly grieved as all the other virtuous citizens would have been if they had foreseen the same things. I did grieve, I did grieve, O conscript fathers, that the republic which had once been saved by your counsels and mine, was fated to perish in a short time. Nor was I so inexperienced in and ignorant of this nature of things, as to be disheartened on account of a fondness for life, which while it endured would wear me out with anguish, and when brought to an end would release me from all trouble. But I was desirous that those most illustrious men, the lights of the republic, should live: so many men of consular rank, so many men of praetorian rank, so many most honourable senators; and besides them all the flower of our nobility and of our youth; and the armies of excellent citizens. And if they were still alive, under ever such hard conditions of peace, (for any sort of peace with our fellow-citizens appeared to me more desirable than civil war,) we should be still this day enjoying the republic.

And if my opinion had prevailed, and if those men, the preservation of whose lives was my main object, elated with the hope of victory, had not been my chief opposers, to say nothing of other results, at all events you would never have continued in this order, or rather in this city. But say you, my speech alienated from me the regard of Pompeius? Was there any one to whom he was more attached? any one with whom he conversed or shared his counsels more frequently? It was, indeed, a great thing that we, differing as we did respecting the general interests of the republic, should continue in uninterrupted friendship. But I saw clearly what his opinions and views were, and he saw mine equally. I was for providing for the safety of the citizens in the first place, in order that we might be able to consult their dignity afterwards. He thought more of consulting their existing dignity. But because each of us had a definite object to pursue, our disagreement was the more endurable. But what that extraordinary and almost godlike man thought of me is known to those men who pursued him to Paphos from the battle of Pharsalia. No mention of me was ever made by him that was not the most honourable that could be, that was not full of the most friendly regret for me; while he confessed that I had had the most foresight, but that he had had more sanguine hopes. And do you dare taunt me with the name of that man whose friend you admit that I was, and whose assassin you confess yourself?

XVI. However, let us say no more of that war, in which you were too fortunate. I will not reply even with those jests to which you have said that I gave utterance in the camp. That camp was in truth full of anxiety, but although men are in great difficulties, still, provided they are men, they sometimes relax their minds. But the fact that the same man finds fault with my melancholy, and also with my jokes, is a great proof that I was very moderate in each particular.

You have said that no inheritances come to me. Would that this accusation of yours were a true one; I should have more of my friends and connexions alive. But how could such a charge ever come into your head? For I have received more than twenty millions of sesterces in inheritances. Although in this particular I admit that you have been more fortunate than I. No one has ever made me his heir except he was a friend of mine, in order that my grief of mind for his loss might be accompanied also with some gain, if it was to be considered as such. But a man whom you never even saw, Lucius Rubrius, of Casinum, made you his heir. And see now how much he loved you, who, though he did not know whether you were white or black, passed over the son of his brother, Quintus Fufius, a most honourable Roman knight, and most attached to him, whom he had on all occasions openly declared his heir, (he never even names him in his will,) and he makes you his heir whom he had never seen, or at all events had never spoken to.

I wish you would tell me, if it is not too much trouble, what sort of countenance Lucius Turselius was of; what sort of height; from what municipal town he came; and of what tribe he was a member. "I know nothing," you will say, "about him, except what farms he had." Therefore, he, disinheriting his brother, made you his heir. And besides these instances, this man has seized on much other property belonging to men wholly unconnected with him, to the exclusion of the legitimate heirs, as if he himself were the heir. Although the thing that struck me with most astonishment of all was, that you should venture to make mention of inheritances, when you yourself had not received the inheritance of your own father.

XVII. And was it in order to collect all these arguments, O you most senseless of men, that you spent so many days in practising declamation in another man's villa? Although, indeed, (as your most intimate friends usually say,) you are in the habit of declaiming, not for the purpose of whetting your genius, but of working off the effects of wine. And, indeed, you employ a master to teach you jokes, a man appointed by your own vote and that of your boon companions; a rhetorician, whom you have allowed to say what ever he pleased against you, a thoroughly facetious gentleman; but there are plenty of materials for speaking against you and against your friends. But just see now what a difference there is between you and your grandfather. He used with great deliberation to bring forth arguments advantageous to the cause he was advocating; you pour forth in a hurry the sentiments which you have been taught by another. And what wages have you paid this rhetorician? Listen, listen, O conscript fathers, and learn the blows which are inflicted on the republic. You have assigned, O Antonius, two thousand acres which is often translated acre also, of land, in the Leontine district, to Sextus Clodius, the rhetorician, and those, too, exempt from every kind of tax, for the sake of putting the Roman people to such a vast expense that you might learn to be a fool. Was this gift, too, O you most audacious of men, found among Caesar's papers? But I will take another opportunity to speak about the Leontine and the Campanian district; where he has stolen lands from the republic to pollute them with most infamous owners. For now, since I have sufficiently replied to all his charges, I must say a little about our corrector and censor himself. And yet I will not say all I could, in order that if I have often to battle with him I may always come to the contest with fresh arms; and the multitude of his vices and atrocities will easily enable me to do so.

XVIII. Shall we then examine your conduct from the time when you were a boy? I think so. Let us begin at the beginning. Do you recollect that, while you were still clad in the praetexta, you became a bankrupt? That was the fault of your father, you will say. I admit that. In truth, such a defence is full of filial affection. But it is peculiarly suited to your own audacity, that you sat among the fourteen rows of the knights, though by the Roscian law there was a place appointed for bankrupts, even if any one had become so.

XIX. But let us say no more of your profligacy and debauchery. There are things which it is not possible for me to mention with honour; but you are all the more free for that, inasmuch as you have not scrupled to be an actor in scenes which a modest enemy cannot bring himself to mention.

Mark now, O conscript fathers, the rest of his life, which I will touch upon rapidly. For my inclination hastens to arrive at those things which he did in the time of the civil war, amid the greatest miseries of the republic, and at those things which he does every day. And I beg of you, though they are far better known to you than they are to me, still to listen attentively, as you are doing, to my relation of them. For in such cases as this, it is not the mere knowledge of such actions that ought to excite the mind, but the recollection of them also. Although we must at once go into the middle of them, lest otherwise we should be too long in coming to the end.

He was very intimate with Clodius at the time of his tribuneship; he, who now enumerates the kindnesses which he did me. He was the firebrand to handle all conflagrations; and even in his house he attempted something. He himself well knows what I allude to. From thence he made a journey to Alexandria, in defiance of the authority of the senate, and against the interests of the republic, and in spite of religious obstacles; but he had Gabinius for his leader, with whom whatever he did was sure to be right. What were the circumstances of his return from thence? what sort of return was it? He went from Egypt to the furthest extremity of Gaul before he returned home. And what was his home? For at that time every man had possession of his own house; and you had no house anywhere, O Antonius. House, do you say? what place was there in the whole world where you could set your foot on anything that belonged to you, except Mienum, which you farmed with your partners, as if it had been Sisapo?

XX. You came from Gaul to stand for the quaestorship. Dare to say that you went to your own father before you came to me. I had already received Caesar's letters, begging me to allow myself to accept of your excuses; and therefore, I did not allow you even to mention thanks. After that, I was treated with respect by you, and you received attentions from me in your canvass for the quaestorship. And it was at that time, indeed, that you endeavoured to slay Publius Clodius in the forum, with the approbation of the Roman people; and though you made the attempt of your own accord, and not at my instigation, still you clearly alleged that you did not think, unless you slew him, that you could possibly make amends to me for all the injuries which you had done me. And this makes me wonder why you should say that Milo did that deed at my instigation; when I never once exhorted you to do it, who of your own accord attempted to do me the same service. Although, if you had persisted in it, I should have preferred allowing the action to be set down entirely to your own love of glory rather than to my influence.

You were elected quaestor. On this, immediately, without any resolution of the senate authorizing such a step, without drawing lots, without procuring any law to be passed, you hastened to Caesar. For you thought the camp the only refuge on earth for indigence, and debt, and profligacy,—for all men, in short, who were in a state of utter ruin. Then, when you had recruited your resources again by his largesses and your own robberies, (if, indeed, a person can be said to recruit, who only acquires something which he may immediately squander,) you hastened, being again a beggar, to the tribuneship, in order that in that magistracy you might, if possible, behave like your friend.

XXI. Listen now, I beseech you, O conscript fathers, not to those things which he did indecently and profligately to his own injury and to his own disgrace as a private individual; but to the actions which he did impiously and wickedly against us and our fortunes,—that is to say, against the whole republic. For it is from his wickedness that you will find that the beginning of all these evils has arisen.

For when, in the consulship of Lucius Lentulus and Marcus Marcellus, you, on the first of January, were anxious to prop up the republic, which was tottering and almost falling, and were willing to consult the interests of Caius Caesar himself, if he would have acted like a man in his senses, then this fellow opposed to your counsels his tribuneship, which he had sold and handed over to the purchaser, and exposed his own neck to that axe under which many have suffered for smaller crimes. It was against you, O Marcus Antonius, that the senate, while still in the possession of its rights, before so many of its luminaries were extinguished, passed that decree which, in accordance with the usage of our ancestors, is at times passed against an enemy who is a citizen. And have you dared, before these conscript fathers, to say anything against me, when I have been pronounced by this order to be the saviour of my country, and when you have been declared by it to be an enemy of the republic? The mention of that wickedness of yours has been interrupted, but the recollection of it has not been effaced. As long as the race of men, as long as the name of the Roman people shall exist, (and that, unless it is prevented from being so by your means, will be everlasting,) so long will that most mischievous interposition of your veto be spoken of. What was there that was being done by the senate either ambitiously or rashly, when you, one single young man, forbade the whole order to pass decrees concerning the safety of the republic? and when you did so, not once only, but repeatedly? nor would you allow any one to plead with you in behalf of the authority of the senate; and yet, what did any one entreat of you, except that you would not desire the republic to be entirely overthrown and destroyed; when neither the chief men of the state by their entreaties, nor the elders by their warnings, nor the senate in a full house by pleading with you, could move you from the determination which you had already sold and as it were delivered to the purchaser? Then it was, after having tried many other expedients previously, that a blow was of necessity struck at you which had been struck at only few men before you, and which none of them had ever survived. Then it was that this order armed the consuls, and the rest of the magistrates who were invested with either military or civil command, against you, and you never would have escaped them, if you had not taken refuge in the camp of Caesar.

XXII. It was you, you, I say, O Marcus Antonius, who gave Caius Caesar, desirous as he already was to throw everything into confusion, the principal pretext for waging war against his country. For what other pretence did he allege? what cause did he give for his own most frantic resolution and action, except that the power of interposition by the veto had been disregarded, the privileges of the tribunes taken away, and Antonius's rights abridged by the senate? I say nothing of how false, how trivial these pretences were; especially when there could not possibly be any reasonable cause whatever to justify any one in taking up arms against his country. But I have nothing to do with Caesar. You must unquestionably allow, that the cause of that ruinous war existed in your person.

O miserable man if you are aware, more miserable still if you are not aware, that this is recorded in writings, is handed down to men's recollection, that our very latest posterity in the most distant ages will never forget this fact, that the consuls were expelled from Italy, and with them Cnaeus Pompeius, who was the glory and light of the empire of the Roman people; that all the men of consular rank, whose health would allow them to share in that disaster and that flight, and the praetors, and men of praetorian rank, and the tribunes of the people, and a great part of the senate, and all the flower of the youth of the city, and, in a word, the republic itself was driven out and expelled from its abode. As, then, there is in seeds the cause which produces trees and plants, so of this most lamentable war you were the seed. Do you, O conscript fathers, grieve that these armies of the Roman people have been slain? It is Antonius who slew them. Do you regret your most illustrious citizens? It is Antonius, again, who has deprived you of them. The authority of this order is overthrown; it is Antonius who has overthrown it. Everything, in short, which we have seen since that time, (and what misfortune is there that we have not seen?) we shall, if we argue rightly, attribute wholly to Antonius. As Helen was to the Trojans, so has that man been to this republic,—the cause of war, the cause of mischief, the cause of ruin. The rest of his tribuneship was like the beginning. He did everything which the senate had laboured to prevent, as being impossible to be done consistently with the safety of the republic. And see, now, how gratuitously wicked he was even in accomplishing his wickedness.

XXIII. He restored many men who had fallen under misfortune. Among them no mention was made of his uncle. If he was severe, why was he not so to every one? If he was merciful, why was he not merciful to his own relations? But I say nothing of the rest. He restored Licinius Lenticula, a man who had been condemned for gambling, and who was a fellow-gamester of his own. As if he could not play with a condemned man; but in reality, in order to pay by a straining of the law in his favour, what he had lost by the dice. What reason did you allege to the Roman people why it was desirable that he should be restored? I suppose you said that he was absent when the prosecution was instituted against him; that the cause was decided without his having been heard in his defence; that there was not by a law any judicial proceeding established with reference to gambling; that he had been put down by violence or by arms; or lastly, as was said in the case of your uncle, that the tribunal had been bribed with money. Nothing of this sort was said. Then he was a good man, and one worthy of the republic. That, indeed, would have been nothing to the purpose, but still, since being condemned does not go for much, I would forgive you if that were the truth. Does not he restore to the full possession of his former privileges the most worthless man possible,—one who would not hesitate to play at dice even in the forum, and who had been convicted under the law which exists respecting gambling,—does not he declare in the most open manner his own propensities?

Then in this same tribuneship, when Caesar while on his way into Spain had given him Italy to trample on, what journeys did he make in every direction! how did he visit the municipal towns! I know that I am only speaking of matters which have been discussed in every one's conversation, and that the things which I am saying and am going to say are better known to every one who was in Italy at that time, than to me, who was not. Still I mention the particulars of his conduct, although my speech cannot possibly come up to your own personal knowledge. When was such wickedness ever heard of as existing upon earth? or such shamelessness? or such open infamy?

XXIV. The tribune of the people was borne along in a chariot, lictors crowned with laurel preceded him; among whom, on an open litter, was carried an actress; whom honourable men, citizens of the different municipalities, coming out from their towns under compulsion to meet him, saluted not by the name by which she was well known on the stage, but by that of Volumnia. A car followed full of pimps; then a lot of debauched companions; and then his mother, utterly neglected, followed the mistress of her profligate son, as if she had been her daughter-in-law. O the disastrous fecundity of that miserable woman! With the marks of such wickedness as this did that fellow stamp every municipality, and prefecture, and colony, and, in short, the whole of Italy.

To find fault with the rest of his actions, O conscript fathers, is difficult, and somewhat unsafe. He was occupied in war; he glutted himself with the slaughter of citizens who bore no resemblance to himself. He was fortunate—if at least there can be any good fortune in wickedness. But since we wish to show a regard for the veterans, although the cause of the soldiers is very different from yours; they followed their chief; you went to seek for a leader; still, (that I may not give you any pretence for stirring up odium against me among them,) I will say nothing of the nature of the war.

When victorious, you returned with the legions from Thessaly to Brundusium. There you did not put me to death. It was a great kindness! For I confess that you could have done it. Although there was no one of those men who were with you at that time, who did not think that I ought to be spared. For so great is men's affection for their country, that I was sacred even in the eyes of your legions, because they recollected that the country had been saved by me. However, grant that you did give me what you did not take away from me; and that I have my life as a present from you, since it was not taken from me by you; was it possible for me, after all your insults, to regard that kindness of yours as I regarded it at first, especially after you saw that you must hear this reply from me?

XXV. You came to Brundusium, to the bosom and embraces of your actress. What is the matter? Am I speaking falsely? How miserable is it not to be able to deny a fact which it is disgraceful to confess! If you had no shame before the municipal towns, had you none even before your veteran army? For what soldier was there who did not see her at

Brundusium? who was there who did not know that she had come so many days' journey to congratulate you? who was there who did not grieve that he was so late in finding out how worthless a man he had been following?

Again you made a tour through Italy, with that same actress for your companion. Cruel and miserable was the way in which you led your soldiers into the towns; shameful was the pillage in every city, of gold and silver, and above all, of wine. And besides all this, while Caesar knew nothing about it, as he was at Alexandria, Antonius, by the kindness of Caesar's friends, was appointed his master of the horse. Then he thought that he could live with Hippia by virtue of his office, and that he might give horses which were the property of the state to Sergius the buffoon. At that time he had selected for himself to live in, not the house which he now dishonours, but that of Marcus Piso. Why need I mention his decrees, his robberies, the possessions of inheritances which were given him, and those too which were seized by him? Want compelled him; he did not know where to turn. That great inheritance from Lucius Rubrius, and that other from Lucius Turselius, had not yet come to him. He had not yet succeeded as an unexpected heir to the place of Cnaeus Pompeius, and of many others who were absent. He was forced to live like a robber, having nothing beyond what he could plunder from others.

However, we will say nothing of these things, which are acts of a more hardy sort of villany. Let us speak rather of his meaner descriptions of worthlessness. You, with those jaws of yours, and those sides of yours, and that strength of body suited to a gladiator, drank such quantities of wine at the marriage of Hippia, that you were forced to vomit the next day in the sight of the Roman people. O action disgraceful not merely to see, but even to hear of! If this had happened to you at supper amid those vast drinking cups of yours, who would not have thought it scandalous? But in an assembly of the Roman people, a man holding a public office, a master of the horse, to whom it would have been disgraceful even to belch, vomiting filled his own bosom and the whole tribunal with fragments of what he had been eating reeking with wine. But he himself confesses this among his other disgraceful acts. Let us proceed to his more splendid offences.

XXVI. Caesar came back from Alexandria, fortunate, as he seemed at least to himself; but in my opinion no one can be fortunate who is unfortunate for the republic. The spear was set up in front of the temple of Jupiter Stator, and the property of Cnaeus Pompeius Magnus—(miserable that I am, for even now that my tears have ceased to flow, my grief remains deeply implanted in my heart,)—the property, I say, of Cnaeus Pompeius the Great was submitted to the pitiless, voice of the auctioneer. On that one occasion the state forgot its slavery, and groaned aloud, and though men's minds were enslaved, as everything was kept under by fear, still the groans of the Roman people were free. While all men were waiting to see who would be so impious, who would be so mad, who would be so declared an enemy to gods and to men as to dare to mix himself up with that wicked auction, no one was found except Antonius, even though there were plenty of men collected round that spear who would have dared anything else. One man alone was found to dare to do that which the audacity of every one else had shrunk from and shuddered at. Were you, then, seized with such stupidity,—or, I should rather say, with such insanity,—as not to see that if you, being of the rank in which you were born, acted as a broker at all, and above all as a broker in the case of Pompeius's property, you would be execrated and hated by the Roman people, and that all gods and all men must at once become and for ever continue hostile to you? But with what violence did that glutton immediately proceed to take possession of the property of that man, to whose valour it had been owing that the Roman people had been more terrible to foreign nations, while his justice had made it dearer to them.

XXVII. When, therefore, this fellow had begun to wallow in the treasures of that great man, he began to exult like a buffoon in a play, who has lately been a beggar, and has become suddenly rich. But, as some poet or other says,—

"Ill gotten gain comes quickly to an end."

It is an incredible thing, and almost a miracle, how he in a few, not months, but days, squandered all that vast wealth. There was an immense quantity of wine, an excessive abundance of very valuable plate, much precious apparel, great quantities of splendid furniture, and other magnificent things in many places, such as one was likely to see belonging to a man who was not indeed luxurious, but who was very wealthy. Of all this in a few days there was nothing left. What Charybdis was ever so voracious? Charybdis, do I say? Charybdis, if she existed at all, was only one animal. The ocean, I swear most solemnly, appears scarcely capable of having swallowed up such numbers of things so widely scattered, and distributed in such different places, with such rapidity. Nothing was shut up, nothing sealed up, no list was made of anything. Whole storehouses were abandoned to the most worthless of men. Actors seized on this, actresses on that, the house was crowded with gamblers, and full of drunken men, people were drinking all day, and that too in many places, there were added to all this expense (for this fellow was not invariably fortunate) heavy gambling losses. You might see in the cellars of the slaves, couches covered with the most richly embroidered counterpanes of Cnaeus Pompeius. Wonder not, then, that all these things were so soon consumed. Such profligacy as that could have devoured not only the patrimony of one individual, however ample it might have been, (as indeed his was) but whole cities and kingdoms.

And then his houses and gardens! Oh the cruel audacity! Did you dare to enter into that house? Did you dare to cross that most sacred threshold? and to show your most profligate countenance to the household gods who protect that abode? A house which for a long time no one could behold, no one could pass by without tears! Are you not ashamed to dwell so long in that house? one in which, stupid and ignorant as you are, still you can see nothing which is not painful to you.

XXVIII. When you behold those beaks of ships in the vestibule, and those warlike trophies, do you fancy that you are entering into a house which belongs to you? It is impossible. Although you are devoid of all sense and all feeling,—as in truth you are,—still you are acquainted with yourself, and with your trophies, and with your friends. Nor do I believe that you either waking or sleeping, can ever act with quiet sense. It is impossible but that, were you ever so drunk and frantic,—as in truth you are,—when the recollection of the appearance of that illustrious man comes across you, you should be roused from sleep by your fears, and often stirred up to madness if awake. I pity even the walls and the roof. For what had that house ever beheld except what was modest, except what proceeded from the purest principles and from the most virtuous practice? For that man was, O conscript fathers, as you yourselves know, not only illustrious abroad, but also admirable at home; and not more praiseworthy for his exploits in foreign countries, than for his domestic arrangements. Now in his house every bedchamber is a brothel, and every dining-room a cookshop. Although he denies this:—Do not, do not make inquiries. He is become economical. He desired that mistress of his to take possession of whatever belonged to her, according to the laws of the Twelve Tables. He has taken his keys from her, and turned her out of doors. What a well-tried citizen! of what proved virtue is he! the most honourable passage in whose life is the one when he divorced himself from this actress.

But how constantly does he harp on the expression "the consul Antonius!" This amounts to say "that most debauched consul," "that most worthless of men, the consul." For what else is Antonius? For if any dignity were implied in the name, then, I imagine, your grandfather would sometimes have called himself "the consul Antonius." But he never did. My colleague too, your own uncle, would have called himself so. Unless you are the only Antonius. But I pass over those offences which have no peculiar connexion with the part you took in harassing the republic; I return to that in which you bore so principal a share,—that is, to the civil war; and it is mainly owing to you that that was originated, and brought to a head, and carried on.

XXIX. Though you yourself took no personal share in it, partly through timidity, partly through profligacy, you had tasted, or rather had sucked in, the blood of fellow-citizens: you had been in the battle of Pharsalia as a leader; you had slain Lucius Domitius, a most illustrious and high-born man; you had pursued and put to death in the most barbarous manner many men who had escaped from the battle, and whom Caesar would perhaps have saved, as he did some others.

And after having performed these exploits, what was the reason why you did not follow Caesar into Africa; especially when so large a portion of the war was still remaining? And accordingly, what place did you obtain about Caesar's person after his return from Africa? What was your rank? He whose quaestor you had been when general, whose master of the horse when he was dictator, to whom you had been the chief cause of war, the chief instigator of cruelty, the sharer of his plunder, his son, as you yourself said, by inheritance, proceeded against you for the money which you owed for the house and gardens, and for the other property which you had bought at that sale. At first you answered fiercely enough, and that I may not appear prejudiced against you in every particular, you used a tolerably just and reasonable argument. "What, does Caius Caesar demand money of me? why should he do so, any more than I should claim it of him? Was he victorious without my assistance? No, and he never could have been. It was I who supplied him with a pretext for civil war, it was I who proposed mischievous laws, it was I who took up arms against the consuls and generals of the Roman people, against the senate and people of Rome, against the gods of the country, against its altars and healths, against the country itself. Has he conquered for himself alone? Why should not those men whose common work the achievement is, have the booty also in common?" You were only claiming your right, but what had that to do with it? He was the more powerful of the two.

Therefore, stopping all your expostulations, he sent his soldiers to you, and to your sureties, when all on a sudden out came that splendid catalogue of yours. How men did laugh! That there should be so vast a catalogue, that their should be such a numerous and various list of possessions, of all of which, with the exception of a portion of Misenum, there was nothing which the man who was putting them up to sale could call his own. And what a miserable sight was the auction. A little apparel of Pompeius's, and that stained, a few silver vessels belonging to the same man, all battered, some slaves in wretched condition, so that we grieved that there was anything remaining to be seen of these miserable relics. This auction, however, the heirs of Lucius Rubrius prevented from proceeding, being armed with a decree of Caesar to that effect. The spendthrift was embarrassed. He did not know which way to turn. It was at this very time that an assassin sent by him was said to have been detected with a dagger in the house of Caesar. And of this Caesar himself complained in the senate, inveighing openly against you. Caesar departs to Spain, having granted you a few days delay for making the payment, on account of your poverty. Even then you do not follow him. Had so good a gladiator as you retired from business so early? Can any one then fear a man who was as timid as this man in upholding his party, that is, in upholding his own fortunes?

XXX. After some time he at last went into Spain; but, as he says, he could not arrive there in safety. How then did Dolabella manage to arrive there? Either, O Antonius, that cause ought never to have been undertaken, or when you had undertaken it, it should have been maintained to the end. Thrice did Caesar fight against his fellow-citizens; in Thessaly, in Africa, and in Spain. Dolabella was present at all these battles. In the battle in Spain he even received a wound. If you ask my opinion, I wish he had not been there. But still, if his design at first was blameable, his consistency and firmness were praiseworthy. But what shall we say of you? In the first place, the children of Cnaeus Pompeius sought to be restored to their country. Well, this concerned the common interests of the whole party. Besides that, they sought to recover their household gods, the gods of their country, their altars, their hearths, the tutelar gods of their family; all of which you had seized upon. And when they sought to recover those things by force of arms which belonged to them by the laws, who was it most natural—(although in unjust and unnatural proceedings what can there be that is natural?)—still, who was it most natural to expect would fight against the children of Cnaeus Pompeius? Who? Why, you who had bought their property. Were you at Narbo to be sick over the tables of your entertainers, while Dolabella was fighting your battles in Spain?

And what a return was that of yours from Narbo? He even asked why I had returned so suddenly from my expedition. I have just briefly explained to you, O conscript fathers, the reason of my return. I was desirous, if I could, to be of service to the republic even before the first of January. For, as to your question, how I had returned; in the first place, I returned by daylight, not in the dark; in the second place, I returned in shoes, and in my Roman gown, not in any Gallic slippers, or barbarian mantle. And even now you keep looking at me; and, as it seems, with great anger. Surely you would be reconciled to me if you knew how ashamed I am of your worthlessness, which you yourself are not ashamed of. Of all the profligate conduct of all the world, I never saw, I never heard of any more shameful than yours. You who fancied yourself a master of the horse, when you were standing for, or I should rather say begging for the consulship for the ensuing year, ran in Gallic slippers and a barbarian mantle about the municipal towns and colonies of Gaul from which we used to demand the consulship when the consulship was stood for and not begged for.

XXXI. But mark now the trifling character of the fellow. When about the tenth hour of the day he had arrived at Red Rocks, he skulked into a little petty wine-shop, and, hiding there, kept on drinking till evening. And from thence getting into a gig and being driven rapidly to the city, he came to his own house with his head veiled. "Who are you?" says the porter. "An express from Marcus." He is at once taken to the woman for whose sake he had come; and he delivered the letter to her. And when she had read it with tears, (for it was written in a very amorous style, but the main subject of the letter was that he would have nothing to do with that actress for the future; that he had discarded all his love for her, and transferred it to his correspondent,) when she, I say, wept plentifully, this soft-hearted man could bear it no longer; he uncovered his head and threw himself on her neck. Oh the worthless man! (for what else can I call him? there is no more suitable expression for me to use,) was it for this that you disturbed the city by nocturnal alarms, and Italy with fears of many days' duration, in order that you might show yourself unexpectedly, and that a woman might see you before she hoped to do so? And he had at home a pretence of love; but out of doors a cause more discreditable still, namely, lest Lucius Plancus should sell up his sureties. But after you had been produced in the assembly by one of the tribunes of the people, and had replied that you had come on your own private business, you made even the people full of jokes against you. But, however, we have said too much about trifles. Let us come to more important subjects.

XXXII. You went a great distance to meet Caesar on his return from Spain. You went rapidly, you returned rapidly in order that we might see that, if you were not brave, you were at least active. You again became intimate with him; I am sure I do not know how. Caesar had this peculiar characteristic; whoever he knew to be utterly ruined by debt, and needy, even if he knew him also to be an audacious and worthless man, he willingly admitted him to his intimacy. You then, being admirably recommended to him by these circumstances, were ordered to be appointed consul, and that too as his own colleague. I do not make any complaint against Dolabella, who was at that time acting under compulsion, and was cajoled and deceived. But who is there who does not know with what great perfidy both of you treated Dolabella in that business? Caesar induced him to stand for the consulship. After having promised it to him, and pledged himself to aid him, he prevented his getting it, and transferred it to himself. And you endorsed his treachery with your own eagerness.

The first of January arrives. We are convened in the senate. Dolabella inveighed against him with much more fluency and premeditation than I am doing now. And what things were they which he said in his anger, O ye good gods! First of all, after Caesar had declared that before he departed he would order Dolabella to be made consul, (and they deny that he was a king who was always doing and saying something of this sort,)—but after Caesar had said this, then this virtuous augur said that he was invested with a pontificate of that sort that he was able, by means of the auspices, either to hinder or to vitiate the comitia, just as he pleased; and he declared that he would do so. And here, in the first place, remark the incredible stupidity of the man. For what do you mean? Could you not just as well have done what you said you had now the power to do by the privileges with which that pontificate had invested you, even if you were not an augur, if you were consul? Perhaps you could even do it more easily. For we augurs have only the power of announcing that the auspices are being observed, but the consuls and other magistrates have the right also of observing them whenever they choose. Be it so. You said this out of ignorance. For one must not demand prudence from a man who is never sober. But still remark his impudence. Many months before, he said in the senate that he would either prevent the comitia from assembling for the election of Dolabella by means of the auspices, or that he would do what he actually did do. Can any one divine beforehand what defect there will be in the auspices, except the man who has already determined to observe the heavens? which in the first place it is forbidden by law to do at the time of the comitia. And if any one has been observing the heavens, he is bound to give notice of it, not after the comitia are assembled, but before they are held. But this man's ignorance is joined to impudence, nor does he know what an augur ought to know, nor do what a modest man ought to do. And just recollect the whole of his conduct during his consulship from that day up to the ides of March. What lictor was ever so humble, so abject? He himself had no power at all; he begged everything of others; and thrusting his head into the hind part of his litter, he begged favours of his colleagues, to sell them himself afterwards.

XXXIII. Behold, the day of the comitia for the election of Dolabella arrives. The prerogative century draws its lot. He is quiet. The vote is declared; he is still silent. The first class is called. Its vote is declared. Then, as is the usual course, the votes are announced. Then the second class. And all this is done faster than I have told it. When the business is over, that excellent augur (you would say he must be Caius Laelius,) says,—"We adjourn it to another day." Oh the monstrous impudence of such a proceeding! What had you seen? what had you perceived? what had you heard? For you did not say that you had been observing the heavens, and indeed you do not say so this day. That defect then has arisen, which you on the first of January had already foreseen would arise, and which you had predicted so long before. Therefore, in truth, you have made a false declaration respecting the auspices, to your own great misfortune, I hope, rather than to that of the republic. You laid the Roman people under the obligations of religion; you as augur interrupted an augur; you as consul interrupted a consul by a false declaration concerning the auspices.

I will say no more, lest I should seem to be pulling to pieces the acts of Dolabella; which must inevitably sometime or other be brought before our college. But take notice of the arrogance and insolence of the fellow. As long as you please, Dolabella is a consul irregularly elected; again, while you please, he is a consul elected with all proper regard to the auspices. If it means nothing when an augur gives this notice in those words in which you gave notice, then confess that you, when you said,—"We adjourn this to another day," were not sober. But if those words have any meaning, then I, an augur, demand of my colleague to know what that meaning is.

But lest by any chance, while enumerating his numerous exploits, our speech should pass over the finest action of Marcus Antonius, let us come to the Lupercalia.

XXXIV. He does not dissemble, O conscript fathers; it is plain that he is agitated; he perspires; he turns pale. Let him do what he pleases, provided he is not sick, and does not behave as he did in the Minucian colonnade. What defence can be made for such beastly behaviour? I wish to hear, that I may see the fruit of those high wages of that rhetorician, of that land given in Leontini. Your colleague was sitting in the rostra, clothed in purple robe, on a golden chair, wearing a crown. You mount the steps; you approach his chair; (if you were a priest of Pan, you ought to have recollected that you were consul too;) you display a diadem. There is a groan over the whole forum. Where did the diadem come from? For you had not picked it up when lying on the ground, but you had brought it from home with you, a premeditated and deliberately planned wickedness. You placed the diadem on his head amid the groans of the people; he rejected it amid great applause. You then alone, O wicked man, were found, both to advise the assumption of kingly power, and to wish to have him for your master who was your colleague; and also to try what the Roman people might be able to bear and to endure. Moreover, you even sought to move his pity; you threw yourself at his feet as a suppliant; begging for what? to be a slave? You might beg it for yourself, when you had lived in such a way from the time that you were a boy that you could bear everything, and would find no difficulty in being a slave; but certainly you had no commission from the Roman people to try for such a thing for them.

Oh how splendid was that eloquence of yours, when you harangued the people stark naked! What could be more foul than this? more shameful than this? more deserving of every sort of punishment? Are you waiting for me to prick you more? This that I am saying must tear you and bring blood enough if you have any feeling at all. I am afraid that I may be detracting from the glory of some most eminent men. Still my indignation shall find a voice. What can be more scandalous than for that man to live who placed a diadem on a man's head, when every one confesses that that man was deservedly slain who rejected it? And, moreover, he caused it to be recorded in the annals, under the head of Lupercalia, "That Marcus Antonius, the consul, by command of the people, had offered the kingdom to Caius Caesar, perpetual dictator; and that Caesar had refused to accept it." I now am not much surprised at your seeking to disturb the general tranquillity; at your hating not only the city but the light of day; and at your living with a pack of abandoned robbers, disregarding the day, and yet regarding nothing beyond the day.

For where can you be safe in peace? What place can there be for you where laws and courts of justice have sway, both of which you, as far as in you lay, destroyed by the substitution of kingly power? Was it for this that Lucius Tarquinius was driven out; that Spurius Cassius, and Spurius Maelius, and Marcus Manlius were slain; that many years afterwards a king might be established at Rome by Marcus Antonius, though the bare idea was impiety? However, let us return to the auspices.

XXXV. With respect to all the things which Caesar was intending to do in the senate on the ides of March, I ask whether you have done anything? I heard, indeed, that you had come down prepared, because you thought that I intended to speak about your having made a false statement respecting the auspices, though it was still necessary for us to respect them. The fortune of the Roman people saved us from that day. Did the death of Caesar also put an end to your opinion respecting the auspices? But I have come to mention that occasion which must be allowed to precede those matters which I had begun to discuss. What a flight was that of yours! What alarm was yours on that memorable day! How, from the consciousness of your wickedness, did you despair of your life! How, while flying, were you enabled secretly to get home by the kindness of those men who wished to save you, thinking you would show more sense than you do! O how vain have at all times been my too true predictions of the future! I told those deliverers of ours in the Capitol, when they wished me to go to you to exhort you to defend the republic, that as long as you were in fear you would promise everything, but that as soon as you had emancipated yourself from alarm you would be yourself again. Therefore, while the rest of the men of consular rank were going backwards and forwards to you, I adhered to my opinion, nor did I see you at all that day, or the next; nor did I think it possible for an alliance between virtuous citizens and a most unprincipled enemy to be made, so as to last, by any treaty or engagement whatever. The third day I came into the temple of Tellus, even then very much against my will, as armed men were blockading all the approaches. What a day was that for you, O Marcus Antonius! Although you showed yourself all on a sudden an enemy to me; still I pity you for having envied yourself.

XXXVI. What a man, O ye immortal gods! and how great a man might you have been, if you had been able to preserve the inclination you displayed that day;—we should still have peace which was made then by the pledge of a hostage, a boy of noble birth, the grandson of Marcus Bambalio. Although it was fear that was then making you a good citizen, which is never a lasting teacher of duty; your own audacity, which never departs from you as long as you are free from fear, has made you a worthless one. Although even at that time, when they thought you an excellent man, though I indeed differed from that opinion, you behaved with the greatest wickedness while presiding at the funeral of the tyrant, if that ought to be called a funeral. All that fine panegyric was yours, that commiseration was yours, that exhortation was yours. It was you—you, I say—who hurled those firebrands, both those with which your friend himself was nearly burnt, and those by which the house of Lucius Bellienus was set on fire and destroyed. It was you who let loose those attacks of abandoned men, slaves for the most part, which we repelled by violence and our own personal exertions; it was you who set them on to attack our houses. And yet you, as if you had wiped off all the soot and smoke in the ensuing days, carried those excellent resolutions in the Capitol, that no document conferring any exemption, or granting any favour, should be published after the ides of March. You recollect yourself, what you said about the exiles; you know what you said about the exemption; but the best thing of all was, that you for ever abolished the name of the dictatorship in the republic. Which act appeared to show that you had conceived such a hatred of kingly power that you took away all fear of it for the future, on account of him who had been the last dictator.

To other men the republic now seemed established, but it did not appear so at all to me, as I was afraid of every sort of shipwreck, as long as you were at the helm. Have I been deceived? or, was it possible for that man long to continue unlike himself? While you were all looking on, documents were fixed up over the whole Capitol, and exemptions were being sold, not merely to individuals, but to entire states. The freedom of the city was also being given now not to single persons only, but to whole provinces. Therefore, if these acts are to stand,—and stand they cannot if the republic stands too,—then, O conscript fathers, you have lost whole provinces; and not the revenues only, but the actual empire of the Roman people has been diminished by a market this man held in his own house.

XXXVII. Where are the seven hundred millions of sesterces which were entered in the account-books which are in the temple of Ops? a sum lamentable indeed, as to the means by which it was procured, but still one which, if it were not restored to those to whom it belonged, might save us from taxes. And how was it, that when you owed forty millions of sesterces on the fifteenth of March, you had ceased to owe them by the first of April? Those things are quite countless which were purchased of different people, not without your knowledge; but there was one excellent decree posted up in the Capitol affecting king Deiotarus, a most devoted friend to the Roman people. And when that decree was posted up, there was no one who, amid all his indignation, could restrain his laughter. For who ever was a more bitter enemy to another than Caesar was to Deiotarus? He was as hostile to him as he was to this order, to the equestrian order, to the people of Massilia, and to all men whom he knew to look on the republic of the Roman people with attachment. But this man, who neither present nor absent could ever obtain from him any favour or justice while he was alive, became quite an influential man with him when he was dead. When present with him in his house he had called for him though he was his host, he had made him give in his accounts of his revenue, he had exacted money from him; he had established one of his Greek retainers in his tetrarchy, and he had taken Armenia from him, which had been given to him by the senate. While he was alive he deprived him of all these things; now that he is dead, he gives them back again. And in what words? At one time he says, "that it appears to him to be just, …" at another, "that it appears not to be unjust…." What a strange combination of words! But while alive, (I know this, for I always supported Deiotarus, who was at a distance,) he never said that anything which we were asking for, for him, appeared just to him. A bond for ten millions of sesterces was entered into in the women's apartment, (where many things have been sold, and are still being sold,) by his ambassadors, well-meaning men, but timid and inexperienced in business, without my advice or that of the rest of the hereditary friends of the monarch. And I advise you to consider carefully what you intend to do with reference to this bond. For the king himself, of his own accord, without waiting for any of Caesar's memoranda, the moment that he heard of his death, recovered his own rights by his own courage and energy. He, like a wise man, knew that this was always the law, that those men from whom the things which tyrants had taken away had been taken, might recover them when the tyrants were slain. No lawyer, therefore, not even he who is your lawyer and yours alone, and by whose advice you do all these things, will say that anything is due to you by virtue of that bond for those things which had been recovered before that bond was executed. For he did not purchase them of you; but, before you undertook to sell him his own property, he had taken possession of it. He was a man—we, indeed, deserve to be despised, who hate the author of the actions, but uphold the actions themselves.

XXXVIII. Why need I mention the countless mass of papers, the innumerable autographs which have been brought forward? writings of which there are imitators who sell their forgeries as openly as if they were gladiators' playbills. Therefore, there are now such heaps of money piled up in that man's house, that it is weighed out instead of being counted. But how blind is avarice! Lately, too, a document has been posted up by which the most wealthy cities of the Cretans are released from tribute; and by which it is ordained that after the expiration of the consulship of Marcus Brutus, Crete shall cease to be a province. Are you in your senses? Ought you not to be put in confinement? Was it possible for there really to be a decree of Caesar's exempting Crete after the departure of Marcus Brutus, when Brutus had no connexion whatever with Crete while Caesar was alive? But by the sale of this decree (that you may not, O conscript fathers, think it wholly ineffectual) you have lost the province of Crete. There was nothing in the whole world which any one wanted to buy that this fellow was not ready to sell.

Caesar too, I suppose, made the law about the exiles which you have posted up. I do not wish to press upon any one in misfortune; I only complain, in the first place, that the return of those men has had discredit thrown upon it, whose cause Caesar judged to be different from that of the rest; and in the second place, I do not know why you do not mete out the same measure to all. For there can not be more than three or four left. Why do not they who are in similar misfortune enjoy a similar degree of your mercy? Why do you treat them as you treated your uncle? about whom you refused to pass a law when you were passing one about all the rest; and whom at the same time you encouraged to stand for the censorship, and instigated him to a canvass, which excited the ridicule and the complaint of every one.

But why did you not hold that comitia? Was it because a tribune of the people announced that there had been an ill-omened flash of lightning seen? When you have any interest of your own to serve, then auspices are all nothing; but when it is only your friends who are concerned, then you become scrupulous. What more? Did you not also desert him in the matter of the septemvirate? "Yes, for he interfered with me." What were you afraid of? I suppose you were afraid that you would be able to refuse him nothing if he were restored to the full possession of his rights. You loaded him with every species of insult, a man whom you ought to have considered in the place of a father to you, if you had had any piety or natural affection at all. You put away his daughter, your own cousin, having already looked out and provided yourself beforehand with another. That was not enough. You accused a most chaste woman of misconduct. What can go beyond this? Yet you were not content with this. In a very full senate held on the first of January, while your uncle was present, you dared to say that this was your reason for hatred of Dolabella, that you had ascertained that he had committed adultery with your cousin and your wife. Who can decide whether it was more shameless of you to make such profligate and such impious statements against that unhappy woman in the senate, or more wicked to make them against Dolabella, or more scandalous to make them in the presence of her father, or more cruel to make them at all?

XXXIX. However, let us return to the subject of Caesar's written papers. How were they verified by you? For the acts of Caesar were for peace's sake confirmed by the senate; that is to say, the acts which Caesar had really done, not those which Antonius said that Caesar had done. Where do all these come from? By whom are they produced and vouched for? If they are false, why are they ratified? If they are true, why are they sold? But the vote which was come to enjoined you, after the first of June, to make an examination of Caesar's acts with the assistance of a council. What council did you consult? Whom did you ever invite to help you? What was the first of June that you waited for? Was it that day on which you, having travelled all through the colonies where the veterans were settled, returned escorted by a band of armed men?

Oh what a splendid progress of yours was that in the months of April and May, when you attempted even to lead a colony to Capua! How you made your escape from thence, or rather how you barely made your escape, we all know. And now you are still threatening that city. I wish you would try, and we should not then be forced to say "barely." However, what a splendid progress of yours that was! Why need I mention your preparations for banquets, why your frantic hard-drinking? Those things are only an injury to yourself; these are injuries to us. We thought that a great blow was inflicted on the republic when the Campanian district was released from the payment of taxes, in order to be given to the soldiery; but you have divided it among your partners in drunkenness and gambling. I tell you, O conscript fathers, that a lot of buffoons and actresses have been settled in the district of Campania. Why should I now complain of what has been done in the district of Leontini? Although formerly these lands of Campania and Leontini were considered part of the patrimony of the Roman people, and were productive of great revenue, and very fertile. You gave your physician three thousand acres; what would you have done if he had cured you? and two thousand to your master of oratory; what would you have done if he had been able to make you eloquent? However, let us return to your progress, and to Italy.

XL. You led a colony to Casilinum, a place to which Caesar had previously led one. You did indeed consult me by letter about the colony of Capua, (but I should have given you the same answer about Casilinum,) whether you could legally lead a new colony to a place where there was a colony already. I said that a new colony could not be legally conducted to an existing colony, which had been established with a due observance of the auspices, as long as it remained in a flourishing state; but I wrote you word that new colonists might be enrolled among the old ones. But you, elated and insolent, disregarding all the respect due to the auspices, led a colony to Casilinum, whither one had been previously led a few years before; in order to erect your standard there, and to mark out the line of the new colony with a plough. And by that plough you almost grazed the gate of Capua, so as to diminish the territory of that flourishing colony. After this violation of all religious observances, you hasten off to the estate of Marcus Varro, a most conscientious and upright man, at Casinum. By what right? with what face do you do this? By just the same, you will say, as that by which you entered on the estates of the heirs of Lucius Rubrius, or of the heirs of Lucius Turselius, or on other innumerable possessions. If you got the right from any auction, let the auction have all the force to which it is entitled; let writings be of force, provided they are the writings of Caesar, and not your own; writings by which you are bound, not those by which you have released yourself from obligation.

But who says that the estate of Varro at Casinum was ever sold at all? who ever saw any notice of that auction? Who ever heard the voice of the auctioneer? You say that you sent a man to Alexandria to buy it of Caesar. It was too long to wait for Caesar himself to come! But whoever heard (and there was no man about whose safety more people were anxious) that any part whatever of Varro's property had been confiscated? What? what shall we say if Caesar even wrote you that you were to give it up? What can be said strong enough for such enormous impudence? Remove for a while those swords which we see around us. You shall now see that the cause of Caesar's auctions is one thing, and that of your confidence and rashness is another. For not only shall the owner drive you from that estate, but any one of his friends, or neighbours, or hereditary connexions, and any agent, will have the right to do so.

XLI. But how many days did he spend revelling in the most scandalous manner in that villa! From the third hour there was one scene of drinking, gambling, and vomiting. Alas for the unhappy house itself! how different a master from its former one has it fallen to the share of! Although, how is he the master at all? but still by how different a person has it been occupied! For Marcus Varro used it as a place of retirement for his studies, not as a theatre for his lusts. What noble discussions used to take place in that villa! what ideas were originated there! what writings were composed there! The laws of the Roman people, the memorials of our ancestors, the consideration of all wisdom, and all learning, were the topics that used to be dwelt on then;—but now, while you were the intruder there, (for I will not call you the master,) every place was resounding with the voices of drunken men; the pavements were floating with wine; the walls were dripping; nobly-born boys were mixing with the basest hirelings; prostitutes with mothers of families. Men came from Casinum, from Aquinum, from Interamna to salute him. No one was admitted. That, indeed, was proper. For the ordinary marks of respect were unsuited to the most profligate of men. When going from thence to Rome he approached Aquinum, a pretty numerous company (for it is a populous municipality) came out to meet him. But he was carried through the town in a covered litter, as if he had been dead. The people of Aquinum acted foolishly, no doubt; but still they were in his road. What did the people of Anagnia do? who, although they were out of his line of road, came down to meet him, in order to pay him their respects, as if he were consul. It is an incredible thing to say, but still it was only too notorious at the time, that he returned nobody's salutation; especially as he had two men of Anagnia with him, Mustela and Laco; one of whom had the care of his swords, and the other of his drinking cups.

Why should I mention the threats and insults with which he inveighed against the people of Teanum Sidicinum, with which he harassed the men of Puteoli, because they had adopted Caius Cassius and the Bruti as their patrons? a choice dictated, in truth, by great wisdom, and great zeal, benevolence, and affection for them; not by violence and force of arms, by which men have been compelled to choose you, and Basilus, and others like you both,—men whom no one would choose to have for his own clients, much less to be their client himself.

XLII. In the mean time, while you yourself were absent, what a day was that for your colleague when he overturned that tomb in the forum, which you were accustomed to regard with veneration! And when that action was announced to you, you—as is agreed upon by all who were with you at the time—fainted away. What happened afterwards I know not. I imagine that terror and arms got the mastery. At all events, you dragged your colleague down from his heaven; and you rendered him, not even now like yourself, but at all events very unlike his own former self.

After that what a return was that of yours to Rome! How great was the agitation of the whole city! We recollected Cinna being too powerful; after him we had seen Sylla with absolute authority, and we had lately beheld Caesar acting as king. There were perhaps swords, but they were sheathed, and they were not very numerous. But how great and how barbaric a procession is yours! Men follow you in battle array with drawn swords; we see whole litters full of shields borne along. And yet by custom, O conscript fathers, we have become inured and callous to these things. When on the first of June we wished to come to the senate, as it had been ordained, we were suddenly frightened and forced to flee. But he, as having no need of a senate, did not miss any of us, and rather rejoiced at our departure, and immediately proceeded to those marvellous exploits of his. He who had defended the memoranda of Caesar for the sake of his own profit, overturned the laws of Caesar—and good laws too—for the sake of being able to agitate the republic. He increased the number of years that magistrates were to enjoy their provinces; moreover, though he was bound to be the defender of the acts of Caesar, he rescinded them both with reference to public and private transactions.

In public transactions nothing is more authoritative than law; in private affairs the most valid of all deeds is a will. Of the laws, some he abolished without giving the least notice; others he gave notice of bills to abolish. Wills he annulled; though they have been at all times held sacred even in the case of the very meanest of the citizens. As for the statues and pictures which Caesar bequeathed to the people, together with his gardens, those he carried away, some to the house which belonged to Pompeius, and some to Scipio's villa.

XLIII. And are you then diligent in doing honour to Caesar's memory? Do you love him even now that he is dead? What greater honour had he obtained than that of having a holy cushion, an image, a temple, and a priest? As then Jupiter, and Mars, and Quirinus have priests, so Marcus Antonius is the priest of the god Julius. Why then do you delay? why are not you inaugurated? Choose a day; select some one to inaugurate you; we are colleagues; no one will refuse O you detestable man, whether you are the priest of a tyrant, or of a dead man! I ask you then, whether you are ignorant what day this is? Are you ignorant that yesterday was the fourth day of the Roman games in the Circus? and that you yourself submitted a motion to the people, that a fifth day should be added besides, in honour of Caesar? Why are we not all clad in the praetexta? Why are we permitting the honour which by your law was appointed for Caesar to be deserted? Had you no objection to so holy a day being polluted by the addition of supplications, while you did not choose it to be so by the addition of ceremonies connected with a sacred cushion? Either take away religion in every case, or preserve it in every case.

You will ask whether I approve of his having a sacred cushion, a temple and a priest? I approve of none of those things. But you, who are defending the acts of Caesar, what reason can you give for defending some, and disregarding others? unless, indeed, you choose to admit that you measure everything by your own gain, and not by his dignity. What will you now reply to these arguments?—(for I am waiting to witness your eloquence; I knew your grandfather, who was a most eloquent man, but I know you to be a more undisguised speaker than he was; he never harangued the people naked; but we have seen your breast, man, without disguise as you are.) Will you make any reply to these statements? will you dare to open your mouth at all? Can you find one single article in this long speech of mine, to which you trust that you can make any answer? However, we will say no more of what is past.

XLIV. But this single day, this very day that now is, this very moment while I am speaking, defend your conduct during this very moment, if you can. Why has the senate been surrounded with a belt of armed men? Why are your satellites listening to me sword in hand? Why are not the folding-doors of the temple of Concord open? Why do you bring men of all nations the most barbarous, Ityreans, armed with arrows, into the forum? He says, that he does so as a guard. Is it not then better to perish a thousand times than to be unable to live in one's own city without a guard of armed men? But believe me, there is no protection in that;—a man must be defended by the affection and good-will of his fellow citizens, not by arms. The Roman people will take them from you, will wrest them from your hands, I wish that they may do so while we are still safe. But however you treat us, as long as you adopt those counsels, it is impossible for you, believe me, to last long. In truth, that wife of yours, who is so far removed from covetousness, and whom I mention without intending any slight to her, has been too long owing her third payment to the state. The Roman people has men to whom it can entrust the helm of the state, and wherever they are, there is all the defence of the republic, or rather, there is the republic itself, which as yet has only avenged, but has not reestablished itself. Truly and surely has the republic most high born youths ready to defend it,—though they may for a time keep in the background from a desire for tranquillity, still they can be recalled by the republic at any time.

The name of peace is sweet, the thing itself is most salutary. But between peace and slavery there is a wide difference. Peace is liberty in tranquillity, slavery is the worst of all evils,—to be repelled, if need be, not only by war, but even by death. But if those deliverers of ours have taken themselves away out of our sight, still they have left behind the example of their conduct. They have done what no one else had done. Brutus pursued Tarquinius with war, who was a king when it was lawful for a king to exist in Rome. Spurius Cassius, Spurius Maelius, and Marcus Manlius were all slain because they were suspected of aiming at regal power. These are the first men who have ever ventured to attack, sword in hand, a man who was not aiming at regal power, but actually reigning. And their action is not only of itself a glorious and godlike exploit, but it is also one put forth for our imitation, especially since by it they have acquired such glory as appears hardly to be bounded by heaven itself. For although in the very consciousness of a glorious action there is a certain reward, still I do not consider immortality of glory a thing to be despised by one who is himself mortal.

XLV. Recollect then, O Marcus Antonius, that day on which you abolished the dictatorship. Set before you the joy of the senate and people of Rome, compare it with this infamous market held by you and by your friends, and then you will understand how great is the difference between praise and profit. But in truth, just as some people, through some disease which has blunted the senses, have no conception of the niceness of food, so men who are lustful, avaricious, and criminal, have no taste for true glory. But if praise cannot allure you to act rightly, still cannot even fear turn you away from the most shameful actions? You are not afraid of the courts of justice. If it is because you are innocent I praise you, if because you trust in your power of overbearing them by violence, are you ignorant of what that man has to fear, who on such an account as that does not fear the courts of justice?

But if you are not afraid of brave men and illustrious citizens, because they are prevented from attacking you by your armed retinue, still, believe me, your own fellows will not long endure you. And what a life is it, day and night to be fearing danger from one's own people! Unless, indeed, you have men who are bound to you by greater kindnesses than some of those men by whom he was slain were bound to Caesar, or unless there are points in which you can be compared with him.

In that man were combined genius, method, memory, literature, prudence, deliberation, and industry. He had performed exploits in war which, though calamitous for the republic, were nevertheless mighty deeds. Having for many years aimed at being a king, he had with great labour, and much personal danger, accomplished what he intended. He had conciliated the ignorant multitude by presents, by monuments, by largesses of food, and by banquets, he had bound his own party to him by rewards, his adversaries by the appearances of clemency. Why need I say much on such a subject? He had already brought a free city, partly by fear, partly by patience, into a habit of slavery.

XLVI. With him I can, indeed, compare you as to your desire to reign, but in all other respects you are in no degree to be compared to him. But from the many evils which by him have been burnt into the republic, there is still this good, that the Roman people has now learnt how much to believe every one, to whom to trust itself, and against whom to guard. Do you never think on these things? And do you not understand that it is enough for brave men to have learnt how noble a thing it is as to the act, how grateful it is as to the benefit done, how glorious as to the fame acquired, to slay a tyrant? When men could not bear him, do you think they will bear you? Believe me, the time will come when men will race with one another to do this deed, and when no one will wait for the tardy arrival of an opportunity.

Consider, I beg you, Marcus Antonius, do some time or other consider the republic: think of the family of which you are born, not of the men with whom you are living. Be reconciled to the republic. However, do you decide on your conduct. As to mine, I myself will declare what that shall be. I defended the republic as a young man, I will not abandon it now that I am old. I scorned the sword of Catiline, I will not quail before yours. No, I will rather cheerfully expose my own person, if the liberty of the city can be restored by my death.

May the indignation of the Roman people at last bring forth what it has been so long labouring with. In truth, if twenty years ago in this very temple I asserted that death could not come prematurely upon a man of consular rank, with how much more truth must I now say the same of an old man? To me, indeed, O conscript fathers, death is now even desirable, after all the honours which I have gained, and the deeds which I have done. I only pray for these two things: one, that dying I may leave the Roman people free. No greater boon than this can be granted me by the immortal gods. The other, that every one may meet with a fate suitable to his deserts and conduct towards the republic.

THE THIRD PHILIPPIC

THE ARGUMENT.

After the composition of the last speech, Octavius, considering that he had reason to be offended with Antonius, formed a plot for his assassination by means of some slaves, which however was discovered. In the mean time Antonius began to declare more and more openly against the conspirators. He erected a statue in the forum to Caesar, with the inscription, "To the most worthy Defender of his Country." Octavius at the same time was trying to win over the soldiers of his uncle Julius, and out-bidding Antonius in all his promises to them, so that he soon collected a formidable army of veterans. But as he had no public office to give him any colour for this conduct, he paid great court to the republican party, in hopes to get his proceedings authorized by the senate; and he kept continually pressing Cicero to return to Rome and support him. Cicero, however, for some time kept aloof, suspecting partly his abilities, on account of his exceeding youth, and partly his sincerity in reconciling himself to his uncle's murderers; however, at last he returned, after expressly stipulating that Octavius should employ all his forces in defence of Brutus and his accomplices.

Antonius left Rome about the end of September, in order to engage in his service four legions of Caesar's, which were on their return from Macedonia. But when they arrived at Brundusium three of them refused to follow him, on which he murdered all their centurions, to the number of three hundred, who were all put to death in his lodgings, in the sight of himself and Fulvia his wife, and then returned to Rome with the one legion which he had prevailed on; while the other three legions declared as yet for neither party. On his arrival in Rome he published many very violent edicts, and summoned the senate to meet on the twenty-fourth of October; then he adjourned it to the twenty-eighth; and a day or two before it met, he heard that two out of the three legions had declared for Octavius, and encamped at Alba. And this news alarmed him so much, that he abandoned his intention of proposing to the senate a decree to declare Octavius a public enemy, and after distributing some provinces among his friends, he put on his military robes, and left the city to take possession of Cisalpine Gaul, which had been assigned to him by a pretended law of the people, against the will of the senate.

On the news of his departure Cicero returned to Rome, where he arrived on the ninth of December. He immediately conferred with Pansa, one of the consuls elect, (Hirtius his colleague was ill,) as to the measures to be taken. He was again addressed with earnest solicitations by the friends of Octavius, who, to confirm his belief in his good intentions, allowed Casca, who had been one of the slayers of Caesar, and had himself given him the first blow, to enter on his office as tribune of the people on the tenth of December.

The new tribunes convoked the senate for the nineteenth, on which occasion Cicero had intended to be absent, but receiving the day before the edict of Decimus Brutus, by which he forbade Antonius to enter his province (immediately after the death of Caesar he had taken possession of Cisalpine Gaul, which had been conferred on him by Caesar), and declared that he would defend it against him by force and preserve it in its duty to the senate, he thought it necessary to procure for Brutus a resolution of the senate in his favour. He went down therefore very early, and, in a very full house, delivered the following speech.

I. We have been assembled at length, O conscript fathers, altogether later than the necessities of the republic required; but still we are assembled, a measure which I, indeed, have been every day demanding, inasmuch as I saw that a nefarious war against our altars and our hearths, against our lives and our fortunes was, I will not say being prepared, but being actually waged by a profligate and desperate man. People are waiting for the first of January. But Antonius is not waiting for that day, who is now attempting with an army to invade the province of Decimus Brutus, a most illustrious and excellent man. And when he has procured reinforcements and equipments there, he threatens that he will come to this city. What is the use then of waiting, or of even a delay for the very shortest time? For although the first of January is at hand, still a short time is a long one for people who are not prepared. For a day, or I should rather say an hour, often brings great disasters, if no precautions are taken. And it is not usual to wait for a fixed day for holding a council, as it is for celebrating a festival. But if the first of January had fallen on the day when Antonius first fled from the city, or if people had not waited for it, we should by this time have no war at all. For we should easily have crushed the audacity of that frantic man by the authority of the senate and the unanimity of the Roman people. And now, indeed, I feel confident that the consuls elect will do so, as soon as they enter on their magistracy. For they are men of the highest courage, of the most consummate wisdom, and they will act in perfect harmony with each other. But my exhortations to rapid and instant action are prompted by a desire not merely for victory, but for speedy victory.

For how long are we to trust to the prudence of an individual to repel so important, so cruel, and so nefarious a war? Why is not the public authority thrown into the scale as quickly as possible?

II. Caius Caesar, a young man, or, I should rather say, almost a boy, endued with an incredible and godlike degree of wisdom and valour, at the time when the frenzy of Antonius was at its height, and when his cruel and mischievous return from Brundusium was an object of apprehension to all, while we neither desired him to do so, nor thought of such a measure, nor ventured even to wish it, (because it did not seem practicable,) collected a most trustworthy army from the invincible body of veteran soldiers, and has spent his own patrimony in doing so. Although I have not used the expression which I ought,—for he has not spent it,—he has invested it in the safety of the republic.

And although it is not possible to requite him with all the thanks to which he is entitled, still we ought to feel all the gratitude towards him which our minds are capable of conceiving. For who is so ignorant of public affairs, so entirely indifferent to all thoughts of the republic, as not to see that, if Marcus Antonius could have come with those forces which he made sure that he should have, from Brundusium to Rome, as he threatened, there would have been no description of cruelty which he would not have practised? A man who in the house of his entertainer at Brundusium ordered so many most gallant men and virtuous citizens to be murdered, and whose wife's face was notoriously besprinkled with the blood of men dying at his and her feet. Who is there of us, or what good man is there at all, whom a man stained with this barbarity would ever have spared; especially as he was coming hither much more angry with all virtuous men than he had been with those whom he had massacred there? And from this calamity Caesar has delivered the republic by his own individual prudence, (and, indeed, there were no other means by which it could have been done.) And if he had not been born in this republic we should, owing to the wickedness of Antonius, now have no republic at all.

For this is what I believe, this is my deliberate opinion, that if that one young man had not checked the violence and inhuman projects of that frantic man, the republic would have been utterly destroyed. And to him we must, O conscript fathers, (for this is the first time, met in such a condition, that, owing to his good service, we are at liberty to say freely what we think and feel,) we must, I say, this day give authority, so that he may be able to defend the republic, not because that defence has been voluntarily undertaken by him but also because it has been entrusted to him by us.

III. Nor (since now after a long interval we are allowed to speak concerning the republic) is it possible for us to be silent about the Martial legion. For what single man has ever been braver, what single man has ever been more devoted to the republic than the whole of the Martial legion? which, as soon as it had decided that Marcus Antonius was an enemy of the Roman people, refused to be a companion of his insanity; deserted him though consul; which, in truth, it would not have done if it had considered him as consul, who, as it saw, was aiming at nothing and preparing nothing but the slaughter of the citizens, and the destruction of the state. And that legion has encamped at Alba. What city could it have selected either more suitable for enabling it to act, or more faithful, or full of more gallant men, or of citizens more devoted to the republic?

The fourth legion, imitating the virtue of this legion, under the leadership of Lucius Egnatuleius, the quaestor, a most virtuous and intrepid citizen, has also acknowledged the authority and joined the army of Caius Caesar.

We, therefore, O conscript fathers, must take care that those things which this most illustrious young man, this most excellent of all men has of his own accord done, and still is doing, be sanctioned by our authority; and the admirable unanimity of the veterans, those most brave men, and of the Martial and of the fourth legion, in their zeal for the reestablishment of the republic, be encouraged by our praise and commendation. And let us pledge ourselves this day that their advantage, and honours, and rewards shall be cared for by us as soon as the consuls elect have entered on their magistracy.

IV. And the things which I have said about Caesar and about his army, are, indeed, already well known to you. For by the admirable valour of Caesar, and by the firmness of the veteran soldiers, and by the admirable discernment of those legions which have followed our authority, and the liberty of the Roman people, and the valour of Caesar, Antonius has been repelled from his attempts upon our lives. But these things, as I have said, happened before; but this recent edict of Decimus Brutus, which has just been issued, can certainly not be passed over in silence. For he promises to preserve the province of Gaul in obedience to the senate and people of Rome. O citizen, born for the republic; mindful of the name he bears; imitator of his ancestors! Nor, indeed, was the acquisition of liberty so much an object of desire to our ancestors when Tarquinius was expelled, as, now that Antonius is driven away, the preservation of it is to us. Those men had learnt to obey kings ever since the foundation of the city, but we from the time when the kings were driven out have forgotten how to be slaves. And that Tarquinius, whom our ancestors expelled, was not either considered or called cruel or impious, but only The Proud. That vice which we have often borne in private individuals, our ancestors could not endure even in a king.

Lucius Brutus could not endure a proud king. Shall Decimus Brutus submit to the kingly power of a man who is wicked and impious? What atrocity did Tarquinius ever commit equal to the innumerable acts of the sort which Antonius has done and is still doing? Again, the kings were used to consult the senate; nor, as is the case when Antonius holds a senate, were armed barbarians ever introduced into the council of the king. The kings paid due regard to the auspices, which this man, though consul and augur, has neglected, not only by passing laws in opposition to the auspices, but also by making his colleague (whom he himself had appointed irregularly, and had falsified the auspices in order to do so) join in passing them. Again, what king was ever so preposterously impudent as to have all the profits, and kindnesses, and privileges of his kingdom on sale? But what immunity is there, what rights of citizenship, what rewards that this man has not sold to individuals, and to cities, and to entire provinces? We have never heard of anything base or sordid being imputed to Tarquinius. But at the house of this man gold was constantly being weighed out in the spinning room, and money was being paid, and in one single house every soul who had any interest in the business was selling the whole empire of the Roman people. We have never heard of any executions of Roman citizens by the orders of Tarquinius, but this man both at Suessa murdered the man whom he had thrown into prison, and at Brundusium massacred about three hundred most gallant men and most virtuous citizens. Lastly, Tarquinius was conducting a war in defence of the Roman people at the very time when he was expelled. Antonius was leading an army against the Roman people at the time when, being abandoned by the legions, he cowered at the name of Caesar and at his army, and neglecting the regular sacrifices, he offered up before daylight vows which he could never mean to perform, and at this very moment he is endeavouring to invade a province of the Roman people. The Roman people, therefore, has already received and is still looking for greater services at the hand of Decimus Brutus than our ancestors received from Lucius Brutus, the founder of this race and name which we ought to be so anxious to preserve.

V. But, while all slavery is miserable, to be slave to a man who is profligate, unchaste, effeminate, never, not even while in fear, sober, is surely intolerable. He, then, who keeps this man out of Gaul, especially by his own private authority, judges, and judges most truly, that he is not consul at all. We must take care, therefore, O conscript fathers, to sanction the private decision of Decimus Brutus by public authority. Nor, indeed, ought you to have thought Marcus Antonius consul at any time since the Lupercalia. For on the day when he, in the sight of the Roman people, harangued the mob, naked, perfumed, and drunk, and laboured moreover to put a crown on the head of his colleague, on that day he abdicated not only the consulship, but also his own freedom. At all events he himself must at once have become a slave, if Caesar had been willing to accept from him that ensign of royalty. Can I then think him a consul, can I think him a Roman citizen, can I think him a freeman, can I even think him a man, who on that shameful and wicked day showed what he was willing to endure while Caesar lived, and what he was anxious to obtain himself after he was dead?

Nor is it possible to pass over in silence the virtue and the firmness and the dignity of the province of Gaul. For that is the flower of Italy, that is the bulwark of the empire of the Roman people, that is the chief ornament of our dignity. But so perfect is the unanimity of the municipal towns and colonies of the province of Gaul, that all men in that district appear to have united together to defend the authority of this order, and the majesty of the Roman people. Wherefore, O tribunes of the people, although you have not actually brought any other business before us beyond the question of protection, in order that the consuls may be able to hold the senate with safety on the first of January, still you appear to me to have acted with great wisdom and great prudence in giving an opportunity of debating the general circumstances of the republic. For when you decided that the senate could not be held with safety without some protection or other, you at the same time asserted by that decision that the wickedness and audacity of Antonius was still continuing its practices within our walls.

VI. Wherefore, I will embrace every consideration in my opinion which I am now going to deliver, a course to which you, I feel sure, have no objection, in order that authority may be conferred by us on admirable generals, and that hope of reward may be held out by us to gallant soldiers, and that a formal decision may be come to, not by words only, but also by actions, that Antonius is not only not a consul, but is even an enemy. For if he be consul, then the legions which have deserted the consul deserve beating to death. Caesar is wicked, Brutus is impious, since they of their own heads have levied an army against the consul. But if new honours are to be sought out for the soldiers on account of their divine and immortal merits, and if it is quite impossible to show gratitude enough to the generals, who is there who must not think that man a public enemy, whose conduct is such that those who are in arms against him are considered the saviours of the republic?

Again, how insulting is he in his edicts! how ignorant! How like a barbarian! In the first place, how has he heaped abuse on Caesar, in terms drawn from his recollection of his own debauchery and profligacy. For where can we find any one who is chaster than this young man? who is more modest? where have we among our youth a more illustrious example of the old-fashioned strictness? Who, on the other hand, is more profligate than the man who abuses him? He reproaches the son of Caius Caesar with his want of noble blood, when even his natural father, if he had been alive, would have been made consul. His mother is a woman of Aricia. You might suppose he was saying a woman of Tralles, or of Ephesus. Just see how we all who come from the municipal towns—that is to say, absolutely all of us—are looked down upon; for how few of us are there who do not come from those towns? and what municipal town is there which he does not despise who looks with such contempt on Aricia; a town most ancient as to its antiquity; if we regard its rights, united with us by treaty; if we regard its vicinity, almost close to us; if we regard the high character of its inhabitants, most honourable? It is from Aricia that we have received the Voconian and Atinian laws; from Aricia have come many of those magistrates who have filled our curule chairs, both in our fathers' recollection and in our own; from Aricia have sprung many of the best and bravest of the Roman knights. But if you disapprove of a wife from Aricia, why do you approve of one from Tusculum? Although the father of this most virtuous and excellent woman, Marcus Atius Balbus, a man of the highest character, was a man of praetorian rank; but the father of your wife,—a good woman, at all events a rich one,—a fellow of the name of Bambalio, was a man of no account at all. Nothing could be lower than he was, a fellow who got his surname as a sort of insult, derived from the hesitation of his speech and the stolidity of his understanding. Oh, but your grandfather was nobly born. Yes, he was that Tuditanus who used to put on a cloak and buskins, and then go and scatter money from the rostra among the people. I wish he had bequeathed his contempt of money to his descendants! You have, indeed, a most glorious nobility of family! But how does it happen that the son of a woman of Aricia appears to you to be ignoble, when you are accustomed to boast of a descent on the mother's side which is precisely the same? Besides, what insanity is it for that man to say anything about the want of noble birth in men's wives, when his father married Numitoria of Fregellae, the daughter of a traitor, and when he himself has begotten children of the daughter of a freedman. However, those illustrious men Lucius Philippus, who has a wife who came from Aricia, and Caius Marcellus, whose wife is the daughter of an Arician, may look to this; and I am quite sure that they have no regrets on the score of the dignity of those admirable women.

VII. Moreover, Antonius proceeds to name Quintus Cicero, my brother's son, in his edict; and is so mad as not to perceive that the way in which he names him is a panegyric on him. For what could happen more desirable for this young man, than to be known by every one to be the partner of Caesar's counsels, and the enemy of the frenzy of Antonius? But this gladiator has dared to put in writing that he had designed the murder of his father and of his uncle. Oh the marvellous impudence, and audacity, and temerity of such an assertion! to dare to put this in writing against that young man, whom I and my brother, on account of his amiable manners, and pure character, and splendid abilities, vie with one another in loving, and to whom we incessantly devote our eyes, and ears, and affections! And as to me, he does not know whether he is injuring or praising me in those same edicts. When he threatens the most virtuous citizens with the same punishment which I inflicted on the most wicked and infamous of men, he seems to praise me as if he were desirous of copying me; but when he brings up again the memory of that most illustrious exploit, then he thinks that he is exciting some odium against me in the breasts of men like himself.

VIII. But what is it that he has done himself? When he had published all these edicts, he issued another, that the senate was to meet in a full house on the twenty-fourth of November. On that day he himself was not present. But what were the terms of his edict? These, I believe, are the exact words of the end of it: "If any one fails to attend, all men will be at liberty to think him the adviser of my destruction and of most ruinous counsels". What are ruinous counsels? those which relate to the recovery of the liberty of the Roman people? Of those counsels I confess that I have been and still am an adviser and prompter to Caesar. Although he did not stand in need of any one's advice, but still I spurned on the willing horse, as it is said. For what good man would not have advised putting you to death, when on your death depended the safety and life of every good man, and the liberty and dignity of the Roman people?

But when he had summoned us all by so severe an edict, why did he not attend himself? Do you suppose that he was detained by any melancholy or important occasion? He was detained drinking and feasting. If, indeed, it deserves to be called a feast, and not rather gluttony. He neglected to attend on the day mentioned in his edict, and he adjourned the meeting to the twenty-eighth. He then summoned us to attend in the Capitol, and at that temple he did arrive himself, coming up through some mine left by the Gauls. Men came, having been summoned, some of them indeed men of high distinction, but forgetful of what was due to their dignity. For the day was such, the report of the object of the meeting such, such too the man who had convened the senate, that it was discreditable for a senate to feel no fear for the result. And yet to those men who had assembled he did not dare to say a single word about Caesar, though he had made up his mind to submit a motion respecting him to the senate. There was a man of consular rank who had brought a resolution ready drawn up. Is it not now admitting that he is himself an enemy, when he does not dare to make a motion respecting a man who is leading an army against him while he is consul? For it is perfectly plain that one of the two must be an enemy, nor is it possible to come to a different decision respecting adverse generals. If then Caius Caesar be an enemy, why does the consul submit no motion to the senate? If he does not deserve to be branded by the senate, then what can the consul say, who, by his silence respecting him, has confessed that he himself is an enemy? In his edicts he styles him Spartacus, while in the senate he does not venture to call him even a bad citizen.

IX. But in the most melancholy circumstances what mirth does he not provoke? I have committed to memory some short phrases of one edict, which he appears to think particularly clever, but I have not as yet found any one who has understood what he intended by them. "That is no insult which a worthy man does." Now, in the first place, what is the meaning of "worthy?" For there are many men worthy of punishment, as he himself is. Does he mean what a man does who is invested with any dignity? if so, what insult can be greater? Moreover, what is the meaning of "doing an insult?" Who ever uses such an expression? Then comes, "Nor any fear which an enemy threatens" What then? is fear usually threatened by a friend? Then came many similar sentences. Is it not better to be dumb, than to say what no one can understand? Now see why his tutor, exchanging pleas for ploughs, has had given to him in the public domain of the Roman people two thousand acres of land in the Leontine district, exempt from all taxes, for making a stupid man still stupider at the public expense.

However, these perhaps are trifling matters. I ask now, why all on a sudden he became so gentle in the senate, after having been so fierce in his edicts? For what was the object of threatening Lucius Cassius, a most fearless tribune of the people, and a most virtuous and loyal citizen, with death if he came to the Senate? of expelling Decimus Caifulenus, a man thoroughly attached to the republic, from the senate by violence and threats of death? of interdicting Titus Canutius, by whom he had been repeatedly and deservedly harassed by most legitimate attacks, not only from the temple itself but from all approach to it? What was the resolution of the senate which he was afraid that they would stop by the interposition of their veto? That, I suppose, respecting the supplication in honour of Marcus Lepidus, a most illustrious man! Certainly there was a great danger of our hindering an ordinary compliment to a man on whom we were every day thinking of conferring some extraordinary honour. However, that he might not appear to have had no reason at all for ordering the senate to meet, he was on the point of bringing forward some motion about the republic, when the news about the fourth legion came; which entirely bewildered him, and hastening to flee away, he took a division on the resolution for decreeing this supplication, though such a proceeding had never been heard of before.

X. But what a setting out was his after this! what a journey when he was in his robe as a general! How did he shun all eyes, and the light of day, and the city, and the forum! How miserable was his flight! how shameful! how infamous! Splendid, too, were the decrees of the senate passed on the evening of that very day; very religiously solemn was the allotment of the provinces; and heavenly indeed was the opportunity, when everyone got exactly what he thought most desirable. You are acting admirably, therefore, O tribunes of the people, in bringing forward a motion about the protection of the senate and consuls, and most deservedly are we all bound to feel and to prove to you the greatest gratitude for your conduct. For how can we be free from fear and danger while menaced by such covetousness and audacity? And as for that ruined and desperate man, what more hostile decision can be passed upon him than has already been passed by his own friends? His most intimate friend, a man connected with me too, Lucius Lentulus, and also Publius Naso, a man destitute of covetousness, have shown that they think that they have no provinces assigned them, and that the allotments of Antonius are invalid. Lucius Philippus, a man thoroughly worthy of his father and grandfather and ancestors, has done the same. The same is the opinion of Marcus Turanius, a man of the greatest integrity and purity of life. The same is the conduct of Publius Oppius; and those very men,—who, influenced by their friendship for Marcus Antonius, have attributed to him more power than they would perhaps really approve of,—Marcus Piso, my own connexion, a most admirable man and virtuous citizen, and Marcus Vehilius, a man of equal respectability, have both declared that they would obey the authority of the senate. Why should I speak of Lucius Cinna? whose extraordinary integrity, proved under many trying circumstances, makes the glory of his present admirable conduct less remarkable; he has altogether disregarded the province assigned to him; and so has Caius Cestius, a man of great and firm mind.

Who are there left then to be delighted with this heavensent allotment? Lucius Antonius and Marcus Antonius! O happy pair! for there is nothing that they wished for more. Caius Antonius has Macedonia. Happy, too, is he! For he was constantly talking about this province. Caius Calvisius has Africa. Nothing could be more fortunate, for he had only just departed from Africa, and, as if he had divined that he should return, he left two lieutenants at Utica. Then Marcus Iccius has Sicily, and Quintus Cassius Spain. I do not know what to suspect. I fancy the lots which assigned these two provinces, were not quite so carefully attended to by the gods.

XI. O Caius Caesar, (I am speaking of the young man,) what safety have you brought to the republic! How unforeseen has it been! how sudden! for if he did these things when flying, what would he have done when he was pursuing? In truth, he had said in a harangue that he would be the guardian of the city; and that he would keep his army at the gates of the city till the first of May. What a fine guardian (as the proverb goes) is the wolf of the sheep! Would Antonius have been a guardian of the city, or its plunderer and destroyer? And he said too that he would come into the city and go out as he pleased. What more need I say? Did he not say, in the hearing of all the people, while sitting in front of the temple of Castor, that no one should remain alive but the conqueror?

On this day, O conscript fathers, for the first time after a long interval do we plant our foot and take possession of liberty. Liberty, of which, as long as I could be, I was not only the defender, but even the saviour. But when I could not be so, I rested; and I bore the misfortunes and misery of that period without abjectness, and not without some dignity. But as for this most foul monster, who could endure him, or how could any one endure him? What is there in Antonius except lust, and cruelty, and wantonness, and audacity? Of these materials he is wholly made up. There is in him nothing ingenuous, nothing moderate, nothing modest, nothing virtuous. Wherefore, since the matter has come to such a crisis that the question is whether he is to make atonement to the republic for his crimes, or we are to become slaves, let us at last, I beseech you, by the immortal gods, O conscript fathers, adopt our fathers' courage, and our fathers' virtue, so as either to recover the liberty belonging to the Roman name and race, or else to prefer death to slavery. We have borne and endured many things which ought not to be endured in a free city, some of us out of a hope of recovering our freedom, some from too great a fondness for life. But if we have submitted to these things, which necessity and a sort of force which may seem almost to have been put on us by destiny have compelled us to endure, though, in point of fact, we have not endured them, are we also to bear with the most shameful and inhuman tyranny of this profligate robber?

XII. What will he do in his passion, if ever he has the power, who, when he is not able to show his anger against any one, has been the enemy of all good men? What will he not dare to do when victorious, who, without having gained any victory, has committed such crimes as these since the death of Caesar? has emptied his well filled house? has pillaged his gardens? has transferred to his own mansion all their ornaments? has sought to make his death a pretext for slaughter and conflagration? who, while he has carried two or three resolutions of the senate which have been advantageous to the republic, has made everything else subservient to his own acquisition of gain and plunder? who has put up exemptions and annuities to sale? who has released cities from obligations? who has removed whole provinces from subjection to the Roman empire? who has restored exiles? who has passed forged laws in the name of Caesar, and has continued to have forged decrees engraved on brass and fixed up in the Capitol, and has set up in his own house a domestic market for all things of that sort? who has imposed laws on the Roman people? and who, with armed troops and guards, has excluded both the people and the magistrates from the forum? who has filled the senate with armed men? and has introduced armed men into the temple of Concord when he was holding a senate there? who ran down to Brundusium to meet the legions, and then murdered all the centurions in them who were well affected to the republic? who endeavoured to come to Rome with his army to accomplish our massacre and the utter destruction of the city?

And he, now that he has been prevented from succeeding in this attempt by the wisdom and forces of Caesar, and the unanimity of the veterans, and the valour of the legions, even now that his fortunes are desperate, does not diminish his audacity, nor, mad that he is, does he cease proceeding in his headlong career of fury. He is leading his mutilated army into Gaul, with one legion, and that too wavering in its fidelity to him, he is waiting for his brother Lucius, as he cannot find any one more nearly like himself than him. But now what slaughter is this man, who has thus become a captain instead of a matador, a general instead of a gladiator, making, wherever he sets his foot! He destroys stores, he slays the flocks and herds, and all the cattle, wherever he finds them, his soldiers revel in their spoil, and he himself, in order to imitate his brother, drowns himself in wine. Fields are laid waste, villas are plundered, matrons, virgins, well born boys are carried off and given up to the soldiery, and Marcus Antonius has done exactly the same wherever he has led his army.

XIII. Will you open your gates to these most infamous brothers? will you ever admit them into the city? will you not rather, now that the opportunity is offered to you, now that you have generals ready, and the minds of the soldiers eager for the service, and all the Roman people unanimous, and all Italy excited with the desire to recover its liberty,—will you not, I say, avail yourself of the kindness of the immortal gods? You will never have an opportunity if you neglect this one. He will be hemmed in in the rear, in the front, and in flank, if he once enters Gaul. Nor must he be attacked by arms alone, but by our decrees also. Mighty is the authority, mighty is the name of the senate when all its members are inspired by one and the same resolution. Do you not see how the forum is crowded? how the Roman people is on tiptoe with the hope of recovering its liberty? which now, beholding us, after a long interval, meeting here in numbers, hopes too that we are also met in freedom. It was in expectation of this day that I avoided the wicked army of Marcus Antonius, at a time when he, while inveighing against me, was not aware for what an occasion I was reserving myself and my strength. If at that time I had chosen to reply to him, while he was seeking to begin the massacre with me, I should not now be able to consult the welfare of the republic. But now that I have this opportunity, I will never, O conscript fathers, neither by day nor by night, cease considering what ought to be thought concerning the liberty of the Roman people, and concerning your dignity. And whatever ought to be planned or done, I not only will never shrink from, but I will offer myself for, and beg to have entrusted to me. This is what I did before while it was in my power; when it was no longer in my power to do so, I did nothing. But now it is not only in my power, but it is absolutely necessary for me, unless we prefer being slaves to fighting with all our strength and courage to avoid being slaves.

The immortal gods have given us these protectors, Caesar for the city, Brutus for Gaul. For if he had been able to oppress the city we must have become slaves at once; if he had been able to get possession of Gaul, then it would not have been long before every good man must have perished and all the rest have been enslaved.

XIV. Now then that this opportunity is afforded to you, O conscript fathers, I entreat you in the name of the immortal gods, seize upon it; and recollect at last that you are the chief men of the most honourable council on the whole face of the earth. Give a token to the Roman people that your wisdom shall not fail the republic, since that too professes that its valour shall never desert it either. There is no need for my warning you: there is no one so foolish as not to perceive that if we go to sleep over this opportunity we shall have to endure a tyranny which will be not only cruel and haughty, but also ignominious and flagitious. You know the insolence of Antonius; you know his friends; you know his whole household. To be slaves to lustful, wanton, debauched, profligate, drunken gamblers, is the extremity of misery combined with the extremity of infamy. And if now (but may the immortal gods avert the omen!) that worst of fates shall befall the republic, then, as brave gladiators take care to perish with honour, let us too, who are the chief men of all countries and nations, take care to fall with dignity rather than to live as slaves with ignominy.

There is nothing more detestable than disgrace; nothing more shameful than slavery. We have been born to glory and to liberty; let us either preserve them or die with dignity. Too long have we concealed what we have felt: now at length it is revealed: every one has plainly shown what are his feelings to both sides, and what are his inclinations. There are impious citizens, measured by the love I bear my country, too many; but in proportion to the multitude of well-affected ones, very few; and the immortal gods have given the republic an incredible opportunity and chance for destroying them. For, in addition to the defences which we already have, there will soon be added consuls of consummate prudence, and virtue, and concord, who have already deliberated and pondered for many months on the freedom of the Roman people. With these men for our advisers and leaders, with the gods assisting us, with ourselves using all vigilance and taking great precautions for the future, and with the Roman people acting with unanimity, we shall indeed be free in a short time, and the recollection of our present slavery will make liberty sweeter.

XV. Moved by these considerations, since the tribunes of the people have brought forward a motion to ensure that the senate shall be able to meet in safety on the first of January, and that we may be able to deliver our sentiments on the general welfare of the state with freedom, I give my vote that Caius Pansa and Aulus Hirtius, the consuls elect, do take care that the senate be enabled to meet in safety on the first of January; and, as an edict has been published by Decimus Brutus, imperator and consul elect, I vote that the senate thinks that Decimus Brutus, imperator and consul, deserves excellently well of the republic, inasmuch as he is upholding the authority of the senate, and the freedom and empire of the Roman people; and as he is also retaining the province of Gallia Citerior, a province full of most virtuous and brave men, and of citizens most devoted to the republic, and his army, in obedience to the senate, I vote that the senate judges that he, and his army, and the municipalities and colonies of the province of Gaul, have acted and are acting properly, and regularly, and in a manner advantageous to the republic. And the senate thinks that it will be for the general interests of the republic that the provinces which are at present occupied by Decimus Brutus and by Lucius Plancus, both imperators, and consuls elect, and also by the officers who are in command of provinces, shall continue to be held by them in accordance with the provisions of the Julian law, until each of these officers has a successor appointed by a resolution of the senate; and that they shall take care to maintain those provinces and armies in obedience to the senate and people of Rome, and as a defence to the republic. And since, by the exertions and valour and wisdom of Caius Caesar, and by the admirable unanimity of the veteran soldiers, who, obeying his authority, have been and are a protection to the republic, the Roman people has been defended, and is at this present time being defended, from the most serious dangers. And as the Martial legion has encamped at Alba, in a municipal town of the greatest loyalty and courage, and has devoted itself to the support of the authority of the senate, and of the freedom of the Roman people; and as the fourth legion, behaving with equal wisdom and with the same virtue, under the command of Lucius Egnatuleius the quaestor, an illustrious citizen, has defended and is still defending the authority of the senate and the freedom of the Roman people; I give my vote, That it is and shall be an object of anxious care to the senate to pay due honour and to show due gratitude to them for their exceeding services to the republic: and that the senate hereby orders that when Caius Pausa and Aulus Hirtius, the consuls elect, have entered on their office, they take the earliest opportunity of consulting this body on these matters, as shall seem to them expedient for the republic, and worthy of their own integrity and loyalty.

THE FOURTH PHILIPPIC

THE ARGUMENT.

After delivering the preceding speech in the senate, Cicero proceeded to the forum, where he delivered the following speech to the people, to give them information of what had been done.

I. The great numbers in which you are here met this day, O Romans, and this assembly, greater than, it seems to me, I ever remember, inspires me with both an exceeding eagerness to defend the republic, and with a great hope of reestablishing it. Although my courage indeed has never failed; what has been unfavourable is the time; and the moment that that has appeared to show any dawn of light, I at once have been the leader in the defence of your liberty. And if I had attempted to have done so before, I should not be able to do so now. For this day, O Romans, (that you may not think it is but a trifling business in which we have been engaged,) the foundations have been laid for future actions. For the senate has no longer been content with styling Antonius an enemy in words, but it has shown by actions that it thinks him one. And now I am much more elated still, because you too with such great unanimity and with such a clamour have sanctioned our declaration that he is an enemy.

And indeed, O Romans, it is impossible but that either the men must be impious who have levied armies against the consul, or else that he must be an enemy against whom they have rightly taken arms. And this doubt the senate has this day removed—not indeed that there really was any; but it has prevented the possibility of there being any. Caius Caesar, who has upheld and who is still upholding the republic and your freedom by his seal and wisdom, and at the expense of his patrimonial estate, has been complimented with the highest praises of the senate. I praise you,—yes, I praise you greatly, O Romans, when you follow with the most grateful minds the name of that most illustrious youth, or rather boy; for his actions belong to immortality, the name of youth only to his age. I can recollect many things; I have heard of many things; I have read of many things; but in the whole history of the whole world I have never known anything like this. For, when we were weighed down with slavery, when the evil was daily increasing, when we had no defence, while we were in dread of the pernicious and fatal return of Marcus Antonius from Brundusium, this young man adopted the design which none of us had ventured to hope for, which beyond all question none of us were acquainted with, of raising an invincible army of his father's soldiers, and so hindering the frenzy of Antonius, spurred on as it was by the most inhuman counsels, from the power of doing mischief to the republic.

II. For who is there who does not see clearly that, if Caesar had not prepared an army, the return of Antonius must have been accompanied by our destruction? For, in truth, he returned in such a state of mind, burning with hatred of you all, stained with the blood of the Roman citizens, whom he had murdered at Suessa and at Brundusium, that he thought of nothing but the utter destruction of the republic. And what protection could have been found for your safety and for your liberty if the army of Caius Caesar had not been composed of the bravest of his father's soldiers? And with respect to his praises and honours,—and he is entitled to divine and everlasting honours for his godlike and undying services,—the senate has just consented to my proposals, and has decreed that a motion be submitted to it at the very earliest opportunity.

Now who is there who does not see that by this decree Antonius has been adjudged to be an enemy? For what else can we call him, when the senate decides that extraordinary honours are to be devised for those men who are leading armies against him? What? did not the Martial legion (which appears to me by some divine permission to have derived its name from that god from whom we have heard that the Roman people descended) decide by its resolutions that Antonius was an enemy before the senate had come to any resolution? For if he be not an enemy, we must inevitably decide that those men who have deserted the consul are enemies. Admirably and seasonably, O Romans, have you by your cries sanctioned the noble conduct of the men of the Martial legion, who have come over to the authority of the senate, to your liberty, and to the whole republic; and have abandoned that enemy and robber and parricide of his country. Nor did they display only their spirit and courage in doing this, but their caution and wisdom also. They encamped at Alba, in a city convenient, fortified, near, full of brave men and loyal and virtuous citizens. The fourth legion imitating the virtue of this Martial legion, under the leadership of Lucius Egnatuleius, whom the senate deservedly praised a little while ago, has also joined the army of Caius Caesar.

III. What more adverse decisions, O Marcus Antonius, can you want? Caesar, who has levied an army against you, is extolled to the skies. The legions are praised in the most complimentary language, which have abandoned you, which were sent for into Italy by you; and which, if you had chosen to be a consul rather than an enemy, were wholly devoted to you. And the fearless and honest decision of those legions is confirmed by the senate, is approved of by the whole Roman people,—unless, indeed, you to-day, O Romans, decide that Antonius is a consul and not an enemy. I thought, O Romans, that you did think as you show you do. What? do you suppose that the municipal towns, and the colonies, and the prefectures have any other opinion? All men are agreed with one mind; so that every one who wishes the state to be saved must take up every sort of arms against that pestilence. What? does, I should like to know, does the opinion of Decimus Brutus, O Romans, which you can gather from his edict, which has this day reached us, appear to any one deserving of being lightly esteemed? Rightly and truly do you say No, O Romans. For the family and name of Brutus has been by some especial kindness and liberality of the immortal gods given to the republic, for the purpose of at one time establishing, and at another of recovering, the liberty of the Roman people. What then has been the opinion which Decimus Brutus has formed of Marcus Antonius? He excludes him from his province. He opposes him with his army. He rouses all Gaul to war, which is already used of its own accord, and in consequence of the judgment which it has itself formed. If Antonius be consul, Brutus is an enemy. Can we then doubt which of these alternatives is the fact?

IV. And just as you now with one mind and one voice affirm that you entertain no doubt, so did the senate just now decree that Decimus Brutus deserved excellently well of the republic, inasmuch as he was defending the authority of the senate and the liberty and empire of the Roman people. Defending it against whom? Why, against an enemy. For what other sort of defence deserves praise? In the next place the province of Gaul is praised, and is deservedly complimented in most honourable language by the senate for resisting Antonius. But if that province considered him the consul, and still refused to receive him, it would be guilty of great wickedness. For all the provinces belong to the consul of right, and are bound to obey him. Decimus Brutus, imperator and consul elect, a citizen born for the republic, denies that he is consul; Gaul denies it; all Italy denies it; the senate denies it; you deny it. Who then think that he is consul except a few robbers? Although even they themselves do not believe what they say; nor is it possible that they should differ from the judgment of all men, impious and desperate men though they be. But the hope of plunder and booty blinds their minds; men whom no gifts of money, no allotment of land, nor even that interminable auction has satisfied; who have proposed to themselves the city, the properties and fortunes of all the citizens as their booty; and who, as long as there is something for them to seize and carry off, think that nothing will be wanting to them; among whom Marcus Antonius (O ye immortal gods, avert, I pray you, and efface this omen,) has promised to divide this city. May things rather happen, O Romans, as you pray that they should, and may the chastisement of this frenzy fall on him and on his friend. And, indeed, I feel sure that it will be so. For I think that at present not only men but the immortal gods have all united together to preserve this republic. For if the immortal gods foreshow us the future, by means of portents and prodigies, then it has been openly revealed to us that punishment is near at hand to him, and liberty to us. Or if it was impossible for such unanimity on the part of all men to exist without the inspiration of the gods, in either case how can we doubt as to the inclinations of the heavenly deities? It only remains, O Romans, for you to persevere in the sentiments which you at present display.

V. I will act, therefore, as commanders are in the habit of doing when their army is ready for battle, who, although they see their soldiers ready to engage, still address an exhortation to them; and in like manner I will exhort you who are already eager and burning to recover your liberty. You have not—you have not, indeed, O Romans, to war against an enemy with whom it is possible to make peace on any terms whatever. For he does not now desire your slavery, as he did before, but he is angry now and thirsts for your blood. No sport appears more delightful to him than bloodshed, and slaughter, and the massacre of citizens before his eyes. You have not, O Romans, to deal with a wicked and profligate man, but with an unnatural and savage beast. And, since he has fallen into a well, let him be buried in it. For if he escapes out of it, there will be no inhumanity of torture which it will be possible to avoid. But he is at present hemmed in, pressed, and besieged by those troops which we already have, and will soon be still more so by those which in a few days the new consuls will levy. Apply yourselves then to this business, as you are doing. Never have you shown greater unanimity in any cause; never have you been so cordially united with the senate. And no wonder. For the question now is not in what condition we are to live, but whether we are to live at all, or to perish with torture and ignominy.

Although nature, indeed, has appointed death for all men: but valour is accustomed to ward off any cruelty or disgrace in death. And that is an inalienable possession of the Roman race and name. Preserve, I beseech you, O Romans, this attribute which your ancestors have left you as a sort of inheritance. Although all other things are uncertain, fleeting, transitory; virtue alone is planted firm with very deep roots; it cannot be undermined by any violence; it can never be moved from its position. By it your ancestors first subdued the whole of Italy; then destroyed Carthage, overthrew Numantia, and reduced the most mighty kings and most warlike nations under the dominion of this empire.

VI. And your ancestors, O Romans, had to deal with an enemy who had also a republic, a senate-house, a treasury, harmonious and united citizens, and with whom, if fortune had so willed it, there might have been peace and treaties on settled principles. But this enemy of yours is attacking your republic, but has none himself; is eager to destroy the senate, that is to say, the council of the whole world, but has no public council himself; he has exhausted your treasury, and has none of his own. For how can a man be supported by the unanimity of his citizens, who has no city at all? And what principles of peace can there be with that man who is full of incredible cruelty, and destitute of faith?

The whole then of the contest, O Romans, which is now before the Roman people, the conqueror of all nations, is with an assassin, a robber, a Spartacus. For as to his habitual boast of being like Catilina, he is equal to him in wickedness, but inferior in energy. He, though he had no army, rapidly levied one. This man has lost that very army which he had. As, therefore, by my diligence, and the authority of the senate, and your own zeal and valour, you crushed Catilina, so you will very soon hear that this infamous piratical enterprise of Antonius has been put down by your own perfect and unexampled harmony with the senate, and by the good fortune and valour of your armies and generals. I, for my part, as far as I am able to labour, and to effect anything by my care, and exertions, and vigilance, and authority, and counsel, will omit nothing which I may think serviceable to your liberty. Nor could I omit it without wickedness after all your most ample and honourable kindness to me. However, on this day, encouraged by the motion of a most gallant man, and one most firmly attached to you, Marcus Servilius, whom you see before you, and his colleagues also, most distinguished men, and most virtuous citizens; and partly, too, by my advice and my example, we have, for the first time after a long interval, fired up again with a hope of liberty.

THE FIFTH PHILIPPIC

THE ARGUMENT.

The new consuls Hirtius and Pansa were much attached to Cicero, had consulted him a great deal, and professed great respect for his opinion; but they were also under great obligations to Julius Caesar and, consequently, connected to some extent with his party and with Antonius, on which account they wished, if possible, to employ moderate measures only against him.

As soon as they had entered on their office, they convoked the senate to meet for the purpose of deliberating on the general welfare of the republic. They both spoke themselves with great firmness, promising to be the leaders in defending the liberties of Rome, and exhorting the senate to act with courage. And then they called on Quintus Fufius Calenus, who had been consul A.U.C. 707, and who was Pansa's father-in-law, to deliver his opinion first. He was known to be a firm friend of Antonius. Cicero wished to declare Antonius a public enemy at once, but Calenus proposed that before they proceeded to acts of open hostility against him, they should send an embassy to him to admonish him to desist from his attempts upon Gaul, and to submit to the authority of the senate. Piso and others supported this motion, on the ground that it was cruel and unjust to condemn a man without giving him a fair chance of submitting, and without hearing what he had to say. It was in opposition to Calenus's motion that Cicero made the following speech, substituting for his proposition one to declare Antonius an enemy, and to offer pardon to those of his army who returned to their duty by the first of February, to thank Decimus Brutus for his conduct in Gaul, to decree a statue to Marcus Lepidus for his services to the republic and his loyalty, to thank Caius Caesar (Octavius) and to grant him a special commission as general, to make him a senator and propraetor and to enable him to stand for any subsequent magistracy as if he had been quaestor, to thank Lucius Egnatuleius, and to vote thanks and promise rewards to the Martial and the fourth legion.

I. Nothing, O conscript fathers, has ever seemed to me longer than these calends of January, and I think that for the last few days you have all been feeling the same thing. For those who are waging war against the republic have not waited for this day. But we, while it would have been most especially proper for us to come to the aid of the general safety with our counsel, were not summoned to the senate. However, the speech just addressed to us by the consuls has removed our complaints as to what is past, for they have spoken in such a manner that the calends of January seem to have been long wished for rather than really to have arrived late.

And while the speeches of the consuls have encouraged my mind, and have given me a hope, not only of preserving our safety, but even of recovering our former dignity, on the other hand, the opinion of the man who has been asked for his opinion first would have disturbed me, if I had not confidence in your virtue and firmness. For this day, O conscript fathers, has dawned upon you, and this opportunity has been afforded you of proving to the Roman people how much virtue, how much firmness and how much dignity exists in the counsels of this order. Recollect what a day it was thirteen days ago, how great was then your unanimity, and virtue, and firmness, and what great praise, what great glory, and what great gratitude you gained from the Roman people. And on that day, O conscript fathers, you resolved that no other alternative was in your power, except either an honourable peace, or a necessary war.

Is Marcus Antonius desirous of peace? Let him lay down his arms, let him implore our pardon, let him deprecate our vengeance; he will find no one more reasonable than me, though, while seeking to recommend himself to impious citizens, he has chosen to be an enemy instead of a friend to me. There is, in truth, nothing which can be given to him while waging war, there will perhaps be something which may be granted to him if he comes before us as a suppliant.

II. But to send ambassadors to a man respecting whom you passed a most dignified and severe decision only thirteen days ago, is not an act of lenity, but, if I am to speak my real opinion, of downright madness. In the first place, you praised those generals who, of their own head, had undertaken war against him, in the next place, you praised the veterans who, though they had been settled in those colonies by Antonius, preferred the liberty of the Roman people to the obligations which they were under to him. Is it not so? Why was the Martial legion? why was the fourth legion praised? For if they have deserted the consul, they ought to be blamed; if they have abandoned an enemy to the republic, then they are deservedly praised.

But as at that time you had not yet got any consuls, you passed a decree that a motion concerning the rewards for the soldiers and the honours to be conferred on the generals should be submitted to you at the earliest opportunity. Are you then going now to arrange rewards for those men who have taken arms against Antonius, and to send ambassadors to Antonius? so as to deserve to be ashamed that the legions should have come to more honourable resolutions than the senate if, indeed, the legions have resolved to defend the senate against Antonius, but the senate decrees to send ambassadors to Antonius. Is this encouraging the spirit of the soldiers, or damping their virtue?

This is what we have gained in the last twelve days, that the man whom no single person except Cotyla was then found to defend, has now advocates even of consular rank. Would that they had all been asked their opinion before me, (although I have my suspicions as to what some of those men who will be asked after me, are intending to say) I should find it easier to speak against them if any argument appeared to have been advanced.

For there is an opinion in some quarters that some one intends to propose to decree Antonius that further Gaul, which Plancus is at present in possession of. What else is that but supplying an enemy with all the arms necessary for civil war; first of all with the sinews of war, money in abundance, of which he is at present destitute, and secondly, with as much cavalry as he pleases? Cavalry do I say? He is a likely man to hesitate, I suppose, to bring with him the barbarian nations,—a man who does not see this is senseless, he who does see it, and still advocates such a measure, is impious. Will you furnish a wicked and desperate citizen with an army of Gauls and Germans, with money, and infantry, and cavalry, and all sorts of resources? All these excuses are no excuse at all.—"He is a friend of mine." Let him first be a friend of his country.— "He is a relation of mine." Can any relationship be nearer than that of one's country, in which even one's parents are comprised? "He has given me money:"—I should like to see the man who will dare to say that. But when I have explained what is the real object aimed at, it will be easy for you to decide which opinion you ought to agree with and adopt.

III. The matter at issue is, whether power is to be given to Marcus Antonius of oppressing the republic, of massacring the virtuous citizens, of plundering the city, of distributing the lands among his robbers, of overwhelming the Roman people in slavery; or, whether he is not to be allowed to do all this. Do you doubt what you are to do? "Oh, but all this does not apply to Antonius." Even Cotyla would not venture to say that. For what does not apply to him? A man who, while he says that he is defending the acts of another, perverts all those laws of his which we might most properly praise. Caesar wished to drain the marshes: this man has given all Italy to that moderate man Lucius Antonius to distribute.—What? has the Roman people adopted this law?—What? could it be passed with a proper regard for the auspices? But this conscientious augur acts in reference to the auspices without his colleagues. Although those auspices do not require any interpretation;—for who is there who is ignorant that it is impious to submit any motion to the people while it is thundering? The tribunes of the people carried laws respecting the provinces in opposition to the acts of Caesar; Caesar had extended the provisions of his law over two years; Antonius over six years. Has then the Roman people adopted this law? What? was it ever regularly promulgated? What? was it not passed before it was even drawn up? Did we not see the deed done before we even suspected that it was going to be done? Where is the Caecilian and Didian law? What is become of the law that such bills should be published on three market days? What is become of the penalty appointed by the recent Junian and Licinian law? Can these laws be ratified without the destruction of all other laws? Has any one had a right of entering the forum? Moreover, what thunder, and what a storm that was! so that even if the consideration of the auspices had no weight with Marcus Antonius, it would seem strange that he could endure and bear such exceeding violence of tempest, and rain, and whirlwind. When therefore he, as augur, says that he carried a law while Jupiter was not only thundering, but almost uttering an express prohibition of it by his clamour from heaven, will he hesitate to confess that it was carried in violation of the auspices? What? does the virtuous augur think that it has nothing to do with the auspices, that he carried the law with the aid of that colleague whose election he himself vitiated by giving notice of the auspices?

IV. But perhaps we, who are his colleagues, may be the interpreters of the auspices? Do we also want interpreters of arms? In the first place, all the approaches to the forum were so fenced round, that even if no armed men were standing in the way, still it would have been impossible to enter the forum except by tearing down the barricades. But the guards were arranged in such a manner, that, as the access of an enemy to a city is prevented, so you might in this instance see the burgesses and the tribunes of the people cut off by forts and works from all entrance to the forum. On which account I give my vote that those laws which Marcus Antonius is said to have carried were all carried by violence, and in violation of the auspices; and that the people is not bound by them. If Marcus Antonius is said to have carried any law about confirming the acts of Caesar and abolishing the dictatorship for ever, and of leading colonies into any lands, then I vote that those laws be passed over again, with a due regard to the auspices, so that they may bind the people. For although they may be good measures which he passed irregularly and by violence, still they are not to be accounted laws, and the whole audacity of this frantic gladiator must be repudiated by our authority. But that squandering of the public money cannot possibly be endured by which he got rid of seven hundred millions of sesterces by forged entries and deeds of gifts, so that it seems an absolute miracle that so vast a sum of money belonging to the Roman people can have disappeared in so short a time. What? are those enormous profits to be endured which the household of Marcus Antonius has swallowed up? He was continually selling forged decrees; ordering the names of kingdoms and states, and grants of exemptions to be engraved on brass, having received bribes for such orders. And his statement always was, that he was doing these things in obedience to the memoranda of Caesar, of which he himself was the author. In the interior of his house there was going on a brisk market of the whole republic. His wife, more fortunate for herself than for her husband, was holding an auction of kingdoms and provinces: exiles were restored without any law, as if by law: and unless all these acts are rescinded by the authority of the senate, now that we have again arrived at a hope of recovering the republic, there will be no likeness of a free city left to us.

Nor is it only by the sale of forged memoranda and autographs that a countless sum of money was collected together in that house, while Antonius, whatever he sold, said that he was acting in obedience to the papers of Caesar; but he even took bribes to make false entries of the resolutions of the senate; to seal forged contracts; and resolutions of the senate that had never been passed were entered on the records of that treasury. Of all this baseness even foreign nations were witnesses. In the meantime treaties were made; kingdoms given away; nations and provinces released from the burdens of the state; and false memorials of all these transactions were fixed up all over the Capitol, amid the groans of the Roman people. And by all these proceedings so vast a sum of money was collected in one house, that if it were all made available, the Roman people would never want money again.

V. Moreover, he passed a law to regulate judicial proceedings, this chaste and upright man, this upholder of the tribunals and the law. And in this he deceived us. He used to say that he appointed men from the front ranks of the army, common soldiers, men of the Alauda, as judges. But he has in reality selected gamesters; he has selected exiles; he has selected Greeks. Oh the fine bench of judges! Oh the admirable dignity of that council! I do long to plead in behalf of some defendant before that tribunal—Cyda of Crete; a prodigy even in that island; the most audacious and abandoned of men. But even suppose he were not so. Does he understand Latin? Is he qualified by birth and station to be a judge? Does he—which is most important—does he know anything about our laws and manners? Is he even acquainted with any of the citizens? Why, Crete is better known to you than Rome is to Cyda. In fact, the selection and appointment of the judges has usually been confined to our own citizens. But who ever knew, or could possibly have known this Gortynian judge? For Lysiades, the Athenian, we most of us do know. For he is the son of Phaedrus, an eminent philosopher. And, besides, he is a witty man, so that he will be able to get on very well with Marcus Curius, who will be one of his colleagues, and with whom he is in the habit of playing. I ask if Lysiades, when summoned as a judge, should not answer to his name, and should have an excuse alleged for him that he is an Areopagite, and that he is not bound to act as a judge at both Rome and Athens at the same time, will the man who presides over the investigation admit the excuse of this Greekling judge, at one time a Greek, and at another a Roman? Or will he disregard the most ancient laws of the Athenians?

And what a bench will it be, O ye good gods! A Cretan judge, and he the most worthless of men. Whom can a defendant employ to propitiate him? How is he to get at him? He comes of a hard nation. But the Athenians are merciful. I dare say that Curius, too, is not cruel, inasmuch as he is a man who is himself at the mercy of fortune every day. There are besides other chosen judges who will perhaps be excused. For they have a legitimate excuse, that they have left their country in banishment, and that they have not been restored since. And would that madman have chosen these men as judges, would he have entered their names as such in the treasury, would he have trusted a great portion of the republic to them, if he had intended to leave the least semblance of a republic?

VI. And I have been speaking of those judges who are known. Those whom you are less acquainted with I have been unwilling to name. Know then that dancers, harp-players, the whole troop, in fact, of Antonius's revellers, have all been pitchforked into the third decury of judges. Now you see the object of passing so splendid and admirable a law, amid excessive rain, storm, wind, tempest, and whirlwind, amid thunder and lightning; it was that we might have those men for our judges whom no one would like to have for guests. It is the enormity of his wickedness, the consciousness of his crimes, the plunder of that money of which the account was kept in the temple of Ops, which have been the real inventors of this third decury. And infamous judges were not sought for, till all hope of safety for the guilty was despaired of, if they came before respectable ones. But what must have been the impudence, what must have been the iniquity of a man who dared to select those men as judges, by the selection of whom a double disgrace was stamped on the republic: one, because the judges were so infamous; the other, because by this step it was revealed and published to the world how many infamous citizens we had in the republic? These then, and all other similar laws, I should vote ought to be annulled, even if they had been passed without violence, and with all proper respect for the auspices. But now why need I vote that they ought to be annulled, when I do not consider that they were ever legally passed?

Is not this, too, to be marked with the deepest ignominy, and with the severest animadversion of this order, so as to be recollected by all posterity, that Marcus Antonius (the first man who has ever done so since the foundation of the city) has openly taken armed men about with him in this city? A thing which the kings never did, nor those men who, since the kings have been banished, have endeavoured to seize on kingly power. I can recollect Cinna; I have seen Sylla; and lately Caesar. For these three men are the only ones since the city was delivered by Lucius Brutus, who have had more power than the entire republic. I cannot assert that no man in their trains had weapons. This I do say, that they had not many, and that they concealed them. But this pest was attended by an army of armed men. Classitius, Mustela, and Tiro, openly displaying their swords, led troops of fellows like themselves through the forum. Barbarian archers occupied their regular place in the army. And when they arrived at the temple of Concord, the steps were crowded, the litters full of shields were arranged; not because he wished the shields to be concealed, but that his friends might not be fatigued by carrying the shields themselves.

VII. And what was most infamous not only to see, but even to hear of, armed men, robbers, assassins were stationed in the temple of Concord; the temple was turned into a prison; the doors of the temple were closed, and the conscript fathers delivered their opinions while robbers were standing among the benches of the senators. And if I did not come to a senate-house in this state, he, on the first of September, said that he would send carpenters and pull down my house. It was an important affair, I suppose, that was to be discussed. He made some motion about a supplication. I attended the day after. He himself did not come. I delivered my opinion about the republic, not indeed with quite so much freedom as usual, but still with more than the threats of personal danger to myself made perhaps advisable. But that violent and furious man (for Lucius Piso had done the same thing with great credit thirty days before) threatened me with his enmity, and ordered me to attend the senate on the nineteenth of September. In the meantime he spent the whole of the intervening seventeen days in the villa of Scipio, at Tibur, declaiming against me to make himself thirsty. For this is his usual object in declaiming. When the day arrived on which he had ordered me to attend, then he came with a regular army in battle array to the temple of Concord, and out of his impure mouth vomited forth an oration against me in my absence. On which day, if my friends had not prevented me from attending the senate as I was anxious to do, he would have begun a massacre by the slaughter of me. For that was what he had resolved to do. And when once he had dyed his sword in blood, nothing would have made him leave off but pure fatigue and satiety. In truth, his brother, Lucius Antonius, was present, an Asiatic gladiator, who had fought as a Mirmillo, at Mylasa; he was thirsting for my blood, and had shed much of his own in that gladiatorial combat. He was now valuing our property in his mind, taking notice of our possessions in the city and in the country; his indigence united with his covetousness was threatening all our fortunes; he was distributing our lands to whomsoever and in whatever shares he pleased; no private individual could get access to him, or find any means to propitiate him, and induce him to act with justice. Every former proprietor had just so much property as Antonius left him after the division of his estate. And although all these proceedings cannot be ratified, if you annul his laws, still I think that they ought all to be separately taken note of, article by article; and that we ought formally to decide that the appointment of septemvirs was null and void; and that nothing is ratified which is said to have been done by them.

VIII. But who is there who can consider Marcus Antonius a citizen, rather than a most foul and barbarous enemy, who, while sitting in front of the temple of Castor, in the hearing of the Roman people, said that no one should survive except those who were victorious? Do you suppose, O conscript fathers, that he spoke with more violence than he would act? And what are we to think of his having ventured to say that, after he had given up his magistracy, he should still be at the city with his army? that he should enter the city as often as he pleased? What else was this but threatening the Roman people with slavery? And what was the object of his journey to Brundusium? and of that great haste? What was his hope, except to lead that vast army to the city, or rather into the city? What a proceeding was that selection of the centurions! What unbridled fury of an intemperate mind! For when those gallant legions had raised an outcry against his promises, he ordered those centurions to come to him to his house, whom he perceived to be loyally attached to the republic, and then he had them all murdered before his own eyes and those of his wife, whom this noble commander had taken with him to the army. What disposition do you suppose that this man will display towards us whom he hates, when he was so cruel to those men whom he had never seen? And how covetous will he be with respect to the money of rich men, when he thirsted for even the blood of poor men? whose property, such as it was, he immediately divided among his satellites and boon companions.

And he in a fury was now moving his hostile standards against his country from Brundusium, when Caius Caesar, by the kind inspiration of the immortal gods, by the greatness of his own heavenly courage, and wisdom, and genius, of his own accord, indeed, and prompted by his own admirable virtue, but still with the approbation of my authority, went down to the colonies which had been founded by his father; convoked the veteran soldiery; in a few days raised an army; and checked the furious advance of this bandit. But after the Martial legion saw this admirable leader, it had no other thoughts but those of securing our liberty. And the fourth legion followed its example.

IX. And Antonius, on hearing of this news, after he had summoned the senate, and provided a man of consular rank to declare his opinion that Caius Caesar was an enemy of his country, immediately fainted away. And afterwards, without either performing the usual sacrifices, or offering the customary vows, he, I will not say went forth, but took to flight in his robe as a general. But which way did he flee? To the province of our most resolute and bravest citizens; men who could never have endured him if he had not come bringing war in his train, an intemperate, passionate, insolent, proud man, always making demands, always plundering, always drunk. But he, whose worthlessness even when quiet was more than any one could endure, has declared war upon the province of Gaul; he is besieging Mutina, a valiant and splendid colony of the Roman people; he is blockading Decimus Brutus, the general, the consul elect, a citizen born not for himself, but for us and the republic. Was then Hannibal an enemy, and is Antonius a citizen? What did the one do like an enemy, that the other has not done, or is not doing, or planning, and thinking of? What was there in the whole of the journey of the Antonii; except depopulation, devastation, slaughter, and rapine? Actions which Hannibal never did, because he was reserving many things for his own use, these men do, as men who live merely for the present hour; they never have given a thought not only to the fortunes and welfare of the citizens, but not even to their own advantage.

Are we then, O ye good gods, to resolve to send ambassadors to this man? Are those men who propose this acquainted with the constitution of the republic, with the laws of war, with the precedents of our ancestors? Do they give a thought to what the majesty of the Roman people and the severity of the senate requires? Do you resolve to send ambassadors? If to beg his mercy, he will despise you; if to declare your commands he will not listen to them; and last of all, however severe the message may be which we give the ambassadors, the very name of ambassadors will extinguish this ardour of the Roman people which we see at present, and break the spirit of the municipal towns and of Italy. To say nothing of these arguments, though they are weighty, at all events that sending of an embassy will cause delay and slowness to the war. Although those who propose it should say, as I hear that some intend to say,—"Let the ambassadors go, but let war be prepared for all the same." Still the very name of ambassadors will damp men's courage, and delay the rapidity of the war.

X. The most important events, O conscript fathers, are often determined by very trivial moving influences in every circumstance that can happen in the republic, and also in war, and especially in civil war, which is usually governed a great deal by men's opinions and by reports. No one will ask what is the commission with which we have sent the ambassadors; the mere name of an embassy, and that sent by us of our own accord, will appear an indication of fear. Let him depart from Mutina; let him cease to attack Brutus; let him retire from Gaul. He must not be begged in words to do so; he must be compelled by arms. For we are not sending to Hannibal to desire him to retire from before Saguntum; to whom the senate formerly sent Publius Valerius Flaccus and Quintus Baebius Tampilus; who, if Hannibal did not comply, were ordered to proceed to Carthage. Whither do we order our ambassadors to proceed, if Antonius does not comply? Are we sending an embassy to our own citizen, to beg him not to attack a general and a colony of the Roman people? Is it so? Is it becoming to us to beg this by means of ambassadors? What is the difference, in the name of the immortal gods, whether he attacks this city itself, or whether he attacks an outpost of this city, a colony of the Roman people, established for the sake of its being a bulwark and protection to us? The siege of Saguntum was the cause of the second Punic war, which Hannibal carried on against our ancestors. It was quite right to send ambassadors to him. They were sent to a Carthaginian, they were sent on behalf of those who were the enemies of Hannibal, and our allies. What is there resembling that case here? We are sending to one of our own citizens to beg him not to blockade a general of the Roman army, not to attack our army and our colony,—in short, not to be an enemy of ours. Come; suppose he obeys, shall we either be inclined, or shall we be able by any possibility, to treat him as one of our citizens?

XI. On the nineteenth of December, you overwhelmed him with your decrees; you ordained that this motion should be submitted to you on the first of January, which you see is submitted now, respecting the honours and rewards to be conferred on those who have deserved or do deserve well of the republic. And the chief of those men you have adjudged to be the man who really has done so, Caius Caesar, who had diverted the nefarious attacks of Marcus Antonius against this city, and compelled him to direct them against Gaul; and next to him you consider the veteran soldiers who first followed Caesar; then those excellent and heavenly-minded legions the Martial and the fourth, to whom you have promised honours and rewards, for having not only abandoned their consul, but for having even declared war against him. And on the same day, having a decree brought before you and published on purpose, you praised the conduct of Decimus Brutus, a most excellent citizen, and sanctioned with your public authority this war which he had undertaken of his own head.

What else, then, did you do on that day except pronounce Antonius a public enemy? After these decrees of yours, will it be possible for him to look upon you with equanimity, or for you to behold him without the most excessive indignation? He has been excluded and cut off and wholly separated from the republic, not merely by his own wickedness, as it seems to me, but by some especial good fortune of the republic. And if he should comply with the demands of the ambassadors and return to Rome, do you suppose that abandoned citizens will ever be in need of a standard around which to rally? But this is not what I am so much afraid of. There are other things which I am more apprehensive of and more alarmed at. He never will comply with the demands of the ambassadors. I know the man's insanity and arrogance; I know the desperate counsels of his friends, to which he is wholly given up. Lucius his brother, as being a man who has fought abroad, leads on his household. Even suppose him to be in his senses himself, which he never will be; still he will not be allowed by these men to act as if he were so. In the mean time, time will be wasted. The preparations for war will cool. How is it that the war has been protracted as long as this, if it be not by procrastination and delay?

From the very first moment after the departure, or rather after the hopeless flight of that bandit, that the senate could have met in freedom, I have always been demanding that we should be called together. The first day that we were called together, when the consuls elect were not present, I laid, in my opinion, amid the greatest unanimity on your part, the foundations of the republic, later, indeed, than they should have been laid, for I could not do so before, but still if no time had been lost after that day, we should have no war at all now. Every evil is easily crushed at its birth, when it has become of long standing, it usually gets stronger. But then everybody was waiting for the first of January, perhaps not very wisely.

XII However, let us say no more of what is past. Are we still to allow any further delay while the ambassadors are on their road to him? and while they are coming back again? and the time spent in waiting for them will make men doubt about the war. And while the fact of the war is in doubt, how can men possibly be zealous about the levies for the army?

Wherefore, O conscript fathers, I give my vote that there should be no mention made of ambassadors I think that the business that is to be done must be done without any delay, and instantly. I say that it is necessary that we should decree that there is sedition abroad, that we should suspend the regular courts of justice, order all men to wear the garb of war, and enlist men in all quarters, suspending all exemptions from military service in the city and in all Italy, except in Gaul. And if this be done, the general opinion and report of your severity will overwhelm the insanity of that wicked gladiator. He will feel that he has undertaken a war against the republic, he will experience the sinews and vigour of a unanimous senate For at present he is constantly saying that it is a mere struggle between parties. Between what parties? One party is defeated, the other is the heart of Caius Caesar's party. Unless, indeed, we believe that the party of Caesar is attacked by Pansa and Hirtius the consuls, and by Caius Caesar's son. But this war has been kindled, not by a struggle between parties, but by the nefarious hopes of the most abandoned citizens, by whom all our estates and properties have been marked down, and already distributed according as every one has thought them desirable.

I have read the letter of Antonius which he sent to one of the septemviri, a thoroughpaced scoundrel, a colleague of his own, "Look out, and see what you take a fancy to, what you do fancy you shall certainly have". See to what a man we are sending ambassadors, against what a man we are delaying to make war, a man who does not even let us draw lots for our fortunes, but hands us over to each man's caprice in such a way, that he has not left even himself anything untouched, or which has not been promised to somebody. With this man, O conscript fathers, we must wage war,—war, I say, and that instantly. We must reject the slow proceedings of ambassadors.

Therefore, that we may not have a number of decrees to pass every day, I give my vote that the whole republic should be committed to the consuls, and that they should have a charge given them to defend the republic, and to take care "that the republic suffer no injury." And I give my vote that those men who are in the army of Antonius be not visited with blame, if they leave him before the first of February.

If you adopt these proposals of mine, O conscript fathers, you will in a short time recover the liberty of the Roman people and our own authority. But if you act with more mildness, still you will pass those resolutions, but perhaps you will pass them too late. As to the general welfare of the republic, on which you, O consuls, have consulted us, I think that I have proposed what is sufficient.

XIII. The next question is about honours. And to this point I perceive that I must speak next. But I will preserve the same order in paying respect to brave men, that is usually preserved in asking their opinions.

Let us, therefore, according to the usages of our ancestors, begin with Brutus, the consul elect, and, to say nothing of his former conduct,—which has indeed been most admirable, but still such as has been praised by the individual judgments of men, rather than by public authority,—what words can we find adequate to his praise at this very time? For such great virtue requires no reward except this one of praise and glory; and even if it were not to receive that, still it would be content with itself, and would rejoice at being laid up in the recollection of grateful citizens, as if it were placed in the full light. The praise then of our deliberate opinion, and of our testimony in his favour, must be given to Brutus. Therefore, O conscript fathers, I give my vote that a resolution of the senate be passed in these words:

"As Decimus Brutus, imperator, consul elect is maintaining the province of Gaul in obedience to the senate and people of Rome, and as he has enlisted and collected in so short a time a very numerous army, being aided by the admirable zeal of the municipal towns and colonies of the province of Gaul, which has deserved and still does deserve admirably well of the republic, he has acted rightly and virtuously, and greatly for the advantage of the republic. And that most excellent service done by Decimus Brutus to the republic, is and always will be grateful to the senate and people of Rome. Therefore, the senate and the Roman people is of opinion that the exertions, and prudence, and virtue of Decimus Brutus, imperator and consul elect, and the incredible zeal and unanimity of the province of Gaul, have been a great assistance to the republic, at a most critical time."

What honour, O conscript fathers, can be too great to be due to such a mighty service as this of Brutus, and to such important aid as he has afforded the republic? For if Gaul had been open to Marcus Antonius—if after having overwhelmed the municipal towns and colonies unprepared to resist him, he had been able to penetrate into that further Gaul—what great danger would have hung over the republic! That most insane of men, that man so headlong and furious in all his courses, would have been likely, I suppose, to hesitate at waging war against us, not only with his own army, but with all the savage troops of barbarism, so that even the wall of the Alps would not have enabled us to check his frenzy. These thanks then will be deservedly paid to Decimus Brutus, who, before any authority of yours had been interposed, acting on his own judgment and responsibility, refused to receive him as consul, but repelled him from Gaul as an enemy, and preferred to be besieged himself rather than to allow this city to be so. Let him therefore have, by your decree, an everlasting testimony to this most important and glorious action, and let Gaul, which always is and has been a protection to this empire and to the general liberty, be deservedly and truly praised for not having surrendered herself and her power to Antonius, but for having opposed him with them.

XIV. And, furthermore, I give my vote that the most ample honours be decreed to Marcus Lepidus, as a reward for his eminent services to the republic. He has at all times wished the Roman people to be free, and he gave the greatest proof of his inclination and opinion on that day, when, while Antonius was placing the diadem on Caesar's head, he turned his face away, and by his groans and sorrow showed plainly what a hatred of slavery he had, how desirous he was for the Roman people to be free, and how he had endured those things which he had endured more because of the necessity of the times, than because they harmonised with his sentiments. And who of us can forget with what great moderation he behaved during that crisis of the city which ensued after the death of Caesar? These are great merits, but I hasten to speak of greater still. For, (O ye immortal gods!) what could happen more to be admired by foreign nations or more to be desired by the Roman people, than, at a time when there was a most important civil war, the result of which we were all dreading, that it should be extinguished by prudence rather than that arms and violence should be able to put everything to the hazard of a battle? And if Caesar had been guided by the same principles in that odious and miserable war, we should have—to say nothing of their father—the two sons of Cnaeus Pompeius, that most illustrious and virtuous man, safe among us, men whose piety and filial affection certainly ought not to have been their ruin. Would that Marcus Lepidus had been able to save them all! He showed that he would have done so, by his conduct in cases where he had the power, when he restored Sextus Pompeius to the state, a great ornament to the republic, and a most illustrious monument of his clemency. Sad was that picture, melancholy was the destiny then of the Roman people. For after Pompeius the father was dead, he who was the light of the Roman people, the son too, who was wholly like his father, was also slain. But all these calamities appear to me to have been effaced by the kindness of the immortal gods, Sextus Pompeius being preserved to the republic.

XV. For which cause, reasonable and important as it is and because Marcus Lepidus, by his humanity and wisdom, has changed a most dangerous and extensive civil war into peace and concord, I give my vote, that a resolution of the senate be drawn up in these words:

"Since the affairs of the republic have repeatedly been well and prosperously conducted by Marcus Lepidus, imperator, and Pontifex Maximus, and since the Roman people is fully aware that kingly power is very displeasing to him; and since by his exertions, and virtue, and prudence, and singular clemency and humanity, a most bitter civil war has been extinguished; and Sextus Pompeius Magnus, the son of Cnaeus, having submitted to the authority of this order and laid down his arms, and, in accordance with the perfect good-will of the senate and people of Rome, has been restored to the state by Marcus Lepidus, imperator, and Pontifex Maximus; the senate and people of Rome, in return for the important and numerous services of Marcus Lepidus to the republic, declares that it places great hopes of future tranquillity and peace and concord, in his virtue, authority, and good fortune; and the senate and people of Rome will ever remember his services to the republic; and it is decreed by the vote of this order, That a gilt equestrian statue be erected to him in the Rostra, or in whatever other place in the forum he pleases."

And this honour, O conscript fathers, appears to me a very great one, in the first place, because it is just;—for it is not merely given on account of our hopes of the future, but it is paid, as it were, in requital of his ample services already done. Nor are we able to mention any instance of this honour having been conferred on any one by the senate by their own free and voluntary judgment before.

XVI. I come now to Caius Caesar, O conscript fathers; if he had not existed, which of us could have been alive now? That most intemperate of men, Antonius, was flying from Brundusium to the city, burning with hatred, with a disposition hostile to all good men, with an army. What was there to oppose to his audacity and wickedness? We had not as yet any generals, or any forces. There was no public council, no liberty; our necks were at the mercy of his nefarious cruelty; we were all preparing to have recourse to flight, though flight itself had no escape for us. Who was it—what god was it, who at that time gave to the Roman people this godlike young man, who, while every means for completing our destruction seemed open to that most pernicious citizen, rising up on a sudden, beyond every one's hope, completed an army fit to oppose to the fury of Marcus Antonius before any one suspected that he was thinking of any such step? Great honours were paid to Cnaeus Pompeius when he was a young man, and deservedly; for he came to the assistance of the republic; but he was of a more vigorous age, and more calculated to meet the eager requirements of soldiers seeking a general. He had also been already trained in other kinds of war. For the cause of Sylla was not agreeable to all men. The multitude of the proscribed, and the enormous calamities that fell on so many municipal towns, show this plainly. But Caesar, though many years younger, armed veterans who were now eager to rest; he has embraced that cause which was most agreeable to the senate, to the people, to all Italy,—in short, to gods and men. And Pompeius came as a reinforcement to the extensive command and victorious army of Lucius Sylla; Caesar had no one to join himself to. He, of his own accord, was the author and executor of his plan of levying an army, and arraying a defence for us. Pompeius found the whole Picene district hostile to the party of his adversaries; but Caesar has levied an army against Antonius from men who were Antonius's own friends, but still greater friends to liberty. It was owing to the influence of Pompeius that Sylla was enabled to act like a king. It is by the protection afforded us by Caesar that the tyranny of Antonius has been put down.

Let us then confer on Caesar a regular military command, without which the military affairs cannot be directed, the army cannot be held together, war cannot be waged. Let him be made proprietor with all the privileges which have ever been attached to that appointment. That honour, although it is a great one for a man of his age, still is not merely of influence as giving dignity, but it confers powers calculated to meet the present emergency. Therefore, let us seek for honours for him which we shall not easily find at the present day.

XVII. But I hope that we and the Roman people shall often have an opportunity of complimenting and honouring this young man. But at the present moment I give my vote that we should pass a decree in this form:

"As Caius Caesar, the son of Caius, Pontiff and Propraetor, has at a most critical period of the republic exhorted the veteran soldiers to defend the liberty of the Roman people, and has enlisted them in his army, and as the Martial legion and the fourth legion, with great zeal for the republic, and with admirable unanimity, under the guidance and authority of Caius Caesar, have defended and are defending the republic and the liberty of the Roman people, and as Caius Caesar, propraetor, has gone with his army as a reinforcement to the province of Gaul, has made cavalry, and archers, and elephants, obedient to himself and to the Roman people, and has, at a most critical time for the republic, come to the aid of the safety and dignity of the Roman people,—on these accounts, it seems good to the senate that Caius Caesar, the son of Caius, pontiff and propraetor, shall be a senator, and shall deliver his opinions from the bench occupied by men of praetorian rank, and that, on occasion of his offering himself for any magistracy, he shall be considered of the same legal standing and qualification as if he had been quaestor the preceding year."

For what reason can there be, O conscript fathers, why we should not wish him to arrive at the highest honours at as early an age as possible? For when, by the laws fixing the age at which men might be appointed to the different magistracies our ancestors fixed a more mature age for the consulship, they were influenced by fears of the precipitation of youth, Caius Caesar, at his first entrance into life, has shown us that, in the case of his eminent and unparalleled virtue, we have no need to wait for the progress of age. Therefore our ancestors, those old men, in the most ancient times, had no laws regulating the age for the different offices, it was ambition which caused them to be passed many years afterwards, in order that there might be among men of the same age different steps for arriving at honours. And it has often happened that a disposition of great natural virtue has been lost before it had any opportunity of benefiting the republic.

But among the ancients, the Rulii, the Decii, the Corvim, and many others, and in more modern times the elder Africanus and Titus Flaminius were made consuls very young, and performed such exploits as greatly to extend the empire of the Roman people, and to embellish its name. What more? Did not the Macedonian Alexander, having begun to perform mighty deeds from his earliest youth, die when he was only in his thirty-third year? And that age is ten years less than that fixed by our laws for a man to be eligible for the consulship. From which it may be plainly seen that the progress of virtue is often swifter than that of age.

XVIII. For as to the fear which those men, who are enemies of Caesar, pretend to entertain, there is not the slightest reason to apprehend that he will be unable to restrain and govern himself, or that he will be so elated by the honours which he receives from us as to use his power with out moderation. It is only natural, O conscript fathers, that the man who has learnt to appreciate real glory, and who feels that he is considered by the senate and by the Roman knights and the whole Roman people a citizen who is dear to, and a blessing to the republic, should think nothing whatever deserving of being compared to this glory. Would that it had happened to Caius Caesar—the father, I mean—when he was a young man, to be beloved by the senate and by every virtuous citizen, but, having neglected to aim at that, he wasted all the power of genius which he had in a most brilliant degree, in a capricious pursuit of popular favour. Therefore, as he had not sufficient respect for the senate and the virtuous part of the citizens, he opened for himself that path for the extension of his power, which the virtue of a free people was unable to bear.

But the principles of his son are widely different; who is not only beloved by every one, but in the greatest degree by the most virtuous men. In him is placed all our hope of liberty, from him already has our safety been received, for him the highest honours are sought out and prepared. While therefore we are admiring his singular prudence, can we at the same time fear his folly? For what can be more foolish than to prefer useless power, such influence as brings envy in its train, and a rash and slippery ambition of reigning, to real, dignified, solid glory? Has he seen this truth as a boy, and when he has advanced in age will he cease to see it? "But he is an enemy to some most illustrious and excellent citizens." That circumstance ought not to cause any fear Caesar has sacrificed all those enmities to the republic; he had made the republic his judge; he has made her the directress of all his counsels and actions. For he is come to the service of the republic in order to strengthen her, not to overturn her. I am well acquainted with all the feelings of the young man: there is nothing dearer to him than the republic, nothing which he considers of more weight than your authority; nothing which he desires more than the approbation of virtuous men; nothing which he accounts sweeter than genuine glory.

Wherefore you not only ought not to fear anything from him, but you ought to expect greater and better things still. Nor ought you to apprehend with respect to a man who has already gone forward to release Decimus Brutus from a siege, that the recollection of his domestic injury will dwell in his bosom, and have more weight with him than the safety of the city. I will venture even to pledge my own faith, O conscript fathers, to you, and to the Roman people, and to the republic, which in truth, if no necessity compelled me to do so, I would not venture to do, and in doing which on slight grounds, I should be afraid of giving rise to a dangerous opinion of my rashness in a most important business; but I do promise, and pledge myself, and undertake, O conscript fathers, that Caius Caesar will always be such a citizen as he is this day, and as we ought above all things to wish and desire that he may turn out.

XIX. And as this is the case, I shall consider that I have said enough at present about Caesar.

Nor do I think that we ought to pass over Lucius Egnatuleius, a most gallant and wise and firm citizen, and one thoroughly attached to the republic, in silence; but that we ought to give him our testimony to his admirable virtue, because it was he who led the fourth legion to Caesar, to be a protection to the consuls, and senate, and people of Rome, and the republic. And for these acts I give my vote:

"That it be made lawful for Lucius Egnatuleius to stand for, and be elected to, and discharge the duties of any magistracy, three years before the legitimate time."

And by this motion, O conscript fathers, Lucius Egnatuleius does not get so much actual advantage as honour. For in a case like this it is quite sufficient to be honourably mentioned.

But concerning the army of Caius Caesar, I give my vote for the passing of a decree in this form:

"The senate decrees that the veteran soldiers who have defended and are defending of Caesar, pontiff and the authority of this order, should, and their children after them, have an exemption from military service. And that Caius Pansa and Aulus Hirtius the consuls, one or both of them, as they think fit, shall inquire what land there is in those colonies in which the veteran soldiers have been settled, which is occupied in defiance of the provisions of the Julian law, in order that that may be divided among these veterans. That they shall institute a separate inquiry about the Campanian district, and devise a plan for increasing the advantages enjoyed by these veteran soldiers; and with respect to the Martial legion, and to the fourth legion, and to those soldiers of the second and thirty-fifth legions who have come over to Caius Pansa and Aulus Hirtius the consuls, and have given in their names, because the authority of the senate and the liberty of the Roman people is and always has been most dear to them, the senate decrees that they and their children shall have exemption from military service, except in the case of any Gallic and Italian sedition; and decrees further, that those legions shall have their discharge when this war is terminated; and that whatever sum of money Caius Caesar, pontiff and propraetor, has promised to the soldiers of those legions individually, shall be paid to them. And that Caius Pansa and Aulus Hirtius the consuls, one or both of them, as it seems good to them, shall make an estimate of the land which can be distributed without injury to private individuals; and that land shall be given and assigned to the soldiers of the Martial legion and of the fourth legion, in the largest shares in which land has ever been given and assigned to soldiers."

I have now spoken, O consuls, on every point concerning which you have submitted a motion to us; and if the resolutions which I have proposed be decreed without delay, and seasonably, you will the more easily prepare those measures which the present time and emergency demand. But instant action is necessary. And if we had adopted that earlier, we should, as I have often said, now have no war at all.

THE SIXTH PHILIPPIC

THE ARGUMENT

In respect of the honours proposed by Cicero in the last speech the senate agreed with him, voting to Octavius honours beyond any that Cicero had proposed. But they were much divided about the question of sending an embassy to Antonius, and the consuls, seeing that a majority agreed with Cicero, adjourned the debate till the next day. The discussion lasted three days, and the senate would at last have adopted all Cicero's measures if one of the tribunes, Salvius, had not put his veto on them. So that at last the embassy was ordered to be sent, and Servius Sulpicius, Lucius Piso, and Lucius Philippus, appointed as the ambassadors, but they were charged merely to order Antonius to abandon the siege of Mutina, and to desist from hostilities against the province of Gaul, and further, to proceed to Decimus Brutus in Mutina, and to give him and his army the thanks of the senate and people.

The length of the debates roused the curiosity of the people, who, being assembled in the forum to learn the result, called on Cicero to come forth and give them an account of what had been done—on which he went to the rostra, accompanied by Publius Appuleius the tribune, and related to them all that had passed in the following speech:

I. I imagine that you have heard, O Romans, what has been done in the senate, and what has been the opinion delivered by each individual. For the matter which has been in discussion ever since the first of January, has been just brought to a conclusion, with less severity indeed than it ought to have been, but still in a manner not altogether unbecoming. The war has been subjected to a delay, but the cause has not been removed. Wherefore, as to the question which Publius Appuleius—a man united to me by many kind offices and by the closest intimacy, and firmly attached to your interests—has asked me, I will answer in such a manner that you may be acquainted with the transactions at which you were not present.

The cause which prompted our most fearless and excellent consuls to submit a motion on the first of January, concerning the general state of the republic, arose from the decree which the senate passed by my advice on the nineteenth of December. On that day, O Romans, were the foundations of the republic first laid. For then, after a long interval, the senate was free in such a manner that you too might become free. On which day, indeed,—even if it had been to bring to me the end of my life,—I received a sufficient reward for my exertions, when you all with one heart and one voice cried out together, that the republic had been a second time saved by me. Stimulated by so important and so splendid a decision of yours in my favour, I came into the senate on the first of January, with the feeling that I was bound to show my recollection of the character which you had imposed upon me, and which I had to sustain.

Therefore, when I saw that a nefarious war was waged against the republic, I thought that no delay ought to be interposed to our pursuit of Marcus Antonius; and I gave my vote that we ought to pursue with war that most audacious man, who, having committed many atrocious crimes before, was at this moment attacking a general of the Roman people, and besieging your most faithful and gallant colony; and that a state of civil war ought to be proclaimed; and I said further, that my opinion was that a suspension of the ordinary forms of justice should be declared, and that the garb of war should be assumed by the citizens, in order that all men might apply themselves with more activity and energy to avenging the injuries of the republic, if they saw that all the emblems of a regular war had been adopted by the senate. Therefore, this opinion of mine, O Romans, prevailed so much for three days, that although no division was come to, still all, except a very few, appeared inclined to agree with me. But to-day—I know not owing to what circumstance—the senate was more indulgent. For the majority decided on our making experiment, by means of ambassadors, how much influence the authority of the senate and your unanimity will have upon Antonius.

II. I am well aware, O Romans, that this decision is disapproved of by you; and reasonably too. For to whom are we sending ambassadors? Is it not to him who, after having dissipated and squandered the public money, and imposed laws on the Roman people by violence and in violation of the auspices,—after having put the assembly of the people to flight and besieged the senate, sent for the legions from Brundusium to oppress the republic? who, when deserted by them, has invaded Gaul with a troop of banditti? who is attacking Brutus? who is besieging Mutina? How can you offer conditions to, or expect equity from, or send an embassy to, or, in short, have anything in common with, this gladiator? although, O Romans, it is not an embassy, but a denunciation of war if he does not obey. For the decree has been drawn up as if ambassadors were being sent to Hannibal. For men are sent to order him not to attack the consul elect, not to besiege Mutina, not to lay waste the province, not to enlist troops, but to submit himself to the power of the senate and people of Rome. No doubt he is a likely man to obey this injunction, and to submit to the power of the conscript fathers and to yours, who has never even had any mastery over himself. For what has he ever done that showed any discretion, being always led away wherever his lust, or his levity, or his frenzy, or his drunkenness has hurried him? He has always been under the dominion of two very dissimilar classes of men, pimps and robbers; he is so fond of domestic adulteries and forensic murders, that he would rather obey a most covetous woman than the senate and people of Rome.

III. Therefore, I will do now before you what I have just done in the senate. I call you to witness, I give notice, I predict beforehand, that Marcus Antonius will do nothing whatever of those things which the ambassadors are commissioned to command him to do; but that he will lay waste the lands, and besiege Mutina and enlist soldiers, wherever he can. For he is a man who has at all times despised the judgment and authority of the senate, and your inclinations and power. Will he do what it has been just now decreed that he shall do,—lead his army back across the Rubicon, which is the frontier of Gaul, and yet at the same time not come nearer Rome than two hundred miles? will he obey this notice? will he allow himself to be confined by the river Rubicon and by the limit of two hundred miles? Antonius is not that sort of man. For if he had been, he would never have allowed matters to come to such a pass, as for the senate to give him notice, as it did to Hannibal at the beginning of the Punic war not to attack Saguntum. But what ignominy it is to be called away from Mutina, and at the same time to be forbidden to approach the city as if he were some fatal conflagration! what an opinion is this for the senate to have of a man! What? As to the commission which is given to the ambassadors to visit Decimus Brutus and his soldiers, and to inform them that their excellent zeal in behalf of, and services done to the republic, are acceptable to the senate and people of Rome, and that that conduct shall tend to their great glory and to their great honour; do you think that Antonius will permit the ambassadors to enter Mutina? and to depart from thence in safety? He never will allow it, believe me. I know the violence of the man, I know his impudence, I know his audacity.

Nor, indeed, ought we to think of him as of a human being, but as of a most ill-omened beast. And as this is the case, the decree which the senate has passed is not wholly improper. The embassy has some severity in it; I only wish it had no delay. For as in the conduct of almost every affair slowness and procrastination are hateful, so above all things does this war require promptness of action. We must assist Decimus Brutus;

we must collect all our forces from all quarters; we cannot lose a single hour in effecting the deliverance of such a citizen without wickedness. Was it not in his power, if he had considered Antonius a consul, and Gaul the province of Antonius, to have given over the legions and the province to Antonius? and to return home himself? and to celebrate a triumph? and to be the first man in this body to deliver his opinion, until he entered on his magistracy? What was the difficulty of doing that? But as he remembered that he was Brutus, and that he was born for your freedom, not for his own tranquillity, what else did he do but—as I may almost say—put his own body in the way to prevent Antonius from entering Gaul? Ought we then to send ambassadors to this man, or legions? However, we will say nothing of what is past. Let the ambassadors hasten, as I see that they are about to do. Do you prepare your robes of war. For it has been decreed, that, if he does not obey the authority of the senate, we are all to betake our selves to our military dress. And we shall have to do so. He will never obey. And we shall lament that we have lost so many days, when we might have been doing something.

IV. I have no fear, O Romans, that when Antonius hears that I have asserted, both in the senate and in the assembly of the people, that he never will submit himself to the power of the senate, he will, for the sake of disproving my words, and making me to appeal to have had no foresight, alter his behaviour and obey the senate. He will never do so. He will not grudge me this part of my reputation, he will prefer letting me be thought wise by you to being thought modest himself. Need I say more? Even if he were willing to do so himself, do you think that his brother Lucius would permit him? It has been reported that lately at Tibur, when Marcus Antonius appeared to him to be wavering, he, Lucius, threatened his brother with death. And do we suppose that the orders of the senate, and the words of the ambassadors, will be listened to by this Asiatic gladiator? It will be impossible for him to be separated from a brother, especially from one of so much authority. For he is another Africanus among them. He is considered of more influence than Lucius Trebellius, of more than Titus Plancus a noble young man. As for Plancus, who, having been condemned by the unanimous vote of every one, amid the overpowering applause of you yourselves, somehow or other got mixed up in this crowd, and returned with a countenance so sorrowful, that he appeared to have been dragged back rather than to have returned, he despises him to such degree, as if he were interdicted from fire and water. At times he says that that man who set the senate house on fire has no right to a place in the senate house. For at this moment he is exceedingly in love with Trebellius. He hated him some time ago, when he was opposing an abolition of debts, but now he delights in him, ever since he has seen that Trebellius himself cannot continue in safety without an abolition of debts. For I think that you have heard, O Romans, what indeed you may possibly have seen, that the sureties and creditors of Lucius Trebellius meet every day. Oh confidence! for I imagine that Trebellius has taken this surname, what can be greater confidence than defrauding one's creditors? than flying from one's house? than, because of one's debts, being forced to go to war? What has become of the applauses which he received on the occasion of Caesar's triumph, and often at the games? Where is the aedileship that was conferred on him by the zealous efforts of all good men? who is there who does not now think that he acted virtuously by accident?

V. However, I return to your love and especial delight, Lucius Antonius, who has admitted you all to swear allegiance to him. Do you deny it? is there any one of you who does not belong to a tribe? Certainly not. But thirty five tribes have adopted him for their patron. Do you again cry out against my statement? Look at that gilt statue of him on the left what is the inscription upon it? "The thirty five tribes to their patron." Is then Lucius Antonius the patron of the Roman people? Plague take him! For I fully assent to your outcry. I won't speak of this bandit whom no one would choose to have for a client, but was there ever a man possessed of such influence, or illustrious for mighty deeds, as to dare to call himself the patron of the whole Roman people, the conqueror and master of all nations? We see in the forum a statue of Lucius Antonius, just as we see one of Quintus Tremulus, who conquered the Hernici, before the temple of Castor. Oh the incredible impudence of the man! Has he assumed all this credit to himself, because as a mumillo at Mylasa he slew the Thracian, his friend? How should we be able to endure him, if he had fought in this forum before the eyes of you all? But, however, this is but one statue. He has another erected by the Roman knights who received horses from the state, and they too inscribe on that, "To their patron". Who was ever before adopted by that order as its patron? If it ever adopted any one as such, it ought to have adopted me. What censor was ever so honoured? what imperator? "But he distributed land among them". Shame on their sordid natures for accepting it! shame on his dishonesty for giving it!

Moreover, the military tribunes who were in the army of Caesar have erected him a statue. What order is that? There have been plenty of tribunes in our numerous legions in so many years. Among them he has distributed the lands of Semurium. The Campus Martius was all that was left, if he had not first fled with his brother. But this allotment of lands was put an end to a little while ago, O Romans, by the declaration of his opinion by Lucius Caesar a most illustrious man and a most admirable senator. For we all agreed with him and annulled the acts of the septemvirs. So all the kindness of Nucula goes for nothing, and the patron Antonius is at a discount. For those who had taken possession will depart with more equanimity. They had not been at any expense, they had not yet furnished or stocked their domains, partly because they did not feel sure of their title, and partly because they had no money.

But as for that splendid statue, concerning which, if the times were better, I could not speak without laughing, "To Lucius Antonius, patron of the middle of Janus" Is it so? Is the middle of Janus a client of Lucius Antonius? Who ever was found in that Janus who would have lent Lucius Antonius a thousand sesterces?

VI. However, we have been spending too much time in trifles. Let us return to our subject and to the war. Although it was not wholly foreign to the subject for some characters to be thoroughly appreciated by you, in order that you might in silence think over who they were against whom you were to wage war.

But I exhort you, O Romans, though perhaps other measures might have been wiser, still now to wait with calmness for the return of the ambassadors. Promptness of action has been taken from our side, but still some good has accrued to it. For when the ambassadors have reported what they certainly will report, that Antonius will not submit to you nor to the senate, who then will be so worthless a citizen as to think him deserving of being accounted a citizen? For at present there are men, few indeed, but still more than there ought to be, or than the republic deserves that there should be, who speak in this way,—"Shall we not even wait for the return of the ambassadors?" Certainly the republic itself will force them to abandon that expression and that pretence of clemency. On which account, to confess the truth to you, O Romans, I have less striven to day, and laboured all the less to day, to induce the senate to agree with me in decreeing the existence of a seditious war, and ordering the apparel of war to be assumed. I preferred having my sentiments applauded by every one in twenty days' time, to having it blamed to day by a few. Wherefore, O Romans, wait now for the return of the ambassadors, and devour your annoyance for a few days. And when they do return, if they bring back peace, believe me that I have been desirous that they should, if they bring back war, then allow me the praise of foresight. Ought I not to be provident for the welfare of my fellow-citizens? Ought I not day and night to think of your freedom and of the safety of the republic? For what do I not owe to you, O Romans, since you have preferred for all the honours of the state a man who is his own father to the most nobly born men in the republic? Am I ungrateful? Who is less so? I, who, after I had obtained those honours, have constantly laboured in the forum with the same exertions as I used while striving for them. Am I inexperienced in state affairs? Who has had more practice than I, who have now for twenty years been waging war against impious citizens?

VII Wherefore, O Romans, with all the prudence of which I am master, and with almost more exertion than I am capable of, will I put forth my vigilance and watchfulness in your behalf In truth, what citizen is there, especially in this rank in which you have placed me, so forgetful of your kindness, so unmindful of his country, so hostile to his own dignity, as not to be roused and stimulated by your wonderful unanimity? I, as consul, have held many assemblies of the people, I have been present at many others, I have never once seen one so numerous as this one of yours now is. You have all one feeling, you have all one desire, that of averting the attempts of Marcus Antonius from the republic, of extinguishing his frenzy and crushing his audacity. All orders have the same wish. The municipal towns, the colonies, and all Italy are labouring for the same end. Therefore you have made the senate, which was already pretty firm of its own accord, firmer still by your authority. The time has come, O Romans, later altogether than for the honour of the Roman people it should have been, but still so that the things are now so ripe that they do not admit of a moment's delay. There has been a sort of fatality, if I may say so, which we have borne as it was necessary to bear it. But hereafter if any disaster happens to us it will be of our own seeking. It is impossible for the Roman people to be slaves, that people whom the immortal gods have ordained should rule over all nations. Matters are now come to a crisis. We are fighting for our freedom. Either you must conquer, O Romans, which indeed you will do if you continue to act with such piety and such unanimity, or you must do anything rather than become slaves. Other nations can endure slavery. Liberty is the inalienable possession of the Roman people.

THE SEVENTH PHILIPPIC

THE ARGUMENT

After the senate had decided on sending them, the ambassadors immediately set out, though Servius Sulpicius was in a very bad state of health. In the meantime the partisans of Antonius in the city, with Calenus at their head were endeavouring to gain over the rest of the citizens, by representing him as eager for an accommodation and they kept up a correspondence with him, and published such of his letters as they thought favourable for their views. Matters being in this state, Cicero, at an ordinary meeting of the senate, made the following speech to counteract the machinations of this party, and to warn the citizens generally of the danger of being deluded by them.

I. We are consulted to-day about matters of small importance, but still perhaps necessary, O conscript fathers. The consul submits a motion to us about the Appian road, and about the coinage, the tribune of the people one about the Luperci. And although it seems easy to settle such matters as those, still my mind cannot fix itself on such subjects, being anxious about more important matters. For our affairs, O conscript fathers, are come to a crisis, and are in a state of almost extreme danger. It is not without reason that I have always feared and never approved of that sending of ambassadors. And what their return is to bring us I know not, but who is there who does not see with how much languor the expectation of it infects our minds? For those men put no restraint on themselves who grieve that the senate has revived so as to entertain hopes of its former authority, and that the Roman people is united to this our order, that all Italy is animated by one common feeling, that armies are prepared, and generals ready for the armies, even already they are inventing replies for Antonius, and defending them. Some pretend that his demand is that all the armies be disbanded. I suppose then we sent ambassadors to him, not that he should submit and obey this our body, but that he should offer us conditions, impose laws upon us, order us to open Italy to foreign nations, especially while we were to leave him in safety from whom there is more danger to be feared than from any nation whatever. Others say that he is willing to give up the nearer Gaul to us, and that he will be satisfied with the further Gaul. Very kind of him! in order that from thence he may endeavour to bring not merely legions, but even nations against this city. Others say that he makes no demands now but such as are quite moderate. Macedonia he calls absolutely his own, since it was from thence that his brother Caius was recalled. But what province is there in which that firebrand may not kindle a conflagration? Therefore those same men, like provident citizens and diligent senators, say that I have sounded the charge, and they undertake the advocacy of peace. Is not this the way in which they argue? "Antonius ought not to have been irritated, he is a reckless and a bold man, there are many bad men besides him." (No doubt, and they may begin and count themselves first). And they warn us to be on our guard against them. Which conduct then is it which shows the more prudent caution chastising wicked citizens when one is able to do so, or fearing them?

II. And these men speak in this way, who on account of their trifling disposition used to be considered friends of the people. From which it may be understood that they in their hearts have at all times been disinclined to a good constitution of the state, and they were not friends of the people from inclination. For how comes it to pass that those men who were anxious to gratify the people in evil things, now, on an occasion which above all others concerns the people's interests, because the same thing would be also salutary for the republic, now prefer being wicked to being friends of the people? This noble cause of which I am the advocate has made me popular, a man who (as you know) have always opposed the rashness of the people. And those men are called, or rather they call themselves, consulars; though no man is worthy of that name except those who can support so high an honour. Will you favour an enemy? Will you let him send you letters about his hopes of success? Will you be glad to produce them? to read them? Will you even give them to wicked citizens to take copies of? Will you thus raise their courage? Will you thus damp the hopes and valour of the good? And then will you think yourself a consular, or a senator, or even a citizen? Caius Pansa, a most fearless and virtuous consul, will take what I say in good part. For I will speak with a disposition most friendly to him; but I should not consider him himself a consul, though a man with whom I am most intimate, unless he was such a consul as to devote all his vigilance, and cares, and thoughts to the safety of the republic.

Although long acquaintance, and habit, and a fellowship and resemblance in the most honourable pursuits, has bound us together from his first entrance into life; and his incredible diligence, proved at the time of the most formidable dangers of the civil war, showed that he was a favourer not only of my safety, but also of my dignity; still, as I said before, if he were not such a consul as I have described, I should venture to deny that he was a consul at all. But now I call him not only a consul, but the most excellent and virtuous consul within my recollection; not but that there have been others of equal virtue and equal inclination, but still they have not had an equal opportunity of displaying that virtue and inclination. But the opportunity of a time of most formidable change has been afforded to his magnanimity, and dignity, and wisdom. And that is the time when the consulship is displayed to the greatest advantage, when it governs the republic during a time which, if not desirable, is at all events critical and momentous. And a more critical time than the present, O conscript fathers, never was.

III. Therefore I, who have been at all times an adviser of peace, and who, though all good men always considered peace, and especially internal peace, desirable, have desired it more than all of them;—for the whole of the career of my industry has been passed in the forum and in the senate-house, and in warding off dangers from my friends; it is by this course that I have arrived at the highest honours, at moderate wealth, and at any dignity which we may be thought to have: I therefore, a nursling of peace, as I may call myself, I who, whatever I am, (for I arrogate nothing to myself,) should undoubtedly not have been such without internal peace: I am speaking in peril: I shudder to think how you will receive it, O conscript fathers: but still, out of regard for my unceasing desire to support and increase your dignity, I beg and entreat you, O conscript fathers, although it may be a bitter thing to hear, or an incredible thing that it should be said by Marcus Cicero, still to receive at first, without offence, what I am going to say, and not to reject it before I have fully explained what it is;—I, who, I will say so over and over again, have always been a panegyrist, have always been an adviser of peace, do not wish to have peace with Marcus Antonius. I approach the rest of my speech with great hope, O conscript fathers, since I have now passed by that perilous point amid your silence.

Why then do I not wish for peace? Because it would be shameful; because it would be dangerous; because it cannot possibly be real. And while I explain these three points to you, I beg of you, O conscript fathers, to listen to my words with the same kindness which you usually show to me.

What is more shameful than inconsistency, fickleness, and levity, both to individuals, and also to the entire senate? Moreover, what can be more inconsistent than on a sudden to be willing to be united in peace with a man whom you have lately adjudged to be an enemy, not by words, but by actions and by many formal decrees? Unless, indeed, when you were decreeing honours to Caius Caesar, well-deserved indeed by and fairly due to him, but still unprecedented and never to be forgotten, for one single reason,—because he had levied an army against Marcus Antonius,—you were not judging Marcus Antonius to be an enemy; and unless Antonius was not pronounced an enemy by you, when the veteran soldiers were praised by your authority, for having followed Caesar; and unless you did not declare Antonius an enemy when you promised exemptions and money and lands to those brave legions, because they had deserted him who was consul while he was an enemy.

IV. What? when you distinguished with the highest praises Brutus, a man born under some omen, as it were, of his race and name, for the deliverance of the republic, and his army, which was waging war against Antonius on behalf of the liberty of the Roman people, and the most loyal and admirable province of Gaul, did you not then pronounce Antonius an enemy? What? when you decreed that the consuls, one or both of them, should go to the war, what war was there if Antonius was not an enemy? Why then was it that most gallant man, my own colleague and intimate friend, Aulus Hirtius the consul, has set out? And in what delicate health he is; how wasted away! But the weak state of his body could not repress the vigour of his mind. He thought it fair, I suppose, to expose to danger in defence of the Roman people that life which had been preserved to him by their prayers. What? when you ordered levies of troops to be made throughout all Italy, when you suspended all exemptions from service, was he not by those steps declared to be an enemy? You see manufactories of arms in the city; soldiers, sword in hand, are following the consul; they are in appearance a guard to the consul, but in fact and reality to us; all men are giving in their names, not only without any shirking, but with the greatest eagerness; they are acting in obedience to your authority. Has not Antonius been declared an enemy by such acts?

"Oh, but we have sent ambassadors to him." Alas, wretched that I am! why am I compelled to find fault with the senate whom I have always praised? Why? Do you think, O conscript fathers, that you have induced the Roman people to approve of the sending ambassadors? Do you not perceive, do you not hear, that the adoption of my opinion is demanded by them? that opinion which you, in a full house, agreed to the day before, though the day after you allowed yourselves to be brought down to a groundless hope of peace. Moreover, how shameful it is for the legions to send out ambassadors to the senate, and the senate to Antonius! Although that is not an embassy; it is a denunciation that destruction is prepared for him if he do not submit to this order. What is the difference? At all events, men's opinions are unfavourable to the measure; for all men see that ambassadors have been sent, but it is not all who are acquainted with the terms of your decree.

V. You must, therefore, preserve your consistency, your wisdom, your firmness, your perseverance. You must go back to the old-fashioned severity, if at least the authority of the senate is anxious to establish its credit, its honour, its renown, and its dignity, things which this order has been too long deprived of. But there was some time ago some excuse for it, as being oppressed; a miserable excuse indeed, but still a fair one; now there is none. We appeared to have been delivered from kingly tyranny; and afterwards we were oppressed much more severely by domestic enemies. We did indeed turn their arms aside; we must now wrest them from their hands. And if we cannot do so, (I will say what it becomes one who is both a senator and a Roman to say,) let us die. For how just will be the shame, how great will be the disgrace, how great the infamy to the republic, if Marcus Antonius can deliver his opinion in this assembly from the consular bench. For, to say nothing of the countless acts of wickedness committed by him while consul in the city, during which time he has squandered a vast amount of public money, restored exiles without any law, sold our revenues to all sorts of people, removed provinces from the empire of the Roman people, given men kingdoms for bribes, imposed laws on the city by violence, besieged the senate, and, at other times, excluded it from the senate-house by force of arms;—to say nothing, I say, of all this, do you not consider this, that he who has attacked Mutina, a most powerful colony of the Roman people—who has besieged a general of the Roman people, who is consul elect—who has laid waste the lands,—do you not consider, I say, how shameful and iniquitous a thing it would be for that man to be received into this order, by which he has been so repeatedly pronounced an enemy for these very reasons?

I have said enough of the shamefulness of such a proceeding; I will now speak next, as I proposed, of the danger of it; which, although it is not so important to avoid as shame, still offends the minds of the greater part of mankind even more.

VI. Will it then be possible for you to rely on the certainty of any peace, when you see Antonius, or rather the Antonii, in the city? Unless, indeed, you despise Lucius: I do not despise even Caius. But, as I think,

Lucius will be the dominant spirit,—for he is the patron of the five-and-thirty tribes, whose votes he took away by his law, by which he divided the magistracies in conjunction with Caius Caesar. He is the patron of the centuries of the Roman knights, which also he thought fit to deprive of the suffrages: he is the patron of the men who have been military tribunes; he is the patron of the middle of Janus. O ye gods! who will be able to support this man's power? especially when he has brought all his dependants into the lands. Who ever was the patron of all the tribes? and of the Roman knights? and of the military tribunes? Do you think that the power of even the Gracchi was greater than that of this gladiator will be? whom I have called gladiator, not in the sense in which sometimes Marcus Antonius too is called gladiator, but as men call him who are speaking plain Latin. He has fought in Asia as a mirmillo. After having equipped his own companion and intimate friend in the armour of a Thracian, he slew the miserable man as he was flying; but he himself received a palpable wound, as the scar proves.

What will the man who murdered his friend in this way, when he has an opportunity, do to an enemy? and if he did such a thing as this for the fun of the thing, what do you think he will do when tempted by the hope of plunder? Will he not again meet wicked men in the decuries? will he not again tamper with those men who have received lands? will he not again seek those who have been banished? will he not, in short, be Marcus Antonius; to whom, on the occasion of every commotion, there will be a rush of all profligate citizens? Even if there be no one else except those who are with him now, and these who in this body now openly speak in his favour, will they be too small in number? especially when all the protection which we might have had from good men is lost, and when those men are prepared to obey his nod? But I am afraid, if at this time we fail to adopt wise counsels, that that party will in a short time appear too numerous for us. Nor have I any dislike to peace; only I do dread war disguised under the name of peace. Wherefore, if we wish to enjoy peace we must first wage war. If we shrink from war, peace we shall never have.

VII. But it becomes your prudence, O conscript fathers, to provide as far forward as possible for posterity. That is the object for which we were placed in this garrison, and as it were on this watch-tower; that by our vigilance and foresight we might keep the Roman people free from fear. It would be a shameful thing, especially in so clear a case as this, for it to be notorious that wisdom was wanting to the chief council of the whole world. We have such consuls, there is such eagerness on the part of the Roman people, we have such an unanimous feeling of all Italy in our favour, such generals, and such armies, that the republic cannot possibly suffer any disaster without the senate being in fault. I, for my part, will not be wanting. I will warn you, I will forewarn you, I will give you notice, I will call gods and men to witness what I do really believe. Nor will I display my good faith alone, which perhaps may seem to be enough, but which in a chief citizen is not enough; I will exert all my care, and prudence, and vigilance.

I have spoken about the danger. I will now proceed to prove to you that it is not possible for peace to be firmly cemented; for of the propositions which I promised to establish this is the last.

VIII. What peace can there be between Marcus Antonius and (in the first place) the senate? with what face will he be able to look upon you, and with what eyes will you, in turn, look upon him? Which of you does not hate him? which of you does not he hate? Come, are you the only people who hate him; and whom he hates? What? what do you think of those men who are besieging Mutina, who are levying troops in Gaul, who are threatening your fortunes? will they ever be friends to you, or you to them? Will he embrace the Roman knights? For, suppose their inclinations respecting, and their opinions of Antonius were very much concealed, when they stood in crowds on the steps of the temple of Concord, when they stimulated you to endeavour to recover your liberty, when they demanded arms, the robe of war, and war, and who, with the Roman people, invited me to meet in the assembly of the people, will these men ever become friends to Antonius? will Antonius ever maintain peace with them? For why should I speak of the whole Roman people? which, in a full and crowded forum, twice, with one heart and one voice, summoned me into the assembly, and plainly showed their excessive eagerness for the recovery of their liberty. So, desirable as it was before to have the Roman people for our comrade, we now have it for our leader.

What hope then is there that there ever can be peace between the Roman people and the men who are besieging Mutina and attacking a general and army of the Roman people? Will there be peace with the municipal towns, whose great zeal is shown by the decrees which they pass, by the soldiers whom they furnish, by the sums which they promise, so that in each town there is such a spirit as leaves no one room to wish for a senate of the Roman people? The men of Firmium deserve to be praised by a resolution of our order, who set the first example of promising money; we ought to return a complimentary answer to the Marrucini, who have passed a vote that all who evade military service are to be branded with infamy. These measures are adopted all over Italy. There is great peace between Antonius and these men, and between them and him! What greater discord can there possibly be? And in discord civil peace cannot by any possibility exist. To say nothing of the mob, look at Lucius Nasidius, a Roman knight, a man of the very highest accomplishments and honour, a citizen always eminent, whose watchfulness and exertions for the protection of my life I felt in my consulship; who not only exhorted his neighbours to become soldiers, but also assisted them from his own resources; will it be possible ever to reconcile Antonius to such a man as this, a man whom we ought to praise by a formal resolution of the senate? What? will it be possible to reconcile him to Caius Caesar, who prevented him from entering the city, or to Decimus Brutus, who has refused him entrance into Gaul? Moreover, will he reconcile himself to, or look mercifully on the province of Gaul, by which he has been excluded and rejected? You will see everything, O conscript fathers, if you do not take care, full of hatred and full of discord, from which civil wars arise. Do not then desire that which is impossible: and beware, I entreat you by the immortal gods, O conscript fathers, that out of hope of present peace you do not lose perpetual peace.

What now is the object of this oration? For we do not yet know what the ambassadors have done. But still we ought to be awake, erect, prepared, armed in our minds, so as not to be deceived by any civil or supplicatory language, or by any pretence of justice. He must have complied with all the prohibitions and all the commands which we have sent him, before he can demand anything. He must have desisted from attacking Brutus and his army, and from plundering the cities and lands of the province of Gaul; he must have permitted the ambassadors to go to Brutus, and led his army back on this side of the Rubicon, and yet not come within two hundred miles of this city. He must have submitted himself to the power of the senate and of the Roman people. If he does this, then we shall have an opportunity of deliberating without any decision being forced upon us either way. If he does not obey the senate, then it will not be the senate that declares war against him, but he who will have declared it against the senate.

But I warn you, O conscript fathers, the liberty of the Roman people, which is entrusted to you, is at stake. The life and fortune of every virtuous man is at stake, against which Antonius has long been directing his insatiable covetousness, united to his savage cruelty. Your authority is at stake, which you will wholly lose if you do not maintain it now.

Beware how you let that foul and deadly beast escape now that you have got him confined and chained. You too, Pansa, I warn, (although you do not need counsel, for you have plenty of wisdom yourself: but still, even the most skilful pilots receive often warnings from the passengers in terrible storms,) not to allow this vast and noble preparation which you have made to fall away to nothing. You have such an opportunity as no one ever had. It is in your power so to avail yourself of this wise firmness of the senate, of this zeal of the equestrian order, of this ardour of the Roman people, as to release the Roman people from fear and danger for ever. As to the matters to which your motion before the senate refers, I agree with Publius Servilius.

THE EIGHTH PHILIPPIC

THE ARGUMENT

After the embassy to Antonius had left Rome the consuls zealously exerted themselves in preparing for war, in case he should reject the demands of the ambassador. Hirtius, though in bad health, left Rome first, at the head of an army containing, among others, the Martial and the fourth legions, intending to join Octavius and hoping with his assistance to prevent his gaining any advantage over Brutus till Pansa could join them. And he gained some advantages over Antonius at once.

About the beginning of February the two remaining ambassadors (for Servius Sulpicius had died just as they arrived at Antonius's camp) returned, bringing word that Antonius would comply with none of the commands of the senate, nor allow them to proceed to Decimus Brutus, and bringing also (contrary to their duty) demands from him, of which the principal were, that his troops were to be rewarded, all the acts of himself and Dolabella to be ratified as also all that he had done respecting Caesar's papers, that no account was to be required of him of the money; in the temple of Ops and that he should have the further Gaul with an army of six legions.

Pansa summoned the senate to receive the report of the ambassador, when Cicero made a severe speech, proposing very vigorous measures against Antonius, which, however, Galenus and his party were still numerous enough to mitigate very greatly; and even Pansa voted against him and in favour of the milder measures though they could not prevail against Cicero to have a second embassy sent to Antonius, and though Cicero carried his point of ordering the citizens to assume the sagum, or robe of war which he also (waving his privilege as a man of consular rank) wore himself. The next day the senate met again, to draw upon form the decrees on which they had resolved the day before, when Cicero addressed the following speech to them, expostulating with them for their wavering the day before.

I. Matters were carried on yesterday, O Caius Pansa, in a more irregular manner than the beginning of your consulship required. You did not appear to me to make sufficient resistance to those men, to whom you are not in the habit of yielding. For while the virtue of the senate was such as it usually is, and while all men saw that there was war in reality, and some thought that the name ought to be kept back, on the division, your inclination inclined to lenity. The course which we proposed therefore was defeated, at your instigation, on account of the harshness of the word war. That urged by Lucius Caesar, a most honourable man, prevailed, which, taking away that one harsh expression, was gentler in its language than in its real intention. Although he, indeed, before he delivered his opinion at all, pleaded his relationship to Antonius in excuse for it. He had done the same in my consulship, in respect of his sister's husband, as he did now in respect of his sister's son, so that he was moved by the grief of his sister, and at the same time he wished to provide for the safety of the republic.

And yet Caesar himself in some degree recommended you, O conscript fathers, not to agree with him, when he said that he should have expressed quite different sentiments, worthy both of himself and of the republic, if he had not been hampered by his relationship to Antonius. He, then, is his uncle, are you his uncles too, you who voted with him?

But on what did the dispute turn? Some men, in delivering their opinion, did not choose to insert the word "war". They preferred calling it "tumult," being ignorant not only of the state of affairs, but also of the meaning of words. For there can be a "war" without a "tumult," but there cannot be a "tumult" without a "war." For what is a "tumult," but such a violent disturbance that an unusual alarm is engendered by it? from which indeed the name "tumult" is derived. Therefore, our ancestors spoke of the Italian "tumult," which was a domestic one, of the Gallic "tumult," which was on the frontier of Italy, but they never spoke of any other. And that a "tumult" is a more serious thing than a "war" may be seen from this, that during a war exemptions from military service are valid, but in a tumult they are not. So that it is the fact, as I have said, that war can exist without a tumult, but a tumult cannot exist without a war. In truth, as there is no medium between war and peace, it is quite plain that a tumult, if it be not a sort of war, must be a sort of peace; and what more absurd can be said or imagined? However, we have said too much about a word; let us rather look to the facts, O conscript fathers, the appreciation of which, I know, is at times injured by too much attention being paid to words.

II. We are unwilling that this should appear to be a war. What is the object, then, of our giving authority to the municipal towns and colonies to exclude Antonius? of our authorizing soldiers to be enlisted without any force, without the terror of any fine, of their own inclination and eagerness? of permitting them to promise money for the assistance of the republic? For if the name of war be taken away, the zeal of the municipal towns will be taken away too. And the unanimous feeling of the Roman people which at present pours itself into our cause, if we cool upon it, must inevitably be damped.

But why need I say more? Decimus Brutus is attacked. Is not that war? Mutina is besieged. Is not even that war? Gaul is laid waste. What peace can be more assured than this? Who can think of calling that war? We have sent forth a consul, a most gallant man, with an army, who, though he was in a weak state from a long and serious illness, still thought he ought not to make any excuse when he was summoned to the protection of the republic. Caius Caesar, indeed, did not wait for our decrees; especially as that conduct of his was not unsuited to his age. He undertook war against Antonius of his own accord; for there was not yet time to pass a decree; and he saw that, if he let slip the opportunity of waging war, when the republic was crushed it would be impossible to pass any decrees at all. They and their arms, then, are now at peace. He is not an enemy whose garrison Hirtius has driven from Claterna; he is not an enemy who is in arms resisting a consul, and attacking a consul elect; and those are not the words of an enemy, nor is that warlike language, which Pansa read just now out of his colleague's letters: "I drove out the garrison." "I got possession of Claterna." "The cavalry were routed." "A battle was fought." "A good many men were slain." What peace can be greater than this? Levies of troops are ordered throughout all Italy; all exemptions from service are suspended; the robe of war is to be assumed to-morrow, the consul has said that he shall come down to the senate house with an armed guard.

Is not this war? Ay, it is such a war as has never been. For in all other wars, and most especially in civil wars, it was a difference as to the political state of the republic which gave rise to the contest. Sylla contended against Sulpicius about the force of laws which Sylla said had been passed by violence. Cinna warred against Octavius because of the votes of the new citizens. Again, Sylla was at variance with Cinna and Marius, in order to prevent unworthy men from attaining power, and to avenge the cruel death of most illustrious men. The causes of all these wars arose from the zeal of different parties, for what they considered the interest of the republic. Of the last civil war I cannot bear to speak. I do not understand the cause of it, I detest the result.

III. This is the fifth civil war, (and all of them have fallen upon our times,) the first which has not only not brought dissensions and discord among the citizens, but which has been signalised by extraordinary unanimity and incredible concord. All of them have the same wish, all defend the same objects, all are inspired with the same sentiments. When I say all, I except those whom no one thinks worthy of being citizens at all. What, then, is the cause of war, and what is the object aimed at? We are defending the temples of the immortal gods, we are defending the walls of the city, we are defending the homes and habitations of the Roman people, the household gods, the altars, the hearths and the sepulchres of our forefathers, we are defending our laws, our courts of justice, our freedom, our wives, our children, and our country. On the other hand, Marcus Antonius labours and fights in order to throw into confusion and overturn all these things, and hopes to have reason to think the plunder of the republic sufficient cause for the war, while he squanders part of our fortunes, and distributes the rest among his parricidal followers.

While, then, the motives for war are so different, a most miserable circumstance is what that fellow promises to his band of robbers. In the first place our houses, for he declares that he will divide the city among them, and after that he will lead them out at whatever gate and settle them on whatever lands they please. All the Caphons, all the Saxas, and the other plagues which attend Antonius, are marking out for themselves in their own minds most beautiful houses, and gardens, and villas, at Tusculum and Alba; and those clownish men—if indeed they are men, and not rather brute beasts—are borne on in their empty hopes as far as the waters and Puteoli. So Antonius has something to promise to his followers. What can we do? Have we anything of the sort? May the gods grant us a better fate! for our express object is to prevent any one at all from hereafter making similar promises. I say this against my will, still I must say it;—the auction sanctioned by Caesar, O conscript fathers, gives many wicked men both hope and audacity. For they saw some men become suddenly rich from having been beggars. Therefore, those men who are hanging over our property, and to whom Antonius promises everything, are always longing to see an auction. What can we do? What do we promise our soldiers? Things much better and more honourable. For promises to be earned by wicked actions are pernicious both to those who expect them, and to those who promise them. We promise to our soldiers freedom, rights, laws, justice, the empire of the world, dignity, peace, tranquillity. The promises then of Antonius are bloody, polluted, wicked, odious to gods and men, neither lasting nor salutary; ours, on the other hand, are honourable, upright, glorious, full of happiness, and full of piety.

IV. Here also Quintus Fufius, a brave and energetic man, and a friend of mine, reminds me of the advantages of peace. As if, if it were necessary to praise peace, I could not do it myself quite as well as he. For is it once only that I have defended peace? Have I not at all times laboured for tranquillity? which is desirable for all good men, but especially for me. For what course could my industry pursue without forensic causes, without laws, without courts of justice? and these things can have no existence when civil peace is taken away. But I want to know what you mean, O Calenus? Do you call slavery peace? Our ancestors used to take up arms not merely to secure their freedom, but also to acquire empire; you think that we ought to throw away our arms, in order to become slaves. What juster cause is there for waging war than the wish to repel slavery? in which, even if one's master be not tyrannical, yet it is a most miserable thing that he should be able to be so if he chooses. In truth, other causes are just, this is a necessary one. Unless, perhaps, you think that this does not apply to you, because you expect that you will be a partner in the dominion of Antonius. And there you make a two-fold mistake: first of all, in preferring your own to the general interest; and in the next place, in thinking that there is anything either stable or pleasant in kingly power. Even if it has before now been advantageous to you, it will not always be so. Moreover, you used to complain of that former master, who was a man; what do you think you will do when your master is a beast? And you say that you are a man who have always been desirous of peace, and have always wished for the preservation of all the citizens. Very honest language; that is, if you mean all citizens who are virtuous, and useful, and serviceable to the republic; but if you wish those who are by nature citizens, but by inclination enemies, to be saved, what difference is there between you and them? Your father, indeed, with whom I as a youth was acquainted, when he was an old man, —a man of rigid virtue and wisdom,—used to give the greatest praise of all citizens who had ever lived to Publius Nasica, who slew Tiberius Gracchus. By his valour, and wisdom, and magnanimity he thought that the republic had been saved. What am I to say? Have we received any other doctrine from our fathers? Therefore, that citizen—if you had lived in those times—would not have been approved of by you, because he did not wish all the citizens to be safe. "Because Lucius Opimius the consul has made a speech concerning the republic, the senators have thus decided on that matter, that Opimius the consul shall defend the republic." The senate adopted these measures in words, Opimius followed them up by his arms. Should you then, if you had lived in those times, have thought him a hasty or a cruel citizen?

or should you have thought Quintus Metellus one, whose four sons were all men of consular rank? or Publius Lentulus the chief of the senate, and many other admirable men, who, with Lucius Opimius the consul, took arms, and pursued Gracchus to the Aventine? and in the battle which ensued, Lentulus received a severe wound, Gracchus was plain, and so was Marcus Fulvius, a man of consular rank, and his two youthful sons. Those men, therefore, are to be blamed; for they did not wish all the citizens to be safe.

V. Let us come to instances nearer our own time. The senate entrusted the defence of the republic to Caius Marius and Lucius Valerius, the consuls; Lucius Saturninus, a tribune of the people, and Caius Glaucia the praetor, were slain. On that day, all the Scauri, and Metelli, and Claudii, and Catuli, and Scaevolae, and Crassi took arms. Do you think either those consuls or those other most illustrious men deserving of blame? I myself wished Catiline to perish. Did you who wish every one to be safe, wish Catiline to be safe? There is this difference, O Calenus, between my opinion and yours. I wish no citizen to commit such crimes as deserve to be punished with death. You think that, even if he has committed them, still he ought to be saved. If there is anything in our own body which is injurious to the rest of the body, we allow that to be burnt and cut out, in order that a limb may be lost in preference to the whole body. And so in the body of the republic, whatever is rotten must be cut off in order that the whole may be saved. Harsh language! This is much more harsh, "Let the worthless, and wicked and impious be saved, let the innocent, the honourable, the virtuous, the whole republic be destroyed." In the case of one individual, O Quintus Fufius, I confess that you saw more than I did. I thought Publius Clodius a mischievous, wicked, lustful, impious, audacious, criminal citizen. You, on the other hand, called him religious, temperate, innocent, modest; a citizen to be preserved and desired. In this one particular I admit that you had great discernment, and that I made a great mistake. For as for your saying that I am in the habit of arguing against you with ill-temper, that is not the case. I confess that I argue with vehemence, but not with ill-temper. I am not in the habit of getting angry with my friends every now and then, not even if they deserve it. Therefore, I can differ from you without using any insulting language, though not without feeling the greatest grief of mind. For is the dissension between you and me a trifling one, or on a trifling subject? Is it merely a case of my favouring this man, and you that man? Yes; I indeed favour Decimus Brutus, you favour Marcus Antonius; I wish a colony of the Roman people to be preserved, you are anxious that it should be stormed and destroyed.

VI. Can you deny this, when you interpose every sort of delay calculated to weaken Brutus, and to improve the position of Antonius? For how long will you keep on saying that you are desirous of peace? Matters are progressing rapidly; the works have been carried on; severe battles are taking place. We sent three chief men of the city to interpose. Antonius has despised, rejected, and repudiated them. And still you continue a persevering defender of Antonius. And Calenus, indeed, in order that he may appear a more conscientious senator, says that he ought not to be a friend to him; since, though Antonius was under great obligations to him, he still had acted against him. See how great is his affection for his country. Though he is angry with the individual, still he defends Antonius for the sake of his country.

When you are so bitter, O Quintus Fufius, against the people of Marseilles, I cannot listen to you with calmness. For how long are you going to attack Marseilles? Does not even a triumph put an end to the war? in which was carried an image of that city, without whose assistance our forefathers never triumphed over the Transalpine nations. Then, indeed, did the Roman people groan. Although they had their own private griefs because of their own affairs, still there was no citizen who thought the miseries of this most loyal city unconnected with himself. Caesar himself, who had been the most angry of all men with them, still, on account of the unusually high character and loyalty of that city, was every day relaxing something of his displeasure. And is there no extent of calamity by which so faithful a city can satiate you? Again, perhaps, you will say that I am losing my temper. But I am speaking without passion, as I always do, though not without great indignation. I think that no man can be an enemy to that city, who is a friend to this one. What your object is, O Calenus, I cannot imagine. Formerly we were unable to deter you from devoting yourself to the gratification of the people; now we are unable to prevail on you to show any regard for their interests. I have argued long enough with Fufius, saying everything without hatred, but nothing without indignation. But I suppose that a man who can bear the complaint of his son in law with indifference, will bear that of his friend with great equanimity.

VII. I come now to the rest of the men of consular rank of whom there is no one, (I say this on my own responsibility,) who is not connected with me in some way or other by kindnesses conferred or received, some in a great, some in a moderate degree, but everyone to some extent or other. What a disgraceful day was yesterday to us! to us consulars, I mean. Are we to send ambassadors again? What? would he make a truce? Before the very face and eyes of the ambassadors he battered Mutina with his engines. He displayed his works and his defences to the ambassadors. The siege was not allowed one moment's breathing time, not even while the ambassadors should be present. Send ambassadors to this man! What for? in order to have great fears for their return? In truth, though on the previous occasion I had voted against the ambassadors being decreed, still I consoled myself with this reflection, that, when they had returned from Antonius despised and rejected, and had reported to the senate not merely that he had not withdrawn from Gaul, as we had voted that he should, but that he had not even retired from before Mutma, and that they had not been allowed to proceed on to Decimus Brutus, all men would be inflamed with hatred and stimulated by indignation, so that we should reinforce Decimus Brutus with arms, and horses, and men. But we have become even more languid since we have become acquainted with, not only the audacity and wickedness of Antonius, but also with his indolence and pride. Would that Lucius Caesar were in health, that Servius Sulpicius were alive. This cause would be pleaded much better by these men, than it is now by me single handed. What I am going to say I say with grief, rather than by way of insult. We have been deserted—we have, I say, been deserted, O conscript fathers, by our chiefs. But, as I have often said before, all those who in a time of such danger have proper and courageous sentiments shall be men of consular rank. The ambassadors ought to have brought us back courage, they have brought us back fear. Not, indeed, that they have caused me any fear—let them have as high an opinion as they please of the man to whom they were sent; from whom they have even brought back commands to us.

VIII. O ye immortal gods! where are the habits and virtues of our forefathers? Caius Popillius, in the time of our ancestors, when he had been sent as ambassador to Antiochus the king, and had given him notice, in the words of the senate, to depart from Alexandria, which he was besieging, on the kings seeking to delay giving his answer, drew a line round him where he was standing with his rod, and stated that he should report him to the senate if he did not answer him as to what he intended to do before he moved out of that line which surrounded him. He did well for he had brought with him the countenance of the senate and the authority of the Roman people, and if a man does not obey that, we are not to receive commands from him in return, but he is to be utterly rejected. Am I to receive commands from a man who despises the commands of the senate? Or am I to think that he has anything in common with the senate, who besieges a general of the Roman people in spite of the prohibition of the senate? But what commands they are! With what arrogance, with what stupidity, with what insolence are they conceived! But what made him charge our ambassadors with them when he was sending Cotyla to us, the ornament and bulwark of his friends, a man of aedilitian rank? if, indeed, he really was an aedile at the time when the public slaves flogged him with thongs at a banquet by command of Antonius.

But what modest commands they are! We must be non-hearted men, O conscript fathers, to deny anything to this man! "I give up both provinces," says he, "I disband my army, I am willing to become a private individual." For these are his very words. He seems to be coming to himself. "I am willing to forget everything, to be reconciled to everybody." But what does he add? "If you give booty and land to my six legions, to my cavalry, and to my praetorian cohort." He even demands rewards for those men for whom, if he were to demand pardon, he would be thought the most impudent of men. He adds further, "Those men to whom the lands have been given which he himself and Dolabella distributed, are to retain them." This is the Campanian and Leontine district, both which our ancestors considered a certain resource in times of scarcity.

IX. He is protecting the interests of his buffoons and gamesters and pimps. He is protecting Capho's and Sasu's interests too, pugnacious and muscular centurions, whom he placed among his troops of male and female buffoons. Besides all this, he demands "that the decrees of himself and his colleague concerning Caesar's writings and memoranda are to stand." Why is he so anxious that every one should have what he has bought, if he who sold it all has the price which he received for it? "And that his accounts of the money in the temple of Ops are not to be meddled with." That is to say, that those seven hundred millions of sesterces are not to be recovered from him. "That the septemviri are to be exempt from blame or from prosecution for what they have done." It was Nucula, I imagine, who put him in mind of that, he was afraid, perhaps, of losing so many clients. He also wishes to make stipulations in favour of "those men who are with him who may have done anything against the laws." He is here taking care of Mustela and Tiro, he is not anxious about himself. For what has he done? has he ever touched the public money, or murdered a man, or had armed men about him? But what reason has he for taking so much trouble about them? For he demands, "that his own judiciary law be not abrogated." And if he obtains that, what is there that he can fear? can he be afraid that any one of his friends may be convicted by Cydas, or Lysiades, or Curius? However, he does not press us with many more demands. "I give up," says he, "Gallia Togata; I demand Gallia Comata"—he evidently wishes to be quite at his ease—'with six legions, and those made up to their full complement out of the army of Decimus Brutus,—not only out of the troops whom he has enlisted himself; "and he is to keep possession of it as long as Marcus Brutus and Carus Cassius, as consuls, or as proconsuls, keep possession of their provinces." In the comitia held by him, his brother Carus (for it is his year) has already been repulsed. "And I myself," says he, "am to retain possession of my province five years." But that is expressly forbidden by the law of Caesar, and you defend the acts of Caesar.

X. Were you, O Lucius Piso, and you, O Lucius Philippus, you chiefs of the city, able, I will not say to endure in your minds but even to listen with your ears to these commands of his? But, I suspect there was some alarm at work, nor, while in his power, could you feel as ambassadors, or as men of consular rank, nor could you maintain our own dignity, or that of the republic. And nevertheless, somehow or other, owing to some philosophy, I suppose, you did what I could not have done,—you returned without any very angry feelings. Marcus Antonius paid you no respect, though you were most illustrious men, ambassadors of the Roman people. As for us, what concessions did not we make to Cotyla the ambassador of Marcus Antonius? though it was against the law for even the gates of the city to be opened to him, yet even this temple was opened to him. He was allowed to enter the senate, here yesterday he was taking down our opinions and every word we said in his note books, and men who had been preferred to the highest honours sold themselves to him in utter disregard of their own dignity.

O ye immortal gods! how great an enterprise is it to uphold the character of a leader in the republic, for it requires one to be influenced not merely by the thoughts but also by the eyes of the citizens. To take to one's house the ambassador of an enemy, to admit him to one's chamber, even to confer apart with him, is the act of a man who thinks nothing of his dignity, and too much of his danger. But what is danger? For if one is engaged in a contest where everything is at stake, either liberty is assured to one if victorious, or death if defeated, the former of which alternatives is desirable, and the latter some time or other inevitable. But a base flight from death is worse than any imaginable death. For I will never be induced to believe that there are men who envy the consistency or diligence of others, and who are indignant at the unceasing desire to assist the republic being approved by the senate and people of Rome. That is what we were all bound to do, and that was not only in the time of our ancestors, but even lately, the highest praise of men of consular rank, to be vigilant, to be anxious, to be always either thinking, or doing, or saying something to promote the interests of the republic.

I, O conscript fathers, recollect that Quintus Scaevola the augur, in the Marsic war, when he was a man of extreme old age, and quite broken down in constitution, every day, as soon as it was daylight, used to give every one an opportunity of consulting him, nor, throughout all that war, did any one ever see him in bed, and, though old and weak, he was the first man to come into the senate house. I wish, above all things, that those who ought to do so would imitate his industry, and, next to that, I wish that they would not envy the exertions of another.

XI. In truth, O conscript fathers, now we have begun to entertain hopes of liberty again, after a period of six years, during which we have been deprived of it, having endured slavery longer than prudent and industrious prisoners usually do, what watchfulness, what anxiety, what exertions ought we to shrink from, for the sake of delivering the Roman people? In truth, O conscript fathers, though men who have had the honours conferred on them that we have, usually wear their gowns, while the rest of the city is in the robe of war, still I decided that at such a momentous crisis, and when the whole republic was in so disturbed a state, we would not differ in our dress from you and the rest of the citizens. For we men of consular rank are not in this war conducting ourselves in such a manner that the Roman people will be likely to look with equanimity on the ensigns of our honour, when some of us are so cowardly as to have cast away all recollection of the kindnesses which they have received from the Roman people, some are so disaffected to the republic that they openly allege that they favour this enemy, and easily bear having our ambassadors despised and insulted by Antonius, while they wish to support the ambassador sent by Antonius. For they said that he ought not to be prevented from returning to Antonius, and they proposed an amendment to my proposition of not receiving him. Well, I will submit to them. Let Varius return to his general, but on condition that he never returns to Rome. And as to the others, if they abandon their errors and return to their duty to the republic, I think they may be pardoned and left unpunished.

Therefore, I give my vote, "That of those men who are with Marcus Antonius, those who abandon his army, and come over either to Caius Pansa or Aulus Hirtius the consuls; or to Decimus Brutus, imperator and consul elect, or to Caius Caesar, propraetor, before the first of March next, shall not be liable to prosecution for having been with Antonius. That, if any one of those men who are now with Antonius shall do anything which appears entitled to honour or to reward, Caius Pansa and Aulus Hirtius the consuls, one or both of them, shall, if they think fit, make a motion to the senate respecting that man's honour or reward, at the earliest opportunity. That, if, after this resolution of the senate, any one shall go to Antonius except Lucius Varius, the senate will consider that that man has acted as an enemy to the republic."

THE NINTH PHILIPPIC

THE ARGUMENT

Servius Sulpicius, as has been already said, had died on his embassy to Marcus Antonius, before Mutina; and the day after the delivery of the preceding speech, Pansa again called the senate together to deliberate on the honours to be paid to his memory. He himself proposed a public funeral, a sepulchre, and a statue. Servilius opposed the statue, as due only to those who had been slain by violence while in discharge of their duties as ambassadors. Cicero delivered the following oration in support of Pansa's proposition, which was carried.

I. I wish, O conscript fathers, that the immortal gods had granted to us to return thanks to Servius Sulpicius while alive, rather than thus to devise honours for him now that he is dead. Nor have I any doubt, but that if that man had been able himself to give us his report of the proceedings of his embassy, his return would have been acceptable to you and salutary to the republic. Not that either Lucius Piso or Lucius Philippus have been deficient in either zeal or care in the performance of so important a duty and so grave a commission; but, as Servius Sulpicius was superior in age to them, and in wisdom to every one, he, being suddenly taken from the business, left the whole embassy crippled and enfeebled.

But if deserved honours have been paid to any ambassador after death, there is no one by whom they can be found to have been ever more fully deserved than by Servius Sulpicius. The rest of those men who have died while engaged on an embassy, have gone forth, subject indeed to the usual uncertainties of life, but without any especial danger or fear of death. Servius Sulpicius set out with some hope indeed of reaching Antonius, but with none of returning. But though he was so very ill that if any exertion were added to his bad state of health, he would have no hope of himself, still he did not refuse to try, even while at his last gasp, to be of some service to the republic. Therefore neither the severity of the winter, nor the snow, nor the length of the journey, nor the badness of the roads, nor his daily increasing illness, delayed him. And when he had arrived where he might meet and confer with the man to whom he had been sent, he departed this life in the midst of his care and consideration as to how he might best discharge the duty which he had undertaken.

As therefore, O Caius Pansa, you have done well in other respects, so you have acted admirably in exhorting us this day to pay honour to Servius Sulpicius, and in yourself making an eloquent oration in his praise. And after the speech which we have heard from you, I should have been content to say nothing beyond barely giving my vote, if I did not think it necessary to reply to Publius Servilius, who has declared his opinion that this honour of a statue ought to be granted to no one who has not been actually slain with a sword while performing the duties of his embassy. But I, O conscript fathers, consider that this was the feeling of our ancestors, that they considered that it was the cause of death, and not the manner of it, which was a proper subject for inquiry. In fact, they thought fit that a monument should be erected to any man whose death was caused by an embassy, in order to tempt men in perilous wars to be the more bold in undertaking the office of an ambassador. What we ought to do, therefore, is, not to scrutinise the precedents afforded by our ancestors, but to explain their intentions from which the precedents themselves arose.

II. Lar Tolumnius, the king of Veii, slew four ambassadors of the Roman people, at Fidenae, whose statues were standing in the rostra till within my recollection. The honour was well deserved. For our ancestors gave those men who had encountered death in the cause of the republic an imperishable memory in exchange for this transitory life. We see in the rostra the statue of Cnaeus Octavius, an illustrious and great man, the first man who brought the consulship into that family, which afterwards abounded in illustrious men. There was no one then who envied him, because he was a new man; there was no one who did not honour his virtue. But yet the embassy of Octavius was one in which there was no suspicion of danger. For having been sent by the senate to investigate the dispositions of kings and of free nations, and especially to forbid the grandson of king Antiochus, the one who had carried on war against our forefathers, to maintain fleets and to keep elephants, he was slain at Laodicea, in the gymnasium, by a man of the name of Leptines. On this a statue was given to him by our ancestors as a recompense for his life, which might ennoble his progeny for many years, and which is now the only memorial left of so illustrious a family. But in his case, and in that of Tullus Cluvius, and Lucius Roseius, and Spurius Antius, and Caius Fulcinius, who were slain by the king of Veii, it was not the blood that was shed at their death, but the death itself which was encountered in the service of the republic, which was the cause of their being thus honoured.

III. Therefore, O conscript fathers, if it had been chance which had caused the death of Servius Sulpicius, I should sorrow indeed over such a loss to the republic, but I should consider him deserving of the honour, not of a monument, but of a public mourning. But, as it is, who is there who doubts that it was the embassy itself which caused his death? For he took death away with him; though, if he had remained among us, his own care, and the attention of his most excellent son and his most faithful wife, might have warded it off. But he, as he saw that, if he did not obey your authority, he should not be acting like himself; but that if he did obey, then that duty, undertaken, for the welfare of the republic, would be the end of his life; preferred dying at a most critical period of the republic, to appearing to have done less service to the republic than he might have done.

He had an opportunity of recruiting his strength and taking care of himself in many cities through which his journey lay. He was met by the liberal invitation of many entertainers as his dignity deserved, and the men too who were sent with him exhorted him to take rest, and to think of his own health. But he, refusing all delay, hastening on eager to perform your commands, persevered in this his constant purpose, in spite of the hindrances of his illness And as Antonius was above all things disturbed by his arrival, because the commands which were laid upon him by your orders had been drawn up by the authority and wisdom of Servius Sulpicius, he showed plainly how he hated the senate by the evident joy which he displaced at the death of the adviser of the senate.

Leptines then did not kill Octavius, nor did the king of Veii slay those whom I have just named, more clearly than Antonius killed Servius Sulpicius. Surely he brought the man death, who was the cause of his death. Wherefore, I think it of consequence, in order that posterity may recollect it, that there should be a record of what the judgment of the senate was concerning this war. For the statue itself will be a witness that the war was so serious an one, that the death of an ambassador in it gained the honour of an imperishable memorial.

IV. But if, O conscript fathers, you would only recollect the excuses alleged by Servius Sulpicius why he should not be appointed to this embassy, then no doubt will be left on your minds that we ought to repair by the honour paid to the dead the injury which we did to him while living. For it is you, O conscript fathers (it is a grave charge to make, but it must be uttered,) it is you, I say, who have deprived Servius Sulpicius of life. For when you saw him pleading his illness as an excuse more by the truth of the fact than by any laboured plea of words, you were not indeed cruel, (for what can be more impossible for this order to be guilty of than that,) but as you hoped that there was nothing that could not be accomplished by his authority and wisdom, you opposed his excuse with great earnestness, and compelled the man, who had always thought your decisions of the greatest weight, to abandon his own opinion. But when there was added the exhortation of Pansa, the consul, delivered with more weight than the ears of Servius Sulpicius had learnt to resist, then at last he led me and his own son aside, and said that he was bound to prefer your authority to his own life. And we, admiring his virtue, did not dare to oppose his determination. His son was moved with extraordinary piety and affection, and my own grief did not fall far short of his agitation, but each of us was compelled to yield to his greatness of mind, and to the dignity of his language, when he, indeed, amid the loud praises and congratulations of you all, promised to do whatever you wished, and not to avoid the danger which might be inclined by the adoption of the opinion of which he himself had been the author. And we the next day escorted him early in the morning as he hastened forth to execute your commands. And he, in truth, when departing, spoke with me in such a manner that his language seemed like an omen of his fate.

V. Restore then, O conscript fathers, life to him from whom you have taken it. For the life of the dead consists in the recollection cherished of them by the living. Take ye care that he, whom you without intending it sent to his death, shall from you receive immortality. And if you by your decree erect a statue to him in the rostia, no forgetfulness of posterity will ever obscure the memory of his embassy. For the remainder of the life of Servius Sulpicius will be recommended to the eternal recollection of all men by many and splendid memorials. The praise of all mortals will for ever celebrate his wisdom, his firmness, his loyalty, his admirable vigilance and prudence in upholding the interests of the public. Nor will that admirable, and incredible, and almost godlike skill of his in interpreting the laws and explaining the principles of equity be buried in silence. If all the men of all ages, who have ever had any acquaintance with the law in this city, were got together into one place, they would not deserve to be compared to Servius Sulpicius. Nor was he more skilful in explaining the law than in laying down the principles of justice. Those maxims which were derived from laws and from the common law, he constantly referred to the original principles of kindness and equity. Nor was he more fond of arranging the conduct of law-suits than of preventing disputes altogether. Therefore he is not in want of this memorial which a statue will provide; he has other and better ones. For this statue will be only a witness of his honourable death; those actions will be the memorial of his glorious life. So that this will be rather a monument of the gratitude of the senate, than of the glory of the man.

The affection of the son, too, will appear to have great influence in moving us to honour the father; for although, being overwhelmed with grief, he is not present, still you ought to be animated with the same feelings as if he were present. But he is in such distress, that no father ever sorrowed more over the loss of an only son than he grieves for the death of his father. Indeed, I think that it concerns also the fame of Servius Sulpicius the son, that he should appear to have paid all due respect to his father. Although Servius Sulpicius could leave no nobler monument behind him than his son, the image of his own manners, and virtues, and wisdom, and piety, and genius; whose grief can either be alleviated by this honour paid to his father by you, or by no consolation at all.

VI. But when I recollect the many conversations which in the days of our intimacy on earth I have had with Servius Sulpicius, it appears to me, that if there be any feeling in the dead, a brazen statue, and that too a pedestrian one, will be more acceptable to him than a gilt equestrian one, such as was first erected to Lucius Sylla. For Servius was wonderfully attached to the moderation of our forefathers, and was accustomed to reprove the insolence of this age. As if, therefore, I were able to consult himself as to what he would wish, so I give my vote for a pedestrian statue of brass, as if I were speaking by his authority and inclination; which by the honour of the memorial will diminish and mitigate the great grief and regret of his fellow-citizens. And it is certain that this my opinion, O conscript fathers, will be approved of by the opinion of Publius Servilius, who has given his vote that a sepulchre be publicly decreed to Servius Sulpicius, but has voted against the statue. For if the death of an ambassador happening without bloodshed and violence requires no honour, why does he vote for the honour of a public funeral, which is the greatest honour that can be paid to a dead man! If he grants that to Servius Sulpicius which was not given to Cnaeus Octavius, why does he think that we ought not to give to the former what was given to the latter? Our ancestors, indeed, decreed statues to many men; public sepulchres to few. But statues perish by weather, by violence, by lapse of time; but the sanctity of the sepulchres is in the soil itself, which can neither be moved nor destroyed by any violence; and while other things are extinguished, so sepulchres become holier by age.

Let, then, that man be distinguished by that honour also, a man to whom no honour can be given which is not deserved. Let us be grateful in paying respect in death to him to whom we can now show no other gratitude. And by that same step let the audacity of Marcus Antonius, waging a nefarious war, be branded with infamy. For when these honours have been paid to Servius Sulpicius, the evidence of his embassy having been insulted and rejected by Antonius will remain for everlasting.

VII. On which account I give my vote for a decree in this form: 'As Servius Sulpicius Rufus, the son of Quintus, of the Lemonian tribe, at a most critical period of the republic, and being ill with a very serious and dangerous disease, preferred the authority of the senate and the safety of the republic to his own life, and struggled against the violence and severity of his illness, in order to arrive at the camp of Antonius, to which the senate had sent him; and as he when he had almost arrived at the camp, being overwhelmed by the violence of the disease, has lost his life in discharging a most important office of the republic; and as his death has been in strict correspondence to a life passed with the greatest integrity and honour, during which he, Servius Sulpicius, has often been of great service to the republic, both as a private individual and in the discharge of various magistracies; and as he, being such a man, has encountered death on behalf of the republic while employed on an embassy;—the senate decrees that a brazen pedestrian statue of Servius Sulpicius be erected in the rostra in compliance with the resolution of this order, and that his children and posterity shall have a place round this statue of five feet in every direction, from which to behold the games and gladiatorial combats, because he died in the cause of the republic; and that this reason be inscribed on the pedestal of the statue; and that Carus Pansa and Aulus Hirtius the consuls, one or both of them, if it seem good to them, shall command the quaestors of the city to let out a contract for making that pedestal and that statue, and erecting them in the rostra; and that whatever price they contract for, they shall take care the amount is given and paid to the contractor, and as in old times the senate has exerted its authority with respect to the obsequies of, and honours paid to brave men, it now decrees that he shall be carried to the tomb on the day of his funeral with the greatest possible solemnity. And as Servius Sulpicius Rufus, the son of Quintus of the Lemonian tribe, has deserved so well of the republic as to be entitled to be complimented with all those distinctions, the senate is of opinion, and thinks it for the advantage of the republic, that the consule aedile should suspend the edict which usually prevails with respect to funerals in the case of the funeral of Servius Sulpicius Rufus, the son of Quintus of the Lemonian tribe, and that Carus Pansa, the consul, shall assign him a place for a tomb in the Esquiline plain, or in whatever place shall seem good to him extending thirty feet in every direction, where Servius Sulpicius may be buried, and that that shall be his tomb, and that of his children and posterity, as having been a tomb most deservedly given to them by the public authority.

THE TENTH PHILIPPIC

THE ARGUMENT

Soon after the delivery of the last speech, despatches were received from Brutus by the consuls, giving an account of his success against Carus Antonius in Macedonia, stating that he had secured Macedonia, Illyricum, and Greece with the armies in those countries, that Carus Antonius had retired to Apollonia with seven cohorts, that a legion under Lucius Piso had surrendered to young Cicero, who was commanding his cavalry, that Dolabella's cavalry had deserted to him, and that Vatinius had surrendered Dyrrachium and its garrison to him. He likewise praised Quintus Hortensius, the proconsul of Macedonia, as having assisted him in gaining over the Grecian provinces and the armies in those districts.

As soon as Pansa received the despatches, he summoned the senate to have them read, and in a set speech greatly extolled Brutus, and moved a vote of thanks to him but Calenus, who followed him, declared his opinion, that as Brutus had acted without any public commission or authority he should be required to give up his army to the proper governors of the provinces, or to whoever the senate should appoint to receive it. After he had sat down, Cicero rose, and delivered the following speech.

I. We all, O Pansa, ought both to feel and to show the greatest gratitude to you, who—though we did not expect that you would hold any senate to day,—the moment that you received the letters of Marcus Brutus, that most excellent citizen, did not interpose even the slightest delay to our enjoying the most excessive delight and mutual congratulation at the earliest opportunity. And not only ought this action of yours to be grateful to us all, but also the speech which you addressed to us after the letters had been read. For you showed plainly, that that was true which I have always felt to be so, that no one envied the virtue of another who was confident of his own. Therefore I, who have been connected with Brutus by many mutual good offices and by the greatest intimacy, need not say so much concerning him for the part that I had marked out for myself your speech has anticipated me in. But, O conscript fathers, the opinion delivered by the man who was asked for his vote before me, has imposed upon me the necessity of saying rather more than I otherwise should have said, and I differ from him so repeatedly at present, that I am afraid (what certainly ought not to be the case) that our continual disagreement may appear to diminish our friendship.

What can be the meaning of this argument of yours, O Calenus? what can be your intention? How is it that you have never once since the first of January been of the same opinion with him who asks you your opinion first? How is it that the senate has never yet been so full as to enable you to find one single person to agree with your sentiments? Why are you always defending men who in no point resemble you? why, when both your life and your fortune invite you to tranquillity and dignity, do you approve of those measures, and defend those measures, and declare those sentiments, which are adverse both to the general tranquillity and to your own individual dignity?

II. For to say nothing of former speeches of yours, at all events I cannot pass over in silence this which excites my most especial wonder. What war is there between you and the Bruti? Why do you alone attack those men whom we are all bound almost to worship? Why are you not indignant at one of them being besieged, and why do you—as far as your vote goes—strip the other of those troops which by his own exertions and by his own danger he has got together by himself, without any one to assist him, for the protection of the republic, not for himself? What is your meaning in this? What are your intentions? Is it possible that you should not approve of the Bruti, and should approve of Antonius? that you should hate those men whom every one else considers most dear? and that you should love with the greatest constancy those whom every one else hates most bitterly? You have a most ample fortune, you are in the highest rank of honour, your son, as I both hear and hope is born to glory,—a youth whom I favour not only for the sake of the republic, but for your sake also. I ask, therefore, would you rather have him like Brutus or like Antonius? and I will let you choose whichever of the three Antonii you please. God forbid! you will say. Why, then, do you not favour those men and praise those men whom you wish your own son to resemble? For by so doing you will be both consulting the interests of the republic, and proposing him an example for his imitation.

But in this instance, I hope, O Quintus Fufius, to be allowed to expostulate with you, as a senator who greatly differs from you, without any prejudice to our friendship. For you spoke in this matter, and that too from a written paper, for I should think you had made a slip from want of some appropriate expression, if I were not acquainted with your ability in speaking. You said "that the letters of Brutus appeared properly and regularly expressed." What else is this than praising Brutus's secretary, not Brutus? You both ought to have great experience in the affairs of the republic, and you have. When did you ever see a decree framed in this manner? or in what resolution of the senate passed on such occasions, (and they are innumerable,) did you ever hear of its being decreed that the letters had been well drawn up? And that expression did not—as is often the case with other men—fall from you by chance, but you brought it with you written down, deliberated on, and carefully meditated on.

III. If any one could take from you this habit of disparaging good men on almost every occasion, then what qualities would not be left to you which every one would desire for himself? Do, then, recollect yourself, do at last soften and quiet that disposition of yours, do take the advice of good men, with many of whom you are intimate, do converse with that wisest of men, your own son in-law, oftener than with yourself, and then you will obtain the name of a man of the very highest character. Do you think it a matter of no consequence, (it is a matter in which I, out of the friendship which I feel you, constantly grieve in your stead,) that this should be commonly said out of doors, and should be a common topic of conversation among the Roman people, that the man who delivered his opinion first did not find a single person to agree with him? And that I think will be the case to day.

You propose to take the legions away from Brutus—which legions? Why, those which he has gained over from the wickedness of Caius Antonius, and has by his own authority gained over to the republic. Do you wish then that he should again appear to be the only person stripped of his authority, and as it were banished by the senate? And you, O conscript fathers, if you abandon and betray Marcus Brutus, what citizen in the world will you ever distinguish? Whom will you ever favour? Unless, indeed, you think that those men who put a diadem on a man's head deserve to be preserved, and those who have abolished the very name of kingly power deserve to be abandoned. And of this divine and immortal glory of Marcus Brutus I will say no more, it is already embalmed in the grateful recollection of all the citizens, but it has not yet been sanctioned by any formal act of public authority. Such patience! O ye good gods! such moderation! such tranquillity and submission under injury! A man who, while he was praetor of the city, was driven from the city, was prevented from sitting as judge in legal proceedings, when it was he who had restored all law to the republic, and, though he might have been hedged round by the daily concourse of all virtuous men, who were constantly flocking round him in marvellous numbers, he preferred to be defended in his absence by the judgment of the good, to being present and protected by their force,—who was not even present to celebrate the games to Apollo, which had been prepared in a manner suitable to his own dignity and to that of the Roman people, lest he should open any road to the audacity of most wicked men.

IV. Although, what games or what days were ever more joyful than those on which at every verse that the actor uttered, the Roman people did honour to the memory of Brutus, with loud shouts of applause? The person of their liberator was absent, the recollection of their liberty was present, in which the appearance of Brutus himself seemed to be visible. But the man himself I beheld on those very days of the games, in the country-house of a most illustrious young man, Lucullus, his relation, thinking of nothing but the peace and concord of the citizens. I saw him again afterwards at Veha, departing from Italy, in order that there might be no pretext for civil war on his account. Oh what a sight was that! grievous, not only to men but to the very waves and shores. That its saviour should be departing from his country, that its destroyers should be remaining in their country! The fleet of Cassius followed a few days afterwards, so that I was ashamed O conscript fathers, to return into the city from which those men were departing. But the design with which I returned you heard at the beginning, and since that you have known by experience. Brutus, therefore, bided his time. For, as long as he saw you endure everything, he himself behaved with incredible patience, after that he saw you roused to a desire of liberty, he prepared the means to protect you in your liberty.

But what a pest, and how great a pest was it which he resisted? For if Caius Antonius had been able to accomplish what he intended in his mind, (and he would have been able to do so if the virtue of Marcus Brutus had not opposed his wickedness,) we should have lost Macedonia, Illyricum, and Greece. Greece would have been a refuge for Antonius if defeated, or a support to him in attacking Italy, which at present, being not only arrayed in arms, but embellished by the military command and authority and troops of Marcus Brutus stretches out her right hand to Italy, and promises it her protection. And the man who proposes to deprive him of his army, is taking away a most illustrious honour, and a most trustworthy guard from the republic. I wish, indeed, that Antonius may hear this news as speedily as possible, so that he may understand that it is not Decimus Brutus whom he is surrounding with his ramparts, but he himself who is really hemmed in.

V. He possesses three towns only on the whole face of the earth. He has Gaul most bitterly hostile to him, he has even those men the people beyond the Po, in whom he placed the greatest reliance, entirely alienated from him, all Italy is his enemy. Foreign nations, from the nearest coast of Greece to Egypt, are occupied by the military command and armies of most virtuous and intrepid citizens. His only hope was in Caius Antonius; who being in age the middle one between his two brothers, rivalled both of them in vices. He hastened away as if he were being driven away by the senate into Macedonia, not as if he were prohibited from proceeding thither. What a storm, O ye immortal gods! what a conflagration! what a devastation! what a pestilence to Greece would that man have been, if incredible and godlike virtue had not checked the enterprise and audacity of that frantic man. What promptness was there in Brutus's conduct! what prudence! what valour! Although the rapidity of the movement of Caius Antonius also is not despicable; for if some vacant inheritance had not delayed him on his march, you might have said that he had flown rather than travelled. When we desire other men to go forth to undertake any public business, we are scarcely able to get them out of the city; but we have driven this man out by the mere fact of our desiring to retain him. But what business had he with Apollonia? what business had he with Dyrrachium? or with Illyricum? What had he to do with the army of Publius Vatinius, our general? He, as he said himself, was the successor of Hortensius. The boundaries of Macedonia are well defined; the condition of the proconsul is well known; the amount of his army, if he has any at all, is fixed. But what had Antonius to do at all with Illyricum and with the legions of Vatinius?

But Brutus had nothing to do with them either. For that, perhaps, is what some worthless man may say. All the legions, all the forces which exist anywhere, belong to the Roman people. Nor shall those legions which have quitted Marcus Antonius be called the legions of Antonius rather than of the republic; for he loses all power over his army, and all the privileges of military command, who uses that military command and that army to attack the republic.

VI. But if the republic itself could give a decision, or if all rights were established by its decrees, would it adjudge the legions of the Roman people to Antonius or to Brutus? The one had flown with precipitation to the plunder and destruction of the allies, in order, wherever he went, to lay waste, and pillage, and plunder everything, and to employ the army of the Roman people against the Roman people itself. The other had laid down this law for himself, that wherever he came he should appear to come as a sort of light and hope of safety. Lastly, the one was seeking aids to overturn the republic; the other to preserve it. Nor, indeed, did we see this more clearly than the soldiers themselves; from whom so much discernment in judging was not to have been expected.

He writes, that Antonius is at Apollonia with seven cohorts, and he is either by this time taken prisoner, (may the gods grant it!) or, at all events, like a modest man, he does not come near Macedonia, lest he should seem to act in opposition to the resolution of the senate. A levy of troops has been held in Macedonia, by the great zeal and diligence of Quintus Hortensius; whose admirable courage, worthy both of himself and of his ancestors, you may clearly perceive from the letters of Brutus. The legion which Lucius Piso, the lieutenant of Antonius, commanded, has surrendered itself to Cicero, my own son. Of the cavalry, which was being led into Syria in two divisions, one division has left the quaestor who was commanding it, in Thessaly, and has joined Brutus; and Cnaeus Domitius, a young man of the greatest virtue and wisdom and firmness, has carried off the other from the Syrian lieutenant in Macedonia. But Publius Vatinius, who has before this been deservedly praised by us, and who is justly entitled to further praise at the present time, has opened the gates of Dyrrachium to Brutus, and has given him up his army.

The Roman people then is now in possession of Macedonia, and Illyricum, and Greece. The legions there are all devoted to us, the light-armed troops are ours, the cavalry is ours, and, above all, Brutus is ours, and always will be ours—a man born for the republic, both by his own most excellent virtues, and also by some especial destiny of name and family, both on his father's and on his mother's side.

VII. Does any one then fear war from this man, who, until we commenced the war, being compelled to do so, preferred lying unknown in peace to flourishing in war? Although he, in truth, never did lie unknown, nor can this expression possibly be applied to such great eminence in virtue. For he was the object of regret to the state; he was in every one's mouth, the subject of every one's conversation. But he was so far removed from an inclination to war, that, though he was burning with a desire to see Italy free, he preferred being wanting to the zeal of the citizens, to leading them to put everything to the issue of war. Therefore, those very men, if there be any such, who find fault with the slowness of Brutus's movements, nevertheless at the same time admire his moderation and his patience.

But I see now what it is they mean: nor, in truth, do they use much disguise. They say that they are afraid how the veterans may endure the idea of Brutus having an army. As if there were any difference between the troops of Aulus Hirtius, of Caius Pansa, of Decimus Brutus, of Caius Caesar, and this army of Marcus Brutus. For if these four armies which I have mentioned are praised because they have taken up arms for the sake of the liberty of the Roman people, what reason is there why this army of Marcus Brutus should not be classed under the same head? Oh, but the very name of Marcus Brutus is unpopular among the veterans.—More than that of Decimus Brutus?—I think not; for although the action is common to both the Bruti, and although their share in the glory is equal, still those men who were indignant at that deed were more angry with Decimus Brutus, because they said, that it was more improper for it to be executed by him. What now are all those armies labouring at, except to effect the release of Decimus Brutus from a siege? And who are the commanders of those armies? Those men, I suppose, who wish the acts of Caius Caesar to be overturned, and the cause of the veterans to be betrayed.

VIII. If Caesar himself were alive, could he, do you imagine, defend his own acts more vigorously than that most gallant man Hirtius defends them? or, is it possible that any one should be found more friendly to the cause than his son? But the one of these, though not long recovered from a very long attack of a most severe disease, has applied all the energy and influence which he had to defending the liberty of those men by whose prayers he considered that he himself had been recalled from death; the other, stronger in the strength of his virtue than in that of his age, has set out with those very veterans to deliver Decimus Brutus. Therefore, those men who are both the most certain and at the same time the most energetic defenders of the acts of Caesar, are waging war for the safety of Decimus Brutus; and they are followed by the veterans. For they see that they must fight to the uttermost for the freedom of the Roman people, not for their own advantages. What reason, then, is there why the army of Marcus Brutus should be an object of suspicion to those men who with the whole of their energies desire the preservation of Decimus Brutus?

But, moreover, if there were anything which were to be feared from Marcus Brutus, would not Pansa perceive it? Or if he did perceive it, would not he, too, be anxious about it? Who is either more acute in his conjectures of the future, or more diligent in warding off danger? But you have already seen his zeal for, and inclination towards Marcus Brutus. He has already told us in his speech what we ought to decree, and how we ought to feel with respect to Marcus Brutus. And he was so far from thinking the army of Marcus Brutus dangerous to the republic, that he considered it the most important and the most trusty bulwark of the republic. Either, then, Pansa does not perceive this (no doubt he is a man of dull intellect), or he disregards it. For he is clearly not anxious that the acts which Caesar executed should be ratified,—he, who in compliance with our recommendation is going to bring forward a bill at the comitia centuriata for sanctioning and confirming them.

IX. Let those, then, who have no fear, cease to pretend to be alarmed, and to be exercising their foresight in the cause of the republic. And let those who really are afraid of everything, cease to be too fearful, lest the pretence of the one party and the inactivity of the other be injurious to us. What, in the name of mischief! is the object of always opposing the name of the veterans to every good cause? For even if I were attached to their virtue, as indeed I am, still, if they were arrogant I should not be able to tolerate their airs. While we are endeavouring to break the bonds of slavery, shall any one hinder us by saying that the veterans do not approve of it? For they are not, I suppose, beyond all counting, who are ready to take up arms in defence of the common freedom! There is no man, except the veteran soldiers, who is stimulated by the indignation of a freeman to repel slavery! Can the republic then stand, relying wholly on veterans, without a great reinforcement of the youth of the state? Whom, indeed, you ought to be attached to, if they be assistants to you in the assertion of your freedom, but whom you ought not to follow if they be the advisers of slavery.

Lastly, (let me at last say one true word, one word worthy of myself!)—if the inclinations of this order are governed by the nod of the veterans, and if all our words and actions are to be referred to their will, death is what we should wish for, which has always, in the minds of Roman citizens, been preferable to slavery. All slavery is miserable; but some may have been unavoidable. Do you think, then, that there is never to be a beginning of our endeavours to recover our freedom? Or, when we would not bear that fortune which was unavoidable, and which seemed almost as if appointed by destiny, shalt we tolerate the voluntary bondage? All Italy is burning with a desire for freedom. The city cannot endure slavery any longer. We have given this warlike attire and these arms to the Roman people much later than they have been demanded of us by them.

X. We have, indeed, undertaken our present course of action with a great and almost certain hope of liberty. But even if I allow that the events of war are uncertain, and that the chances of Mars are common to both sides, still it is worth while to fight for freedom at the peril of one's life. For life does not consist wholly in breathing, there is literally no life at all for one who is a slave. All nations can endure slavery. Our state cannot. Nor is there any other reason for this, except that those nations shrink from toil and pain, and are willing to endure anything so long as they may be free from those evils, but we have been trained and bred up by our forefathers in such a manner, as to measure all our designs and all our actions by the standard of dignity and virtue. The recovery of freedom is so splendid a thing that we must not shun even death when seeking to recover it. But if immortality were to be the result of our avoidance of present danger, still slavery would appear still more worthy of being avoided, in proportion as it is of longer duration. But as all sorts of deaths surround us on all sides night and day, it does not become a man, and least of all a Roman, to hesitate to give up to his country that breath which he owes to nature.

Men flock together from all quarters to extinguish a general conflagration. The veterans were the first to follow the authority of Caesar and to repel the attempts of Antonius, afterwards the Martial legion checked his frenzy, the fourth legion crushed it. Being thus condemned by his own legions, he burst into Gaul, which he knew to be adverse and hostile to him both in word and deed. The armies of Aulus Hirtius and Caius Caesar pursued him, and afterwards the levies of Pansa roused the city and all Italy. He is the one enemy of all men. Although he has with him Lucius his brother, a citizen very much beloved by the Roman people, the regret for whose absence the city is unable to endure any longer! What can be more foul than that beast? what more savage? who appears born for the express purpose of preventing Marcus Antonius from being the basest of all mortals. They have with them Trebellius, who, now that all debts are cancelled, is become reconciled to them, and Titus Plancus, and other like them, who are striving with all their hearts, and whose sole object is, to appear to have been restored against the will of the republic. Saxa and Capho, themselves rustic and clownish men, men who never have seen and who never wish to see this republic firmly established, are tampering with the ignorant classes; men who are not upholding the acts of Caesar but those of Antonius, who are led away by the unlimited occupation of the Campanian district, and who I marvel are not somewhat ashamed when they see that they have actors and actresses for their neighbours.

XI. Why then should we be displeased that the army of Marcus Brutus is thrown into the scale to assist us in overwhelming these pests of the commonwealth? It is the army, I suppose, of an intemperate and turbulent man. I am more afraid of his being too patient, although in all the counsels and actions of that man there never has been anything either too much or too little. The whole inclinations of Marcus Brutus, O conscript fathers, the whole of his thoughts, the whole of his ideas, are directed towards the authority of the senate and the freedom of the Roman people. These are the objects which he proposes to himself, these are what he desires to uphold. He has tried what he could do by patience, as he did nothing he has thought it necessary to encounter force by force. And, O conscript fathers, you ought at this time to grant him the same honours which on the nineteenth of December you conferred by my advice on Decimus Brutus and Caius Caesar, whose designs and conduct in regard to the republic, while they also were but private individuals, was approved of and praised by your authority. And you ought to do the same now with respect to Marcus Brutus, by whom an unhoped for and sudden reinforcement of legions and cavalry, and numerous and trusty bands of allies, have been provided for the republic.

Quintus Hortensius also ought to have a share of your praise, who, being governor of Macedonia, joined Brutus as a most faithful and untiring assistant in collecting that army. For I think that a separate motion ought to be made respecting Marcus Appuleius, to whom Brutus bears witness in his letters that he has been a prime assistant to him in his endeavours to get together and equip his army. And since this is the case,

"As Caius Pansa the consul has addressed to us a speech concerning the letters which have been received from Quintus Caepio Brutus, proconsul, and have been read in this assembly, I give my vote in this matter thus.

"Since, by the exertions and wisdom and industry and valour of Quintus Caepio Brutus, proconsul, at a most critical period of the republic, the province of Macedonia, and Illyircum, and all Greece, and the legions and armies and cavalry, have been preserved in obedience to the consuls and senate and people of Rome, Quintus Caepio Brutus, proconsul, has acted well, and in a manner advantageous to the republic and suitable to his own dignity and to that of his ancestors, and to the principles according to which alone the affairs of the republic can be properly managed, and that conduct is and will be grateful to the senate and people of Rome.

"And moreover, as Quintus Caepio Brutus, proconsul, is occupying and defending and protecting the province of Macedonia, and Illyricum, and all Greece, and is preserving them in safety, and as he is in command of an army which he himself has levied and collected, he is at liberty, if he has need of any, to exact money for the use of the military service, which belongs to the public, and can lawfully be exacted, and to use it, and to borrow money for the exigencies of the war from whomsoever he thinks fit, and to exact coin, and to endeavour to approach Italy as near as he can with his forces. And as it has been understood from the letters of Quintus Caepio Brutus, proconsul, that the republic has been greatly benefited by the energy and valour of Quintus Hortensius, proconsul, and that all his counsels have been in harmony with those of Quintus Caepio Brutus, proconsul, and that that harmony has been of the greatest service to the republic, Quintus Hortensius has acted well and becomingly, and in a manner advantageous to the republic. And the senate decrees that Quintus Hortensius, proconsul, shall occupy the province of Macedonia with his quaestors, or proquaestors and lieutenants, until he shall have a successor regularly appointed by resolution of the senate."

THE ELEVENTH PHILIPPIC

THE ARGUMENT

A short time after the delivery of the preceding speech, news came to Rome of Dolabella (the colleague of Antonius) having been very successful in Asia. He had left Rome before the expiration of his consulship to take possession of Syria, which Antonius had contrived to have allotted him, and he hoped to prevail on the inhabitants of the province of Asia also to abandon Trebonius, (who had been one of the slayers of Caesar, and was governor of Asia) and submit to him. Trebonius was residing at Smyrna, and Dolabella arrived before the walls of that town with very few troops, requesting a free passage through Trebonius's province. Trebonius refused to admit him into the town, but promised that he would permit him to enter Ephesus. Dolabella, however, effected an entry into Smyrna by a nocturnal surprise, and seized Trebonius, whom he murdered with great cruelty.

As soon as the news of this event reached Rome, the consul summoned the senate, which at once declared Dolabella a public enemy, and confiscated his estate. Calenus was the mover of this decree. But besides this motion there was another question to be settled namely, who was to be appointed to conduct the war against Dolabella. Some proposed to send Publius Servilus; others, that the two consuls should be sent, and should have the two provinces of Asia and Syria allotted to them, and this last proposition Pansa himself was favourable to, and it was supported not only by his friends, but also by the partisans of Antonius, who thought it would draw off the consuls from their present business of relieving Decimus Brutus. But Cicero thought that it would be an insult to Cassius, who was already in those countries, to supersede him as it were, by sending any one else to command there, and so he exerted all his influence to procure a decree entrusting the command to him, though Servilia, the mother-in-law of Cassius, and other of Cassius's friends, begged him not to disoblige Pansa. He persevered, however and made the following speech in support of his opinion.

It appears that Cicero failed in his proposition through the influence of Pansa, but before any orders came from Rome, Cassius had defeated Dolabella near Laodicea, and he killed himself to avoid falling into the hands of his conqueror.

I. AMID the great grief, O conscript fathers, or rather misery which we have suffered at the cruel and melancholy death of Caius Trebonius, a most virtuous citizen and a most moderate man, there is still a circumstance or two in the case which I think will turn out beneficial to the republic. For we have now thoroughly seen what great barbarity these men are capable of who have taken up wicked arms against their country. For these two, Dolabella and Antonius, are the very blackest and foulest monsters that have ever lived since the birth of man; one of whom has now done what he wished; and as to the other, it has been plainly shown what he intended. Lucius Cinna was cruel; Caius Marius was unrelenting in his anger; Lucius Sylla was fierce; but still the inhumanity of none of these men ever went beyond death; and that punishment indeed was thought too cruel to be inflicted on citizens.

Here now you have a pair equal in wickedness; unprecedented, unheard of, savage, barbarous. Therefore those men whose vehement mutual hatred and quarrel you recollect a short time ago, have now been united in singular unanimity and mutual attachment by the singularity of their wicked natures and most infamous lives. Therefore, that which Dolabella has now done in a case in which he had the power, Antonius threatens many with. But the former, as he was a long way from our counsels and armies, and as he was not yet aware that the senate had united with the Roman people, relying on the forces of Antonius, has committed those wicked actions which he thought were already put in practice at Rome by his accomplice in wickedness. What else then do you think that this man is contriving or wishing, or what other object do you think he has in the war? All of us who have either entertained the thoughts of freemen concerning the republic, or have given utterance to opinions worthy of ourselves, he decides to be not merely opposed to him, but actual enemies. And he plans inflicting bitterer punishments on us than on the enemy; he thinks death a punishment imposed by nature, but torments and tortures the proper inflictions of anger. What sort of enemy then must we consider that man who, if he be victorious, requires one to think death a kindness if he spares one the tortures with which it is in his power to accompany it?

II. Wherefore, O conscript fathers, although you do not need any one to exhort you, (for you yourself have of your own accord warmed up with the desire of recovering your freedom,) still defend, I warn you, your freedom with so much the more zeal and courage, in proportion as the punishments of slavery with which you see the conquered are threatened are more terrible. Antonius has invaded Gaul; Dolabella, Asia;

each a province with which he had no business whatever. Brutus has opposed himself to the one, and at the peril of his own life has checked the onset of that frantic man wishing to harass and plunder everything, has prevented his further progress, and has cut him off from his return. By allowing himself to be besieged he has hemmed in Antonius on each side.

The other has forced his way into Asia. With what object? If it was merely to proceed into Syria, he had a road open to him which was sure, and was not long. What was the need of sending forward some Marsian, they call him Octavius, with a legion; a wicked and necessitous robber; a man to lay waste the lands, to harass the cities, not from any hope of acquiring any permanent property, which they who know him say that he is unable to keep (for I have not the honour of being acquainted with this senator myself,) but just as present food to satisfy his indigence? Dolabella followed him, without any one having any suspicion of war. For how could any one think of such a thing? Very friendly conferences with Trebonius ensued; embraces, false tokens of the greatest good-will, were there full of simulated affection; the pledge of the right hand, which used to be a witness of good faith, was violated by treachery and wickedness; then came the nocturnal entry into Smyrna, as if into an enemy's city—Smyrna, which is a city of our most faithful and most ancient allies; then the surprise of Trebonius, who, if he were surprised by one who was an open enemy, was very careless; if by one who up to that moment maintained the appearance of a citizen, was miserable. And by his example fortune wished us to take a lesson of what the conquered party had to fear. He handed over a man of consular rank, governing the province of Asia with consular authority, to an exiled armourer; he would not slay him the moment that he had taken him, fearing, I suppose, that his victory might appear too merciful; but after having attacked that most excellent man with insulting words from his impious mouth, then he examined him with scourges and tortures concerning the public money, and that for two days together. Afterwards he cut off his head, and ordered it to be fixed on a javelin and carried about, and the rest of his body, having been dragged through the street and town, he threw into the sea.

We, then, have to war against this enemy by whose most foul cruelty all the savageness of barbarous nations is surpassed. Why need I speak of the massacre of Roman citizens? of the plunder of temples? Who is there who can possibly deplore such circumstances as their atrocity deserves? And now he is ranging all over Asia, he is triumphing about as a king, he thinks that we are occupied in another quarter by another war, as if it were not one and the same war against this outrageous pair of impious men.

III. You see now an image of the cruelty of Marcus Antonius in Dolabella, this conduct of his is formed on the model of the other. It is by him that the lessons of wickedness have been taught to Dolabella. Do you think that Antonius, if he had the power, would be more merciful in Italy than Dolabella has proved in Asia? To me, indeed, this latter appears to have gone as far as the insanity of a savage man could go; nor do I believe that Antonius either would omit any description of punishment, if he had only the power to inflict it.

Place then before your eyes, O conscript fathers, that spectacle, miserable indeed, and tearful, but still indispensable to rouse your minds properly: the nocturnal attack upon the most beautiful city in Asia; the irruption of armed men into Trebonius's house, when that unhappy man saw the swords of the robbers before he heard what was the matter, the entrance of Dolabella, raging,—his ill omened voice, and infamous countenance,—the chains, the scourges, the rack, the armourer who was both torturer and executioner, all which they say that the unhappy Trebonius endured with great fortitude. A great praise, and in my opinion indeed the greatest of all, for it is the part of a wise man to resolve beforehand that whatever can happen to a brave man is to be endured with patience if it should happen. It is indeed a proof of altogether greater wisdom to act with such foresight as to prevent any such thing from happening, but it is a token of no less courage to bear it bravely if it should befall one.

And Dolabella was indeed so wholly forgetful of the claims of humanity, (although, indeed, he never had any particular recollection of it,) as to vent his insatiable cruelty, not only on the living man, but also on the dead carcass, and, as he could not sufficiently glut his hatred, to feed his eyes also on the lacerations inflicted, and the insults offered to his corpse.

IV. O Dolabella, much more wretched than he whom you intended to be the most wretched of all men! Trebonius endured great agonies, many men have endured greater still, from severe disease, whom, however, we are in the habit of calling not miserable, but afflicted. His sufferings, which lasted two days, were long, but many men have had sufferings lasting many years, nor are the tortures inflicted by executioners more terrible than those caused by disease are sometimes. There are other tortures,—others, I tell you, O you most abandoned and insane man, which are far more miserable. For in proportion as the vigour of the mind exceeds that of the body, so also are the sufferings which rack the mind more terrible than those which are endured by the body. He, therefore, who commits a wicked action is more wretched than he who is compelled to endure the wickedness of another. Trebonius was tortured by Dolabella, and so, indeed, was Regulus by the Carthaginians. If on that account the Carthaginians were considered very cruel for such behaviour to an enemy, what must we think of Dolabella, who treated a citizen in such a manner? Is there any comparison? or can we doubt which of the two is most miserable? he whose death the senate and Roman people wish to avenge, or he who has been adjudged an enemy by the unanimous vote of the senate? For in every other particular of their lives, who could possibly, without the greatest insult to Trebonius, compare the life of Trebonius to that of Dolabella? Who is ignorant of the wisdom, and genius, and humanity, and innocence of the one, and of his greatness of mind as displayed in his exertions for the freedom of his country? The other, from his very childhood, has taken delight in cruelty; and, moreover, such has been the shameful nature of his lusts, that he has always delighted in the very fact of doing those things which he could not even be reproached with by a modest enemy.

And this man, O ye immortal gods, was once my relation! For his vices were unknown to one who did not inquire into such things nor perhaps should I now be alienated from him if he had not been discovered to be an enemy to you, to the walls of his country, to this city, to our household gods, to the altars and hearths of all of us,—in short, to human nature and to common humanity. But now, having received this lesson from him, let us be the more diligent and vigilant in being on our guard against Antonius.

V. Indeed, Dolabella had not with him any great number of notorious and conspicuous robbers. But you see there are with Antonius, and in what numbers. In the first place, there is his brother Lucius—what a firebrand, O ye immortal gods! what an incarnation of crime and wickedness! what a gulf, what a whirlpool of a man! What do you think that man incapable of swallowing up in his mind, or gulping down in his thoughts! Who do you imagine there is whose blood he is not thirsting for? who, on whose possessions and fortunes he is not fixing his most impudent eyes, his hopes, and his whole heart? What shall we say of Censorinus? who, as far as words go, said indeed that he wished to be the city praetor, but who, in fact, was unwilling to be so? What of Bestia, who professes that he is a candidate for the consulship in the place of Brutus?

May Jupiter avert from us this most detestable omen! But how absurd is it for a man to stand for the consulship who cannot be elected praetor! unless, indeed, he thinks his conviction may be taken as an equivalent to the praetorship. Let this second Caesar, this great Vopiscus, a man of consummate genius, of the highest influence, who seeks the consulship immediately after having been aedile, be excused from obedience to the laws. Although, indeed, the laws do not bind him, on account, I suppose, of his exceeding dignity. But this man has been acquitted five times when I have defended him. To win a sixth city victory is difficult, even in the case of a gladiator. However, this is the fault of the judges, not mine. I defended him with perfect good faith, they were bound to retain a most illustrious and excellent citizen in the republic, who now, however, appears to have no other object except to make us understand that those men whose judicial decisions we annulled, decided rightly and in a manner advantageous to the republic.

Nor is this the case with respect to this man alone; there are other men in the same camp honestly condemned and shamefully restored; what counsel do you imagine can be adopted by those men who are enemies to all good men, that is not utterly cruel? There is besides a fellow called Saxa; I don't know who he is, some man whom Caesar imported from the extremity of Celtiberia and gave us for a tribune of the people. Before that, he was a measurer of ground for camps; now he hopes to measure out and value the city. May the evils which this foreigner predicts to us fall on his own head, and may we escape in safety! With him is the veteran Capho; nor is there any man whom the veteran troops hate more cordially; to these men, as if in addition to the dowry which they had received during our civil disasters, Antonius had given the Campanian district, that they might have it as a sort of nurse for their other estates. I only wish they would be contented with them! We would bear it then, though it would not be what ought to be borne, but still it would be worth our while to bear anything, as long as we could escape this most shameful war.

VI. What more? Have you not before your eyes those ornaments of the camp of Marcus Antonius? In the first place, these two colleagues of the Antonii and Dolabella, Nucula and Lento the dividers of all Italy according to that law which the senate pronounced to have been earned by violence, one of whom has been a writer of farces, and the other an actor of tragedies. Why should I speak of Domitius the Apulian? whose property we have lately seen advertised, so great is the carelessness of his agents. But this man lately was not content with giving poison to his sister's son, he actually drenched him with it. But it is impossible for these men to live in any other than a prodigal manner, who hope for our property while they are squandering their own. I have seen also an auction of the property of Publius Decius, an illustrious man, who, following the example of his ancestors, devoted himself for the debts of another. But at that auction no one was found to be a purchaser. Ridiculous man to think it possible to escape from debt by selling other people's property! For why should I speak of Trebellius? on whom the furies of debts seem to have wrecked their vengeance, for we have seen one table avenging another. Why should I speak of Plancus? whom that most illustrious citizen Aquila has driven from Pollentia,—and that too with a broken leg, and I wish he had met with that accident earlier, so as not to be liable to return hither.

I had almost passed over the light and glory of that army, Caius Annius Cimber, the son of Lysidicus, a Lysidicus himself in the Greek meaning of the word, since he has broken all laws, unless perhaps it is natural for a Cimbrian to slay a German? When Antonius has such numbers with him, and those too men of that sort, what crime will he shrink from, when Dolabella has polluted himself with such atrocious murders without at all an equal troop of robbers to support him? Wherefore, as I have often at other times differed against my will from Quintus Fufius, so on this occasion I gladly agree with his proposition. And from this you may see that my difference is not with the man, but with the cause which he sometimes advocates.

Therefore, at present I not only agree with Quintus Fufius, but I even return thanks to him, for he has given utterance to opinions which are upright, and dignified, and worthy of the republic. He has pronounced Dolabella a public enemy, he has declared his opinion that his property ought to be confiscated by public authority. And though nothing could be added to this, (for, indeed, what could he propose more severe or more pitiless?) nevertheless, he said that if any of those men who were asked their opinion after him proposed any more severe sentence, he would vote for it. Who can avoid praising such severity as this?

VII. Now, since Dolabella has been pronounced a public enemy, he must be pursued by war. For he himself will not remain quiet. He has a legion with him, he has troops of runaway slaves, he has a wicked band of impious men, he himself is confident, intemperate, and bent on falling by the death of a gladiator. Wherefore, since, as Dolabella was voted an enemy by the decree which was passed yesterday, war must be waged, we must necessarily appoint a general.

Two opinions have been advanced, neither of which do I approve. The one, because I always think it dangerous unless it be absolutely necessary, the other, because I think it wholly unsuited to the emergency. For an extraordinary commission is a measure suited rather to the fickle character of the mob, one which does not at all become our dignity or this assembly. In the war against Antiochus, a great and important war, when Asia had fallen by lot to Lucius Scipio as his province, and when he was thought to have hardly spirit and hardly vigour enough for it, and when the senate was inclined to entrust the business to his colleague Caius Laelius, the father of this Laelius, who was surnamed the Wise; Publius Africanus, the elder brother of Lucius Scipio, rose up, and entreated them not to cast such a slur on his family, and said that in his brother there was united the greatest possible valour, with the most consummate prudence, and that he too, notwithstanding his age, and all the exploits which he had performed, would attend his brother as his lieutenant. And after he had said this, nothing was changed in respect to Scipio's province, nor was any extraordinary command sought for any more in that war than in those two terrible Punic wars which had preceded it, which were carried on and conducted to their termination either by the consuls or by dictators, or than in the war with Pyrrhus, or in that with Philippus, or afterwards in the Achaean war, or in the third Punic war, for which last the Roman people took great care to select a suitable general, Publius Scipio, but at the same time it appointed him to the consulship in order to conduct it.

VIII. War was to be waged against Aristonicus in the consulship of Publius Licunius and Lucius Valerius. The people was consulted as to whom it wished to have the management of that war. Crassus, the consul and Pontifex Maximus, threatened to impose a fine upon Flaccus his colleague the priest of Mars, if he deserted the sacrifices. And though the people remitted the fine, still they ordered the priest to submit to the commands of the pontiff. But even then the Roman people did not commit the management of the war to a private individual, although there was Africanus, who the year before had celebrated a triumph over the people of Numantia, and who was far superior to all men in martial renown and military skill; yet he only gained the votes of two tribunes. And accordingly the Roman people entrusted the management of the war to Crassus the consul rather than to the private individual Africanus. As to the commands given to Cnaeus Pompeius, that most illustrious man, that first of men, they were carried by some turbulent tribunes of the people. For the war against Sertorius was only given by the senate to a private individual because the consuls refused it, when Lucius Philippus said that he sent the general in the place of the two consuls, not as proconsul.

What then is the object of these comitia? Or what is the meaning of this canvassing which that most wise and dignified citizen, Lucius Caesar, has introduced into the senate? He has proposed to vote a military command to one who is certainly a most illustrious and unimpeachable man, but still only a private individual. And by doing so he has imposed a heavy burden upon us. Suppose I agree, shall I by so doing countenance the introduction of the practice of canvassing into the senate house? Suppose I vote against it, shall I appear as if I were in the comitia to have refused an honour to a man who is one of my greatest friends? But if we are to have the comitia in the senate, let us ask for votes, let us canvass, let a voting tablet be given us, just as one is given to the people. Why do you, O Caesar, allow it to be so managed that either a most illustrious man, if your proposition be not agreed too, shall appear to have received a repulse, or else that one of us shall appear to have been passed over, if, while we are men of equal dignity, we are not considered worthy of equal honour?

But (for this is what I hear is said,) I myself gave by my own vote an extraordinary commission to Caius Caesar. Ay, indeed, for he had given me extraordinary protection, when I say me, I mean he had given it to the senate and to the Roman people. Was I to refuse giving an extraordinary military command to that man from whom the republic had received protection which had never even been thought of, but that still was of so much consequence that without it she could not have been safe? There were only the alternatives of taking his army from him, or giving him such a command. For on what principle or by what means can an army be retained by a man who has not been invested with any military command? We must not, therefore, think that a thing has been given to a man which has, in fact, not been taken away from him. You would, O conscript fathers, have taken a command away from Caius Caesar, if you had not given him one. The veteran soldiers, who, following his authority and command and name, had taken up arms in the cause of the republic, desired to be commanded by him. The Martial legion and the fourth legion had submitted to the authority of the senate, and had devoted themselves to uphold the dignity of the republic, in such a way as to feel that they had a right to demand Caius Caesar for their commander. It was the necessity of the war that invested Caius Caesar with military command, the senate only gave him the ensigns of it. But I beg you to tell me, O Lucius Caesar,—I am aware that I am arguing with a man of the greatest experience,—when did the senate ever confer a military command on a private individual who was in a state of inactivity, and doing nothing?

IX. However, I have been speaking hitherto to avoid the appearance of gratuitously opposing a man who is a great friend of mine, and who has showed me great kindness. Although, can one deny a thing to a person who not only does not ask for it, but who even refuses it? But, O conscript fathers, that proposition is unsuited to the dignity of the consuls, unsuited to the critical character of the times, namely, the proposition that the consuls, for the sake of pursuing Dolabella, shall have the provinces of Asia and Syria allotted to them. I will explain why it is inexpedient for the republic, but first of all, consider what ignominy it fixes on the consuls. When a consul elect is being besieged, when the safety of the republic depends upon his liberation, when mischievous and parricidal citizens have revolted from the republic, and when we are carrying on a war in which we are fighting for our dignity, for our freedom, and for our lives, and when, if any one falls into the power of Antonius, tortures and torments are prepared for him, and when the struggle for all these objects has been committed and entrusted to our most admirable and gallant consuls,—shall any mention be made of Asia and Syria so that we may appear to have given any injurious cause for others to entertain suspicion of us, or to bring us into unpopularity? They do indeed propose it, "after having liberated Brutus,"—for those were the last words of the proposal, say rather, after having deserted, abandoned, and betrayed him.

But I say that any mention whatever of any provinces has been made at a most unseasonable time. For although your mind, O Caius Pausa, be ever so intent, as indeed it is, on effecting the liberation of the most true and illustrious of all men, still the nature of things would compel you inevitably sometimes to turn your thoughts to the idea of pursuing Antonius, and to divert some portion of your care and attention to Asia and Syria. But if it were possible, I could wish you to have more minds than one, and yet to direct them all upon Mutina. But since that is impossible, I do wish you, with that most virtuous and all accomplished mind which you have got, to think of nothing but Brutus. And that indeed, is what you are doing; that is what you are especially striving at, but still no man can I will not say do two things, especially two most important things, at one time but he cannot even do entire justice to them both in his thoughts. It is our duty rather to spur on and inflame that excellent eagerness of yours, and not to transfer any portion of it to another object of care in a different direction.

X. Add to these considerations the way men talk, the way in which they nourish suspicion, the way in which they take dislikes. Imitate me whom you have always praised; for I rejected a province fully appointed and provided by the senate, for the purpose of discarding all other thoughts, and devoting all my efforts to extinguishing the conflagration that threatened to consume my country. There was no one except me alone, to whom, indeed, you would, in consideration of our intimacy, have been sure to communicate anything which concerned your interests, who would believe that the province had been decreed to you against your will. I entreat you, check, as is due to your eminent wisdom, this report, and do not seem to be desirous of that which you do not in reality care about. And you should take the more care of this point, because your colleague, a most illustrious man, cannot fall under the same suspicion. He knows nothing of all that is going on here, he suspects nothing, he is conducting the war, he is standing in battle array, he is fighting for his blood and for his life, he will hear of the province being decreed to him before he could imagine that there had been time for such a proceeding. I am afraid that our armies too, which have devoted themselves to the republic, not from any compulsory levy, but of their own voluntary zeal, will be checked in their ardour, if they suppose that we are thinking of anything but instant war.

But if provinces appear to the consuls as things to be desired, as they often have been desired by many illustrious men, first restore us Brutus, the light and glory of the state, whom we ought to preserve like that statue which fell from heaven, and is guarded by the protection of Vesta, which, as long as it is safe, ensures our safety also. Then we will raise you, if it be possible, even to heaven on our shoulders, unquestionably we will select for you the most worthy provinces. But at present let us apply ourselves to the business before us. And the question is, whether we will live as freemen, or die, for death is certainly to be preferred to slavery. What more need I say? Suppose that proposition causes delay in the pursuit of Dolabella? For when will the consul arrive? Are we waiting till there is not even a vestige of the towns and cities of Asia left? "But they will send some one of their officers"—That will certainly be a step that I shall quite approve of, I who just now objected to giving any extraordinary military command to even so illustrious a man if he were only a private individual. "But they will send a man worthy of such a charge." Will they send one more worthy than Publius Servilius? But the city has not such a man. What then he himself thinks ought to be given to no one, not even by the senate, can I approve of that being conferred by the decision of one man? We have need, O conscript fathers, of a man ready and prepared, and of one who has a military command legally conferred on him, and of one who, besides this, has authority, and a name, and an army, and a courage which has been already tried in his exertions for the deliverance of the republic.

XI Who then is that man? Either Marcus Brutus, or Caius Cassius, or both of them. I would vote in plain words, as there are many precedents for, one consul or both, if we had not already hampered Brutus sufficiently in Greece, and if we had not preferred having his reinforcement approach nearer to Italy rather than move further off towards Asia, not so much in order to receive succour ourselves from that army, as to enable that army to receive aid across the water. Besides, O conscript fathers, even now Caius Antonius is detaining Marcus Brutus, for he occupies Apollonia, a large and important city, he occupies, as I believe, Byllis, he occupies Amantia, he is threatening Epirus, he is pressing on Illyricum, he has with him several cohorts, and he has cavalry. If Brutus be transferred from this district to any other war, we shall at all events lose Greece. We must also provide for the safety of Brundusium and all that coast of Italy. Although I marvel that Antonius delays so long, for he is accustomed usually to put on his marching dress and not to endure the fear of a siege for any length of time. But if Brutus has finished that business, and perceives that he can better serve the republic by pursuing Dolabella than by remaining in Greece, he will act of his own head, as he has hitherto done, nor amid such a general conflagration will he wait for the orders of the senate when instant help is required. For both Brutus and Cassius have in many instances been a senate to themselves. For it is quite inevitable that in such a confusion and disturbance of all things men should be guided by the present emergency rather than by precedent. Nor will this be the first time that either Brutus or Cassius has considered the safety and deliverance of his country his most holy law and his most excellent precedent. Therefore, if there were no motion submitted to us about the pursuit of Dolabella, still I should consider it equivalent to a decree, when there were men of such a character for virtue, authority, and the greatest nobleness, possessing armies, one of which is already known to us, and the other has been abundantly heard of.

XII Brutus then, you may be sure, has not waited for our decrees, as he was sure of our desires. For he is not gone to his own province of

Crete, he has flown to Macedonia, which belonged to another, he has accounted everything his own which you have wished to be yours, he has enlisted new legions, he has received old ones, he has gained over to his own standard the cavalry of Dolabella, and even before that man was polluted with such enormous parricide, he, of his own head, pronounced him his enemy. For if he were not one, by what right could he himself have tempted the cavalry to abandon the consul? What more need I say? Did not Caius Cassius, a man endowed with equal greatness of mind and with equal wisdom, depart from Italy with the deliberate object of preventing Dolabella from obtaining possession of Syria? By what law? By what right? By that which Jupiter himself has sanctioned, that everything which was advantageous to the republic should be considered legal and just.

For law is nothing but a correct principle drawn from the inspiration of the gods, commanding what is honest, and forbidding the contrary. Cassius, therefore, obeyed this law when he went into Syria, a province which belonged to another, if men were to abide by the written laws, but which, when these were trampled under foot, was his by the law of nature. But in order that they may be sanctioned by your authority also, I now give my vote, that,

"As Publius Dolabella, and those who have been the ministers of and accomplices and assistants in his cruel and infamous crime, have been pronounced enemies of the Roman people by the senate, and as the senate has voted that Publius Dolabella shall be pursued with war, in order that he who has violated all laws of men and gods by a new and unheard of and inexpiable wickedness and has committed the most infamous treason against his country, may suffer the punishment which is his due, and which he has well deserved at the hands of gods and men, the senate decrees that Caius Cassius, proconsul, shall have the government of Syria as one appointed to that province with all due form, and that he shall receive their armies from Quintus Marcus Crispus, proconsul, from Lucius Statius Murcus, proconsul, from Aulus Allienus, lieutenant, and that they shall deliver them up to him, and that he, with these troops and with any more which he may have got from other quarters, shall pursue Dolabella with war both by sea and land; that, for the sake of carrying on war, he shall have authority and power to buy ships, and sailors, and money, and whatever else may be necessary or useful for the carrying on of the war, in whatever places it seems fitting to him to do so, throughout Syria, Asia, Bithynia, and Pontus; and that, in whatever province he shall arrive for the purpose of carrying on that war, in that province as soon as Caius Cassius, proconsul, shall arrive in it, the power of Caius Cassius, proconsul, shall be superior to that of him who may be the regular governor of the province at the time. That king Deiotarus the father, and also king Deiotarus the son, if they assist Caius Cassius, proconsul, with their armies and treasures, as they have heretofore often assisted the generals of the Roman people, will do a thing which will be grateful to the senate and people of Rome; and that also, if the rest of the kings and tetrarchs and governors in those districts do the same, the senate and people of Rome will not be forgetful of their loyalty and kindness; and that Caius Pansa and Aulus Hirtius the consuls, one or both of them, as it seems good to them, as soon as they have re-established the republic, shall at the earliest opportunity submit a motion to this order about the consular and praetorian provinces; and that, in the meantime, the provinces should continue to be governed by those officers by whom they are governed at present, until a successor be appointed to each by a resolution of the senate."

XIII. By this resolution of the senate you will inflame the existing ardour of Cassius, and you will give him additional arms; for you cannot be ignorant of his disposition, or of the resources which he has at present. His disposition is such as you see; his resources, which you have heard stated to you, are those of a gallant and resolute man, who, even while Trebonius was alive, would not permit the piratical crew of Dolabella to penetrate into Syria. Allienus, my intimate friend and connexion, who went thither after the death of Trebonius, will not permit himself to be called the lieutenant of Dolabella. The army of Quintus Caecilius Bassus, a man indeed without any regular appointment, but a brave and eminent man, is vigorous and victorious. The army of Deiotarus the king, both father and son, is very numerous, and equipped in our fashion. Moreover, in the son there is the greatest hope, the greatest vigour of genius and a good disposition, and the most eminent valour. Why need I speak of the father, whose good-will towards the Roman people is coeval with his life; who has not only been the ally of our commanders in their wars, but has also served himself as the general of his own troops. What great things have Sylla, and Murena, and Servilius, and Lucullus said of that man; what complimentary, what honourable and dignified mention have they often made of him in the senate! Why should I speak of Cnaeus Pompeius, who considered Deiotarus the only friend and real well-wisher from his heart, the only really loyal man to the Roman people in the whole world? We were generals, Marcus Bibulus and I, in neighbouring provinces bordering on his kingdom; and we were assisted by that same monarch both with cavalry and infantry. Then followed this most miserable and disastrous civil war; in which I need not say what Deiotarus ought to have done, or what would have been the most proper course which he could have adopted, especially as victory decided for the party opposed to the wishes of Deiotarus. And if in that war he committed any error, he did so in common with the senate. If his judgment was the right one, then even though defeated it does not deserve to be blamed. To these resources other kings and other levies of troops will be added. Nor will fleets be wanting to us; so greatly do the Tyrians esteem Cassius, so mighty is his name in Syria and Phoenicia.

XIV. The republic, O conscript fathers, has a general ready against Dolabella, in Caius Cassius, and not ready only, but also skilful and brave. He performed great exploits before the arrival of Bibulus, a most illustrious man, when he defeated the most eminent generals of the Parthians and their innumerable armies, and delivered Syria from their most formidable invasion. I pass over his greatest and most extraordinary glory; for as the mention of it is not yet acceptable to every one, we had better preserve it in our recollection than by bearing testimony to it with our voice.

I have noticed, O conscript fathers, that some people have said before now, that even Brutus is too much extolled by me, that Cassius is too much extolled; and that by this proposition of mine absolute power and quite a principality is conferred upon Cassius. Whom do I extol? Those who are themselves the glory of the republic. What? have I not at all times extolled Decimus Brutus whenever I have delivered my opinion at all? Do you then find fault with me? or should I rather praise the Antonii, the disgrace and infamy not only of their own families, but of the Roman name? or should I speak in favour of Censorenus, an enemy in time of war, an assassin in time of peace? or should I collect all the other ruined men of that band of robbers? But I am so far from extolling those enemies of tranquility, of concord, of the laws, of the courts of justice, and of liberty, that I cannot avoid hating them as much as I love the republic. "Beware," says one, "how you offend the veterans." For this is what I am most constantly told. But I certainly ought to protect the rights of the veterans; of those at least who are well disposed; but surely I ought not to fear them. And those veterans who have taken up arms in the cause of the republic, and have followed Caius Caesar, remembering the kindnesses which they received from his father, and who at this day are defending the republic to their own great personal danger,—those I ought not only to defend, but to seek to procure additional advantages for them. But those also who remain quiet, such as the sixth and eighth legion, I consider worthy of great glory and praise. But as for those companions of Antonius, who after they have devoured the benefits of Caesar, besiege the consul elect, threaten this city with fire and sword, and have given themselves up to Saxa and Capho, men born for crime and plunder, who is there who thinks that those men ought to be defended? Therefore the veterans are either good men, whom we ought to load with distinctions, or quiet men, whom we ought to preserve, or impious ones, against whose frenzy we have declared war and taken up legitimate arms.

XV. Who then are the veterans whom we are to be fearful of offending? Those who are desirous to deliver Decimus Brutus from siege? for how can those men, to whom the safety of Brutus is dear, hate the name of Cassius? Or those men who abstain from taking arms on either side? I have no fear of any of those men who delight in tranquility becoming a mischievous citizen. But as for the third class, whom I call not veteran soldiers, but infamous enemies, I wish to inflict on them the most bitter pain. Although, O conscript fathers, how long are we to deliver our opinions as it may please the veterans? why are we to yield so much to their haughtiness? why are we to make their arrogance of such importance as to choose our generals with reference to their pleasure? But I (for I must speak, O conscript fathers, what I feel,) think that we ought not so much to regard the veterans, as to look at what the young soldiers, the flower of Italy—at what the new legions, most eager to effect the deliverance of their country—at what all Italy will think of your wisdom. For there is nothing which flourishes for ever. Age succeeds age. The legions of Caesar have flourished for a long time; but now those who are flourishing are the legions of Pansa, and the Legions of Hirtius, and the legions of the son of Caesar, and the legions of Plancus. They surpass the veterans in number, they have the advantage of youth, moreover, they surpass them also in authority. For they are engaged in waging that war which is approved of by all nations. Therefore, rewards have been promised to these latter. To the former they have been already paid,—let them enjoy them. But let these others have those rewards given to them which we have promised them. For that is what I hope that the immortal gods will consider just.

And as this is the case, I give my vote for the proposition which I have made to you, O conscript fathers, being adopted by you.

THE TWELFTH PHILIPPIC

THE ARGUMENT

Decimus Brutus was in such distress in Mutina, that his friends began to be alarmed, fearing that, if he fell into the hands of Antonius, he would be treated as Trebonius had been. And, as the friends of Antonius gave out that he was now more inclined to come to terms with the senate, a proposition was made and supported by Pansa to send a second embassy to him. And even Cicero at first consented to it, and allowed himself to be nominated with Servilius and three other senators, all of consular rank, but on more mature reflection he was convinced that he had been guilty of a blunder, and that the object of Antonius and his friends was only to gain time for Ventidius to join him with his three legions. Accordingly, at the next meeting of the senate, he delivered the following speech, retracting his former sanction of the proposed embassy. And he spoke so strongly against it, that the measure was abandoned and Pansa soon afterwards marched with his army to join Hirtius and Octavius, with the intention of forcing Antonius to a battle.

I. Although, O conscript fathers it seems very unbecoming for that man whose counsels you have so often adopted in the most important affairs, to be deceived and deluded, and to commit mistakes, yet I console myself, since I made the mistake in company with you, and in company also with a consul of the greatest wisdom. For when two men of consular rank had brought us hope of an honorable peace, they appeared as being friends and extremely intimate with Marcus Antonius, to be aware of some weak point about him with which we were unacquainted. His wife and children are in the house of one, the other is known every day to send letters to, to receive letters from, and openly to favour Antonius.

These men, then, appeared likely to have some reason for exhorting us to peace, which they had done for some time. The consul, too, added the weight of his exhortation, and what a consul! If we look for prudence, one who was not easily to be deceived; if for virtue and courage, one who would never admit of peace unless Antonius submitted and confessed himself to be vanquished, if for greatness of mind, one who would prefer death to slavery. You, too, O conscript fathers, appeared to be induced to think not of accepting but of imposing conditions, not so much because you were forgetful of your most important and dignified resolutions, as because you had hopes suggested you of a surrender on the part of Antonius, which his friends preferred to call peace. My own hopes, and I imagine yours also, were increased by the circumstance of my hearing that the family of Antonius was overwhelmed with distress, and that his wife was incessantly lamenting. And in this assembly, too, I saw that the partisans, on whose countenance my eyes are always dwelling, looked more sorrowful than usual. And if that is not so, why on a sudden has mention been made of peace by Piso and Calenus of all people in the world, why at this particular moment, why so unexpectedly? Piso declares that he knows nothing, that he has not heard anything. Calenus declares that no news has been brought. And they make that statement now, after they think that we are involved in a pacific embassy. What need have we, then, of any new determination, if no new circumstances have arisen to call for one?

II. We have been deceived,—we have, I say, been deceived, O conscript fathers. It is the cause of Antonius that has been pleaded by his friends, and not the cause of the public. And I did indeed see that, though through a sort of mist, the safety of Decimus Brutus had dazzled my eyesight. But if in war, substitutes were in the habit of being given, I would gladly allow myself to be hemmed in, so long as Decimus Brutus might be released. But we were caught by this expression of Quintus Fufius; "Shall we not listen to Antonius, even if he retires from Mutina? Shall we not, even if he declares that he will submit himself to the authority of the senate?" It seemed harsh to say that. Thus it was that we were broken, we yielded. Does he then retire from Mutina? "I don't know." Is he obeying the senate? "I think so" says Calenus, "but so as to preserve his own dignity at the same time." You then, O conscript fathers, are to make great exertions for the express purpose of losing your own dignity, which is very great, and of preserving that of Antonius, which neither has nor can have any existence, and of enabling him to recover that by your conduct, which he has lost by his own. "But, however, that matter is not open for consideration now, an embassy has been appointed." But what is there which is not open for consideration to a wise man, as long as it can be remodelled? Any man is liable to a mistake; but no one but a downright fool will persist in error. For second thoughts, as people say, are best. The mist which I spoke of just now is dispelled, light has arisen, the case is plain—we see everything, and that not by our own acuteness, but we are warned by our friends.

You heard just now what was the statement made by a most admirable man. I found, said he, his house, his wife, his children, all in great distress.

Good men marvelled at me, my friends blamed me for having been led by the hope of peace to undertake an embassy. And no wonder, O Publius Servilius. For by your own most true and most weighty arguments Antonius was stripped, I do not say of all dignity, but of even every hope of safety. Who would not wonder if you were to go as an ambassador to him? I judge by my own case, for with regard to myself I see how the same design as you conceived is found fault with. And are we the only people blamed? What? did that most gallant man speak so long and so precisely a little while ago without any reason? What was he labouring for, except to remove from himself a groundless suspicion of treachery? And whence did that suspicion arise? From his unexpected advocacy of peace, which he adopted all on a sudden, being taken in by the same error that we were.

But if an error has been committed, O conscript fathers, owing to a groundless and fallacious hope, let us return into the right road. The best harbour for a penitent is a change of intention.

III. For what, in the name of the immortal gods! what good can our embassy do to the republic? What good, do I say? What will you say if it will even do us harm? Will do us harm? What if it already has done us harm? Do you suppose that that most energetic and fearless desire shown by the Roman people for recovery of their liberty has been damped and weakened by hearing of this embassy for peace? What do you think the municipal towns feel? and the colonies? What do you think will be the feelings of all Italy? Do you suppose that it will continue to glow with the same zeal with which it burnt before to extinguish this common conflagration? Do we not suppose that those men will repent of having professed and displayed so much hatred to Antonius, who promised us money and arms, who devoted themselves wholly, body, heart, and soul, to the safety of the republic? How will Capua, which at the present time feels like a second Rome, approve of this design of yours? That city pronounced them impious citizens, cast them out, and kept them out. Antonius was barely saved from the hands of that city, which made a most gallant attempt to crush him. Need I say more? Are we not by these proceedings cutting the sinews of our own legions, for what man can engage with ardour in a war, when the hope of peace is suggested to him? Even that godlike and divine Martial legion will grow languid at and be cowed by the receipt of this news, and will lose that most noble title of Martial, their swords will fall to the ground, their weapons will drop from their hands. For, following the senate, it will not consider itself bound to feel more bitter hatred against Antonius than the senate.

I am ashamed for this legion, I am ashamed for the fourth legion, which, approving of our authority with equal virtue, abandoned Antonius, not looking upon him as their consul and general, but as an enemy and attacker of their country. I am ashamed for that admirable army which is made up of two armies, which has now been reviewed, and which has started for Mutina, and which, if it hears a word of peace, that is to say, of our fear, even if it does not return, will at all events halt. For who, when the senate recals him and sounds a retreat, will be eager to engage in battle?

IV. For what can be more unreasonable than for us to pass resolutions about peace without the knowledge of those men who wage the war? And not only without their knowledge, but even against their will? Do you think that Aulus Hirtius, that most illustrious consul, and that Carus Caesar, a man born by the especial kindness of the gods for this especial crisis, whose letters, announcing their hope of victory, I hold in my hand, are desirous of peace? leader; and still we cannot bear the countenances or support the language of those men who are left behind in the city out of their number. What do you think will be the result when such numbers force their way into the city at one time? when we have laid aside our arms and they have not laid aside theirs? Must we not be defeated for everlasting, in consequence of our own counsels?

Place before your eyes Marcus Antonius, as a man of consular rank, add to him Lucius, hoping to obtain the consulship, join to them all the rest, and those too not confined to our order, who are fixing then thoughts on honours and commands. Do not despise the Tiros, and the Numisii, or the Mustellae, or the Seii. A peace made with those men will not be peace, but a covenant of slavery. That was in admirable expression of Lucius Piso, a most honourable man, and one which has been deservedly praised by you O Pansa, not only in this order, but also in the assembly of the people. He said, that he would depart from Italy, and leave his household gods and his native home, if (but might the gods avert such a disaster!) Antonius overwhelmed the republic.

VII. I ask, therefore, of you, O Lucius Piso, whether you would not think the republic overwhelmed if so many men of such impiety, of such audacity, and such guilt, were admitted into it? Can you think that men whom we could hardly bear when they were not yet polluted with such parricidal treasons; will be able to be borne by the city now that they are immersed in every sort of wickedness? Believe me, we must either adopt your plan, and retire, depart, embrace a life of indigence and wandering, or else we must offer our throats to those robbers, and perish in our country. What has become, O Carus Pansa, of those noble exhortations of yours, by which the senate was roused, and the Roman people stimulated, not only hearing but also learning from you that there is nothing more disgraceful to a Roman than slavery? Was it for this that we assumed the garb of war, and took arms and roused up all the youth all over Italy, in order that while we had a most flourishing and numerous army, we might send ambassadors to treat for peace? If that peace is to be received by others, why do we not wait to be entreated for it? If our ambassadors are to beg it, what is it that we are afraid of? Shall I make one of this embassy, or shall I be mixed up with this design, in which, even if I should dissent from the rest of my colleagues, the Roman people will not know it? The result will be that if anything be granted or conceded, it will be my danger if Antonius commits any offences, since the power to commit them will seem to have been put in his hands by me.

But even if it had been proper to entertain any idea of peace with the piratical crew of Marcus Antonius, still I was the last person who ought to have been selected to negotiate such a peace. I never voted for sending ambassadors. Before the return of the last ambassadors I ventured to say, that peace itself, even if they did bring it, ought to be repudiated, since war would be concealed under the name of peace; I was the chief adviser of the adoption of the garb of war, I have invariably called that man a public enemy, when others have been calling him only an adversary, I have always pronounced this to be a war, while others have styled it only a tumult Nor have I done this in the senate alone; I have always acted in the same way before the people. Nor have I spoken against himself only, but also against the accomplices in and agents of his crimes, whether present here, or there with him. In short, I have at all times inveighed against the whole family and party of Antonius. Therefore, as those impious citizens began to congratulate one another the moment the hope of peace was presented to them, as if they had gained the victory, so also they abused me as unjust, they made complaints against me, they distrusted Servilius also, they recollected that Antonius had been damaged by his avowed opinions and propositions, they recollected that Lucius Caesar, though a brave and consistent senator, is still his uncle, that Calenus is his agent, that Piso is his intimate friend, they think that you yourself, O Pansa, though a most vigorous and fearless consul, are now become more mercifully inclined. Not that it really is so, or that it possibly can be so. But the fact of a mention of peace having been made by you, has given rise to a suspicion in the hearts of many, that you have changed your mind a little. The friends of Antonius are annoyed at my being included among these persons, and we must no doubt yield to them, since we have once begun to be liberal.

VIII. Let the ambassadors go, with all our good wishes, but let those men go at whom Antonius may take no offence. But if you are not anxious about what he may think, at all events. O conscript fathers, you ought to have some regard for me. At least spare my eyes, and make some allowance for a just indignation. For with what countenance shall I be able to behold, (I do not say, the enemy of my country, for my hatred of him on that score I feel in common with you all,) but how shall I bear to look upon that man who is my own most bitter personal enemy, as his most furious harangues against me plainly declare him? Do you think that I am so completely made of iron as to be able unmoved to meet him, or look at him? who lately, when in an assembly of the people he was making presents to those men who appeared to him the most audacious of his band of parricidal traitors, said that he gave my property to Petissius of Urbinum, a man who, after the shipwreck of a very splendid patrimony, was dashed against these rocks of Antonius. Shall I be able to bear the sight of Lucius Antonius? a man from whose cruelty I could not have escaped if I had not defended myself behind the walls and gates and by the zeal of my own municipal town. And this same Asiatic gladiator, this plunderer of Italy, this colleague of Lenti and Nucula, when he was giving some pieces of gold to Aquila the centurion, said that he was giving him some of my property. For, if he had said he was giving him some of his own, he thought that the eagle itself would not have believed it. My eyes cannot—my eyes, I say, will not bear the sight of Saxa, or Capho, or the two praetors, or the tribune of the people, or the two tribunes elect, or Bestia, or Trebellius, or Titus Plancus. I cannot look with equanimity on so many, and those such foul, such wicked enemies; nor is that feeling caused by any fastidiousness of mine, but by my affection for the republic. But I will subdue my feelings, and keep my own inclinations under restraint. If I cannot eradicate my most just indignation, I will conceal it. What? Do you not think, O Conscript fathers, that I should have some regard for my own life? But that indeed has never been an object of much concern to me, especially since Dolabella has acted in such a way that death is a desirable thing, provided it come without torments and tortures. But in your eyes and in those of the Roman people my life ought not to appear of no consequence. For I am a man,—unless indeed I am deceived in my estimate of myself,— who by my vigilance, and anxiety, by the opinions which I have delivered, and by the dangers too of which I have encountered great numbers, by reason of the most bitter hatred which all impious men bear me, have at least, (not to seem to say anything too boastful,) conducted myself so as to be no injury to the republic. And as this is the case, do you think that I ought to have no consideration for my own danger?

IX. Even here, when I was in the city and at home, nevertheless many attempts were made against me, in a place where I have not only the fidelity of my friends but the eyes also of the entire city to guard me. What do you think will be the case when I have gone on a journey, and that too a long one? Do you think that I shall have no occasion to fear plots then? There are three roads to Mutina, a place which my mind longs to see, in order that I may behold as speedily as possible that pledge of freedom of the Roman people Decimus Brutus, in whose embrace I would willingly yield up my parting breath, when all my actions for the last many months, and all my opinions and propositions have resulted in the end which I proposed to myself. There are, as I have said, three roads, the Flaminian road, along the Adriatic, the Aurelian road, along the Mediterranean coast, the Midland road, which is called the Cassian.

Now, take notice, I beg of you, whether my suspicion of danger to myself is at variance with a reasonable conjecture. The Cassian road goes through Etruria. Do we not know then, O Pansa, over what places the authority of Lenti Caesennius, as a septemvir, prevails at present? He certainly is not on our side either in mind or body. But if he is at home, or not far from home, he is certainly in Etruria, that is, in my road. Who, then, will undertake to me that Lenti will be content with exacting one life alone? Tell me besides, O Pansa, where Ventidius is,—a man to whom I have always been friendly before he became so openly an enemy to the republic and to all good men. I may avoid the Cassian road, and take the Flaminian. What if, as it is said, Ventidius has arrived at Ancona? Shall I be able in that case to reach Ariminum in safety? The Aurelian road remains and here too I shall find a, protector, for on that road are the possessions of Publius Clodius. His whole household will come out to meet me, and will invite me to partake of their hospitality, on account of my notorious intimacy with their master?

X. Shall I then trust myself to those roads—I who lately, on the day of the feast of Terminus, did not dare even to go into the suburbs and return by the same road on the same day? I can scarcely defend myself within the walls of my own house without the protection of my friends; therefore I remain in the city; and if I am allowed to do so I will remain. This is my proper place, this is my beat, this is my post as a sentinel, this is my station as a defender of the city. Let others occupy camps and kingdoms, and engage in the conduct of the war; let them show the active hatred of the enemy; we, as we say, and as we have always hitherto done, will, in common with you, defend the city and the affairs of the city. Nor do I shrink from this office; although I see the Roman people shrink from it for me. No one is less timid than I am; no one more cautious. The facts speak for themselves. This is the twentieth year that I have been a mark for the attempts of all wicked men; therefore, they have paid to the republic (not to say to me) the penalty of their wickedness. As yet the republic has preserved me in safety for itself. I am almost afraid to say what I am going to say; for I know that any accident may happen to a man; but still, when I was once hemmed in by the united force of many most influential men, I yielded voluntarily, and fell in such a manner as to be able to rise again in the most honourable manner.

Can I, then, appear as cautious and as prudent as I ought to be if I commit myself to a journey so full of enemies and dangers to me? Those men who are concerned in the government of the republic ought at their death to leave behind them glory, and not reproaches for their fault, or grounds for blaming their folly. What good man is there who does not mourn for the death of Trebonius? Who is there who does not grieve for the loss of such a citizen and such a man? But there are men who say, (hastily indeed, but still they do say so,) that he deserves to be grieved for less because he did not take precautions against a desperately wicked man. In truth, a man who professes to be himself a defender of many men, wise men say, ought in the first place to show himself able to protect his own life. I say, that when one is fenced round by the laws and by the fear of justice, a man is not bound to be afraid of everything, or to take precautions against all imaginable designs; for who would dare to attack a man in daylight, on a military road, or a man who was well attended, or an illustrious man? But these considerations have no bearing on the present time, nor in my case; for not only would a man who offered violence to me have no fear of punishment, but he would even hope to obtain glory and rewards from those bands of robbers.

XI. These dangers I can guard against in the city; it is easy for me to look around and see where I am going out from, whither I am going, what there is on my right hand, and on my left. Shall I be able to do the same on the roads of the Apennines? in which, even if there should be no ambush, as there easily may be, still my mind will be kept in such a state of anxiety as not to be able to attend to the duties of an embassy. But suppose I have escaped all plots against me, and have passed over the Apennines; still I have to encounter a meeting and conference with Antonius. What place am I to select? If it is outside the camp, the rest may look to themselves,—I think that death would come upon me instantly. I know the frenzy of the man; I know his unbridled violence. The ferocity of his manners and the savageness of his nature is not usually softened even by wine. Then, inflamed by anger and insanity, with his brother Lucius, that foulest of beasts, at his side, he will never keep his sacrilegious and impious hands from me. I can recollect conferences with most bitter enemies, and with citizens in a state of the most bitter disagreement.

Cnaeus Pompeius, the son of Sextus, being consul, in my presence, when I was serving my first campaign in his army, had a conference with Publius Vettius Scato, the general of the Marsians, between the camps. And I recollect that Sextus Pompeius, the brother of the consul, a very learned and wise man, came thither from Rome to the conference. And when Scato had saluted him, "What," said he, "am I to call you?"—"Call me," said he, "one who is by inclination a friend, by necessity an enemy." That conference was conducted with fairness; there was no fear, no suspicion; even their mutual hatred was not great; for the allies were not seeking to take our city from us, but to be themselves admitted to share the privileges of it. Sylla and Scipio, one attended by the flower of the nobility, the other by the allies, had a conference between Cales and Teanum, respecting the authority of the senate, the suffrages of the people, and the privileges of citizenship; and agreed upon conditions and stipulations. Good faith was not strictly observed at that conference; but still there was no violence used, and no danger incurred.

XII. But can we be equally safe among Antonius's piratical crew? We cannot; or, even if the rest can, I do not believe that I can. What will be the case if we are not to confer out of the camp? What camp is to be chosen for the conference? He will never come into our camp:—much less will we go to his. It follows then, that all demands must be received and sent to and fro by means of letters. We then shall be in our respective camps. On all his demands I shall have but one opinion; and when I have stated it here, in your hearing, you may think that I have gone, and that I have come back again.—I shall have finished my embassy. As far as my sentiments can prevail I shall refer every demand which Antonius makes to the senate. For, indeed, we have no power to do otherwise; nor have we received any commission from this assembly, such as, when a war is terminated, is usually, in accordance with the precedents of your ancestors, entrusted to the ambassadors. Nor, in fact, have we received any particular commission from the senate at all.

And, as I shall pursue this line of conduct in the council, where some, as I imagine, will oppose it, have I not reason to fear that the ignorant mob may think that peace is delayed by my means? Suppose now that the new legions do not disapprove of my resolution. For I am quite sure that the Martial legion and the fourth legion will not approve of anything which is contrary to dignity and honour. What then? have we no regard for the opinion of the veterans? For even they themselves do not wish to be feared by us.—Still, how will they receive my severity? For they have heard many false statements concerning me; wicked men have circulated among them many calumnies against me. Their advantage indeed, as you all are most perfect witnesses of, I have always promoted by my opinion, by my authority, and by my language. But they believe wicked men, they believe seditious men, they believe their own party. They are, indeed, brave men; but by reason of their exploits which they have performed in the cause of the freedom of the Roman people and of the safety of the republic they are too ferocious and too much inclined to bring all our counsels under the sway of their own violence. Their deliberate reflection I am not afraid of, but I confess I dread their impetuosity.

If I escape all these great dangers too, do you think my return will be completely safe? For when I have, according to my usual custom, defended your authority, and have proved my good faith towards the republic, and my firmness; then I shall have to fear, not those men alone who hate me, but those also who envy me. Let my life then be preserved for the republic, let it be kept for the service of my country as long as my dignity or nature will permit; and let death either be the necessity of fate, or, if it must be encountered earlier, let it be encountered with glory.

This being the case, although the republic has no need (to say the least of it) of this embassy, still if it be possible for me to go on it in safety, I am willing to go. Altogether, O conscript fathers, I shall regulate the whole of my conduct in this affair, not by any consideration of my own danger, but by the advantage of the republic. And, as I have plenty of time, I think that it behoves me to deliberate upon that over and over again, and to adopt that line of conduct which I shall judge to be most beneficial to the republic.

THE THIRTEENTH PHILIPPIC

THE ARGUMENT

Antonius wrote a long letter to Hirtius and to Octavius, to persuade them that they were acting against their true interests and dignity in combining with the slayers of Julius Caesar against him. But they, instead of answering this letter, sent it to Cicero at Rome. At the same time Lepidus wrote a public letter to the senate to exhort them to measures of peace; and to a reconciliation with Antonius; and took no notice of the public honours which had been decreed to him in compliance with Cicero's motion. The senate was much displeased at this. They agreed, however, to a proposal of Servilius—to thank Lepidus for his love of peace, but to desire him to leave that to them; as there could be no peace till Antonius had laid down his arms. But Antonius's friends were encouraged by Lepidus's letter to renew their suggestions of a treaty; which caused Cicero to deliver the following speech to the senate for the purpose of counteracting the influence of their arguments.

I. From the first beginning, O conscript fathers, of this war which we have undertaken against those impious and wicked citizens, I have been afraid lest the insidious proposals of peace might damp our zeal for the recovery of our liberty. But the name of peace is sweet; and the thing itself not only pleasant but salutary. For a man seems to have no affection either for the private hearths of the citizens, nor for the public laws, nor for the rights of freedom, who is delighted with discord and the slaughter of his fellow-citizens, and with civil war; and such a man I think ought to be erased from the catalogue of men, and exterminated from all human society. Therefore, if Sylla, or Marius, or both of them, or Octavius, or Cinna, or Sylla for the second time, or the other Marius and Carbo, or if any one else has ever wished for civil war, I think that man a citizen born for the detestation of the republic. For why should I speak of the last man who stirred up such a war; a man whose acts, indeed, we defend, while we admit that the author of them was deservedly slain? Nothing, then, is more infamous than such a citizen or such a man; if indeed he deserves to be considered either a citizen or a man, who is desirous of civil war.

But the first thing that we have to consider, O conscript fathers, is whether peace can exist with all men, or whether there be any war incapable of reconciliation, in which any agreement of peace is only a covenant of slavery. Whether Sylla was making peace with Scipio, or whether he was only pretending to do so, there was no reason to despair, if an agreement had been come to, that the city might have been in a tolerable state. If Cinna had been willing to agree with Octavius, the safety of the citizens might still have had an existence in the republic. In the last war, if Pompeius had relaxed somewhat of his dignified firmness, and Caesar a good deal of his ambition, we might have had both a lasting peace, and some considerable remainder of the republic.

II. But what is the state of things now? Is it possible for there to be peace with Antonius? with Censorinus, and Ventidius, and Trebellius, and Bestia, and Nucula, and Munatius, and Lento, and Saxa? I have just mentioned a few names as a specimen; you yourselves see the countless numbers and savage nature of the rest of the host. Add, besides the wrecks of Caesar's party, the Barbae Cassii, the Barbatii, the Pollios; add the companions and fellow-gamblers of Antonius, Eutrapelus, and Mela, and Coelius, and Pontius, and Crassicius, and Tiro, and Mustela, and Petissius; I say nothing of the main body, I am only naming the leaders. To these are added the legionaries of the Alauda and the rest of the veterans, the seminary of the judges of the third decury; who, having exhausted their own estates, and squandered all the fruits of Caesar's kindness, have now set their hearts on our fortunes. Oh that trustworthy right hand of Antonius, with which he has murdered many citizens! Oh that regularly ratified and solemn treaty which we made with the Antonii! Surely if Marcus shall attempt to violate it, the conscientious piety of Lucius will call him back from such wickedness. If there is any room allowed these men in this city, there will be no room for the city itself. Place before your eyes, O conscript fathers, the countenances of those men, and especially the countenances of the Antonii. Mark their gait, their look, their face, their arrogance; mark those friends of theirs who walk by their side, who follow them, who precede them. What breath reeking of wine, what insolence, what threatening language do you not think there will be there? Unless, indeed, the mere fact of peace is to soften them, and unless you expect that, especially when they come into this assembly, they will salute every one of us kindly, and address us courteously.

III. Do you not recollect, in the name of the immortal gods! what resolutions you have given utterance to against those men? You have repealed the acts of Marcus Antonius; you have taken down his laws; you have voted that they were carried by violence, and with a disregard of the auspices; you have called out the levies throughout all Italy; you have pronounced that colleague and ally of all wickedness a public enemy. What peace can there be with this man? Even if he were a foreign enemy, still, after such actions as have taken place, it would be scarcely possible, by any means whatever, to have peace. Though seas and mountains, and vast regions lay between you, still you would hate such a man without seeing him. But these men will stick to your eyes, and when they can, to your very throats; for what fences will be strong enough for us to restrain savage beasts?—Oh, but the result of war is uncertain. It is at all events in the power of brave men, such as you ought to be, to display your valour, (for certainly brave men can do that,) and not to fear the caprice of fortune.

But since it is not only courage but wisdom also which is expected from this order, (although these qualities appear scarcely possible to be separated, still let us separate them here,) courage bids us fight, inflames our just hatred, urges us to the conflict, summons us to danger. What says wisdom? She uses more cautious counsels, she is provident for the future, she is in every respect more on the defensive. What then does she think? for we must obey her, and we are bound to consider that the best thing which is arranged in the most prudent manner. If she enjoins me to think nothing of more consequence than my life, not to fight at the risk of my life, but to avoid all danger, I will then ask her whether I am also to become a slave when I have obeyed all these injunctions? If she says, yes, I for one will not listen to that Wisdom, however learned she may be, but if the answer is, Preserve your life and your safety, Preserve your fortune, "Preserve your estate, still, however, considering all these things of less value than liberty, therefore enjoy these things if you can do so consistently with the freedom of the republic, and do not abandon liberty for them, but sacrifice them for liberty, as proofs of the injury you have sustained,"—then I shall think that I really am listening to the voice of Wisdom, and I will obey her as a god. Therefore, if when we have received those men we can still be free, let us subdue our hatred to them, and endure peace, but if there can be no tranquillity while those men are in safety, then let us rejoice that an opportunity of fighting them is put in our power. For so, either (these men being conquered) we shall enjoy the republic victorious, or, if we be defeated (but may Jupiter avert that disaster), we shall live, if not with an actual breath, at all events in the renown of our valour.

IV. But Marcus Lepidus, having been a second time styled Imperator, Pontifex Maximus, a man who deserved excellently well of the republic in the last civil war, exhorts us to peace. No one, O conscript fathers, has greater weight with me than Marcus Lepidus, both on account of his personal virtues and by reason of the dignity of his family. There are also private reasons which influence me, such as great services he has done me, and some kindnesses which I have done him. But the greatest of his services I consider to be his being of such a disposition as he is towards the republic, which has at all times been dearer to me than my life. For when by his influence he inclined Magnus Pompeius, a most admirable young man, the son of one of the greatest of men, to peace, and without arms released the republic from imminent danger of civil war, by so doing he laid me under as great obligations as it was in the power of any man to do. Therefore I proposed to decree to him the most ample honours that were in my power, in which you agreed with me, nor have I ceased both to think and speak in the highest terms of him. The republic has Marcus Lepidus bound to it by many pledges. He is a man of the highest rank, of the greatest honours, he has the most honourable priesthood, and has received numberless distinctions in the city. There are monuments of himself, and of his brother, and of his ancestors; he has a most excellent wife, children such as any man might desire, an ample family estate, untainted with the blood of his fellow-citizens. No citizen has been injured by him; many have been delivered from misery by his kindness and pity. Such a man and such a citizen may indeed err in his opinion, but it is quite impossible for him in inclination to be unfriendly to the republic.

Marcus Lepidus is desirous of peace. He does well especially if he can make such a peace as he made lately, owing to which the republic will behold the son of Cnaeus Pompeius, and will receive him in her bosom and embrace; and will think, that not he alone, but that she also is restored to herself with him. This was the reason why you decreed to him a statue in the rostra with an honourable inscription, and why you voted him a triumph in his absence. For although he had performed great exploits in war, and such as well deserved a triumph, still for that he might not have had that given to him which was not given to Lucius aemilius, nor to aemilianus Scipio, nor to the former Africanus, nor to Marius, nor to Pompeius, who had the conduct of greater wars than he had, but because he had put an end to a civil war in perfect silence, the first moment that it was in his power, on that account you conferred on him the greatest honours.

V. Do you think, then, O Marcus Lepidus, that the Antonii will be to the republic such citizens as she will find Pompeius? In the one there is modesty, gravity, moderation, integrity; in them (and when I speak of them, I do not mean to omit one of that band of pirates), there is lust, and wickedness, and savage audacity capable of every crime. I entreat of you, O conscript fathers, which of you fails to see this which Fortune herself, who is called blind, sees? For, saving the acts of Caesar, which we maintain for the sake of harmony, his own house will be open to Pompeius, and he will redeem it for the same sum for which Antonius bought it. Yes, I say the son of Cnaeus Pompeius will buy back his house. O melancholy circumstance! But these things have been already lamented long and bitterly enough. You have voted a sum of money to Cnaeus Pompeius, equal to that which his conquering enemy had appropriated to himself of his father's property in the distribution of his booty. But I claim permission to manage this distribution myself, as due to my connexion and intimacy with his father. He will buy back the villas, the houses, and some of the estates in the city which Antonius is in possession of. For as for the silver plate, the garments, the furniture, and the wine which that glutton has made away with, those things he will lose without forfeiting his equanimity. The Alban and Firmian villas he will recover from Dolabella; the Tusculan villa he will also recover from Antonius. And these Ansers who are joining in the attack on Mutina and in the blockade of Decimus Brutus will be driven from his Falernian villa. There are many others, perhaps, who will be made to disgorge their plunder, but their names escape my memory. I say, too, that those men who are not in the number of our enemies, will be made to restore the possessions of Pompeius to his son for the price at which they bought them. It was the act of a sufficiently rash man, not to say an audacious one, to touch a single particle of that property; but who will have the face to endeavour to retain it, when its most illustrious owner is restored to his country? Will not that man restore his plunder, who enfolding the patrimony of his master in his embrace, clinging to the treasure like a dragon, the slave of Pompeius, the freedman of Caesar, has seized upon his estates in the Lucanian district? And as for those seven hundred millions of sesterces which you, O conscript fathers, promised to the young man, they will be recovered in such a manner that the son of Cnaeus Pompeius will appear to have been established by you in his patrimony. This is what the senate must do; the Roman people will do the rest with respect to that family which was at one time one of the most honourable it ever saw. In the first place, it will invest him with his father's honour as an augur, for which rank I will nominate him and promote his election, in order that I may restore to the son what I received from the father.

Which of these men will the Roman people most willingly sanction as the augur of the all-powerful and all-great Jupiter, whose interpreters and messengers we have been appointed,—Pompeius or Antonius? It seems indeed, to me, that Fortune has managed this by the divine aid of the immortal gods, that, leaving the acts of Caesar firmly ratified, the son of Cnaeus Pompeius might still be able to recover the dignities and fortunes of his father.

VI. And I think, O conscript fathers, that we ought not to pass over that fact either in silence,—that those illustrious men who are acting as ambassadors, Lucius Paullus, Quintus Thermus, and Caius Fannius, whose inclinations towards the republic you are thoroughly acquainted with, and also with the constancy and firmness of that favourable inclination, report that they turned aside to Marseilles for the purpose of conferring with Pompeius, and that they found him in a disposition very much inclined to go with his troops to Mutina, if he had not been afraid of offending the minds of the veterans. But he is a true son of that father who did quite as many things wisely as he did bravely. Therefore you perceive that his courage was quite ready, and that prudence was not wanting to him.

And this, too, is what Marcus Lepidus ought to take care of,—not to appear to act in any respect with more arrogance than suits his character. For if he alarms us with his army, he is forgetting that that army belongs to the senate, and to the Roman people, and to the whole republic, not to himself. "But he has the power to use it as if it were his own." What then? Does it become virtuous men to do everything which it is in their power to do? Suppose it be a base thing? Suppose it be a mischievous thing? Suppose it be absolutely unlawful to do it?

But what can be more base, or more shameful, or more utterly unbecoming, than to lead an army against the senate, against one's fellow-citizens, against one's country? Or what can deserve greater blame than doing that which is unlawful? But it is not lawful for any one to lead an army against his country? if indeed we say that that is lawful which is permitted by the laws or by the usages and established principles of our ancestors. For it does not follow that whatever a man has power to do is lawful for him to do; nor, if he be not hindered, is he on that account permitted to do so. For to you, O Lepidus, as to your ancestors, your country has given an army to be employed in her cause. With this army you are to repel the enemy, you are to extend the boundaries of the empire, you are to obey the senate and people of Rome, if by any chance they direct you to some other object.

VII. If these are your thoughts, then are you really Marcus Lepidus the Pontifex Maximus, the great-grandson of Marcus Lepidus, Pontifex Maximus. If you judge that everything is lawful for men to do that they have the power to do, then beware lest you seem to prefer acting on precedents set by those who have no connexion with you, and these, too, modern precedents, to being guided by the ancient examples in your own family. But if you interpose your authority without having recourse to arms, in that case indeed I praise you more; but beware lest this thing itself be quite unnecessary. For although there is all the authority in you that there ought to be in a man of the highest rank, still the senate itself does not despise itself; nor was it ever more wise, more firm, more courageous. We are all hurried on with the most eager zeal to recover our freedom. Such a general ardour on the part of the senate and people of Rome cannot be extinguished by the authority of any one: we hate a man who would extinguish it; we are angry with him, and resist him; our arms cannot be wrested from our hands; we are deaf to all signals for retreat, to all recal from the combat. We hope for the happiest success; we will prefer enduring the bitterest disaster to being slaves. Caesar has collected an invincible army. Two perfectly brave consuls are present with their forces. The various and considerable reinforcements of Lucius Plancus, consul elect, are not wanting. The contest is for the safety of Decimus Brutus. One furious gladiator, with a band of most infamous robbers, is waging war against his country, against our household gods, against our altars and our hearths, against four consuls. Shall we yield to him? Shall we listen to the conditions which he proposes? Shall we believe it possible for peace to be made with him?

VIII. But there is danger of our being overwhelmed. I have no fear that the man who cannot enjoy his own most abundant fortunes, unless all the good men are saved, will betray his own safety. It is nature which first makes good citizens, and then fortune assists them. For it is for the advantage of all good men that the republic should be safe; but that advantage appears more clearly in the case of those who are fortunate. Who is more fortunate than Lentulus, as I said before, and who is more sensible? The Roman people saw his sorrow and his tears at the Lupercal festival. They saw how miserable, how overwhelmed he was when Antonius placed a diadem on Caesar's head and preferred being his slave to being his colleague. And even if he had been able to abstain from his other crimes and wickednesses, still on account of that one single action I should think him worthy of all punishment. For even if he himself was calculated to be a slave, why should he impose a master on us? And if his childhood had borne the lusts of those men who were tyrants over him, was he on that account to prepare a master and a tyrant to lord it over our children? Therefore since that man was slain, he himself has behaved to all others in the same manner as he wished him to behave to us.

For in what country of barbarians was there ever so foul and cruel a tyrant as Antonius, escorted by the arms of barbarians, has proved in this city? When Caesar was exercising the supreme power, we used to come into the senate, if not with freedom, at all events with safety. But under this arch-pirate, (for why should I say tyrant?) these benches were occupied by Itureans. On a sudden he hastened to Brundusium, in order to come against this city from thence with a regular army. He deluged Suessa, a most beautiful town, now of municipal citizens, formerly of most honourable colonists, with the blood of the bravest soldiers. At Brundusium he massacred the chosen centurions of the Martial legion in the lap of his wife, who was not only most avaricious but also most cruel. After that with what fury, with what eagerness did he hurry on to the city, that is to say, to the slaughter of every virtuous man! But at that time the immortal gods brought to us a protector whom we had never seen nor expected.

IX. For the incredible and godlike virtue of Caesar checked the cruel and frantic onslaught of that robber, whom then that madman believed that he was injuring with his edicts, ignorant that all the charges which he was falsely alleging against that most righteous young man, were all very appropriate to the recollections of his own childhood. He entered the city, with what an escort, or rather with what a troop! when on the right hand and on the left, amid the groans of the Roman people, he was threatening the owners of property, taking notes of the houses, and openly promising to divide the city among his followers. He returned to his soldiers; then came that mischievous assembly at Tibur. From thence he hurried to the city; the senate was convened at the Capitol. A decree with the authority of the consuls was prepared for proscribing the young man; when all on a sudden (for he was aware that the Martial legion had encamped at Alba) news is brought him of the proceedings of the fourth legion.

Alarmed at that, he abandoned his intention of submitting a motion to the senate respecting Caesar. He departed not by the regular roads, but by the by-lanes, in the robe of a general; and on that very self-same day he trumped up a countless number of resolutions of the senate; all of which he published even before they were drawn up. From thence it was not a journey, but a race and flight into Gaul. He thought that Caesar was pursuing him with the fourth legion, with the martial legion, with the veterans, whose very name he could not endure for fright. Then, as he was making his way into Gaul, Decimus Brutus opposed him; who preferred being himself surrounded by the waves of the whole war, to allowing him either to retreat or advance; and who put Mutina on him as a sort of bridle to his exultation. And when he had blockaded that city with his works and fortifications, and when the dignity of a most flourishing colony, and the majesty of a consul elect, were both insufficient to deter him from his parricidal treason, then, (I call you, and the Roman people, and all the gods who preside over this city, to witness,) against my will, and in spite of my resistance and remonstrance, three ambassadors of consular rank were sent to that robber, to that leader of gladiators, Marcus Antonius.

Who ever was such a barbarian? Who was ever so savage? so brutal? He would not listen to them; he gave them no answer; and he not only despised and showed that he considered of no importance those men who were with him, but still more us, by whom these men had been sent. And afterwards what wickedness, or what crime was there which that traitor abstained from? He blockaded your colonists, and the army of the Roman people, and your general, and your consul elect. He lays waste the lands of a nation of most excellent citizens. Like a most inhuman enemy he threatens all virtuous men with crosses and tortures.

X. Now what peace, O Marcus Lepidus, can exist with this man? when it does not seem that there is even any punishment which the Roman people can think adequate to his crimes?

But if any one has hitherto been able to doubt the fact, that there can be nothing whatever in common between this order and the Roman people and that most detestable beast, let him at least cease to entertain such a doubt, when he becomes acquainted with this letter which I have just received, it having been sent to me by Hirtius the consul. While I read it, and while I briefly discuss each paragraph, I beg, O conscript fathers, that you will listen to me most attentively, as you have hitherto done.

"Antonius to Hirtius and Caesar."

He does not call himself imperator, nor Hirtius consul, nor Caesar pro-praetor. This is cunningly done enough. He preferred laying aside a title to which he had no right himself, to giving them their proper style.

"When I heard of the death of Caius Trebonius, I was not more rejoiced than grieved."

Take notice why he says he rejoiced, why he says that he was grieved;

and then you will be more easily able to decide the question of peace.

"It was a matter of proper rejoicing that a wicked man had paid the penalty due to the bones and ashes of a most illustrious man, and that the divine power of the gods had shown itself before the end of the current year, by showing the chastisement of that parricide already inflicted in some cases, and impending in others."

O you Spartacus! for what name is more fit for you? you whose abominable wickedness is such as to make even Catiline seem tolerable. Have you dared to write that it is a matter of rejoicing that Trebonius has suffered punishment? that Trebonius was wicked? What was his crime, except that on the ides of March he withdrew you from the destruction which you had deserved? Come; you rejoice at this; let us see what it is that excites your indignation.

"That Dolabella should at this time have been pronounced a public enemy because he has slain an assassin; and that the son of a buffoon should appear dearer to the Roman people than Caius Caesar, the father of his country, are circumstances to be lamented."

Why should you be sad because Dolabella has been pronounced a public enemy? Why? Are you not aware that you yourself—by the fact of an enlistment having taken place all over Italy, and of the consuls being sent forth to war, and of Caesar having received great honours, and of the garb of war having been assumed—have also been pronounced an enemy? And what reason is there, O you wicked man, for lamenting that Dolabella has been declared an enemy by the senate? a body which you indeed think of no consequence at all; but you make it your main object in waging war utterly to destroy the senate, and to make all the rest of those who are either virtuous or wealthy follow the fate of the highest order of all. But he calls him the son of a buffoon. As if that noble Roman knight the father of Trebonius were unknown to us. And does he venture to look down on any one because of the meanness of his birth, when he has himself children by Fadia?

XL "But it is the bitterest thing of all that you, O Aulus Hirtius, who have been distinguished by Caesar's kindness, and who have been left by him in a condition which you yourself marvel at. "

I cannot indeed deny that Aulus Hirtius was distinguished by Caesar, but such distinctions are only of value when conferred on virtue and industry. But you, who cannot deny that you also were distinguished by Caesar, what would you have been if he had not showered so many kindnesses on you? Where would your own good qualities have borne you? Where would your birth have conducted you? You would have spent the whole period of your manhood in brothels, and cookshops, and in gambling and drinking, as you used to do when you were always burying your brains and your beard in the laps of actresses.

"And you too, O boy—"

He calls him a boy whom he has not only experienced and shall again experience to be a man, but one of the bravest of men. It is indeed the name appropriate to his age; but he is the last man in the world who ought to use it, when it is his own madness that has opened to this boy the path to glory.

"You who owe everything to his name—"

He does indeed owe everything, and nobly is he paying it. For if he was the father of his country, as you call him, (I will see hereafter what my opinion of that matter is,) why is not this youth still more truly our father, to whom it certainly is owing that we are now enjoying life, saved out of your most guilty hands!

"Are taking pains to have Dolabella legally condemned."

A base action, truly! by which the authority of this most honourable order is defended against the insanity of a most inhuman gladiator.

"And to effect the release of this poisoner from blockade."

Do you dare to call that man a poisoner who has found a remedy against your own poisoning tricks? and whom you are besieging in such a manner, O you new Hannibal, (or if there was ever any abler general than he,) as to blockade yourself, and to be unable to extricate yourself from your present position, should you be ever so desirous to do so? Suppose you retreat; they will all pursue you from all sides. Suppose you stay where you are; you will be caught. You are very right, certainly, to call him a poisoner, by whom you see that your present disastrous condition has been brought about.

"In order that Cassius and Brutus may become as powerful as possible."

Would you suppose that he is speaking of Censorinus, or of Ventidius, or of the Antonii themselves. But why should they be unwilling that those men should become powerful, who are not only most excellent and nobly born men, but who are also united with them in the defence of the republic?

"In fact, you look upon the existing circumstances as you did on the former ones."

What can he mean?

"You used to call the camp of Pompeius the senate."

XII. Should we rather call your camp the senate? In which you are the only man of consular rank, you whose whole consulship is effaced from every monument and register; and two praetors, who are afraid that they will lose something by us,—a groundless fear. For we are maintaining all the grants made by Caesar; and men of praetorian rank, Philadelphus Annius, and that innocent Gallius; and men of aedilitian rank, he on whom I have spent so much of my lungs and voice, Bestia, and that patron of good faith and cheater of his creditors, Trebellius, and that bankrupt and ruined man Quintus Caelius, and that support of the friends of Antonius Cotyla Varius, whom Antonius for his amusement caused at a banquet to be flogged with thongs by the public slaves. Men of septemviral rank, Lento and Nucula, and then that delight and darling of the Roman people, Lucius Antonius. And for tribunes, first of all two tribunes elect, Tullus Hostilius, who was so full of his privileges as to write up his name on the gate of Rome; and who, when he found himself unable to betray his general, deserted him. The other tribune elect is a man of the name of Viseius; I know nothing about him; but I hear that he is (as they say) a bold robber; who, however, they say was once a bathing man at Pisaurum, and a very good hand at mixing the water. Then there are others too, of tribunitian rank: in the first place, Titus Plancus; a man who, if he had had any affection for the senate, would never have burnt the senate-house. Having been condemned for which wickedness, he returned to that city by force of arms from which he was driven by the power of the law. But, however, this is a case common to him and to many others who are very unlike him. But this is quite true which men are in the habit of saying of this Plancus in a proverbial way, that it is quite impossible for him to die unless his legs are broken. They are broken, and still he lives. But this, like many others, is a service that has been done us by Aquila.

XIII. There is also in that camp Decius, descended, as I believe, from the great Decius Mus; accordingly he gained the gifts of Caesar. And so after a long interval the recollection of the Decii is renewed by this illustrious man. And how can I pass over Saxa Decidius, a fellow imported from the most distant nations, in order that we might see that man tribune of the people whom we had never beheld as a citizen? There is also one of the Sasernae; but all of them have such a resemblance to one another, that I may make a mistake as to their first names. Nor must I omit Exitius, the brother of Philadelphus the quaestor; lest, if I were to be silent about that most illustrious young man, I should seem to be envying Antonius. There is also a gentleman of the name of Asinius, a voluntary senator, having been elected by himself. He saw the senate-house open after the death of Caesar, he changed his shoes, and in a moment became a conscript father. Sextus Albedius I do not know, but still I have not fallen in with any one so fond of evil-speaking, as to deny that he is worthy of a place in the senate of Antonius.

I dare say that I have passed over some names; but still I could not refrain from mentioning those who did occur to me. Relying then on this senate, he looks down on the senate which supported Pompeius, in which ten of us were men of consular rank; and if they were all alive now this war would never have arisen at all. Audacity would have succumbed to authority. But what great protection there would have been in the rest may be understood from this, that I, when left alone of all that band, with your assistance crushed and broke the audacity of that triumphant robber.

XIV. But if Fortune had not taken from us not only Servius Sulpicius, and before him, his colleague Marcus Marcellus,—what citizens! What men! If the republic had been able to retain the two consuls, men most devoted to their country, who were driven together out of Italy; and Lucius Afranius, that consummate general; and Publius Lentulus, a citizen who displayed his extraordinary virtue on other occasions, and especially in the securing my safe return; and Bibulus, whose constant and firm attachment to the republic has at all times been deservedly praised; and Lucius Domitius, that most excellent citizen; and Appius Claudius, a man equally distinguished for nobleness of birth and for attachment to the state; and Publius Scipio, a most illustrious man, closely resembling his ancestors. Certainly with these men of consular rank, the senate which supported Pompeius was not to be despised.

Which, then, was more just, which was more advantageous for the republic, that Cnaeus Pompeius, or that Antonius the brother who bought all Pompeius's property, should live? And then what men of praetorian rank were there with us! the chief of whom was Marcus Cato, being indeed the chief man of any nation in the world for virtue. Why need I speak of the other most illustrious men? you know them all. I am more afraid lest you should think me tedious for enumerating so many, than ungrateful for passing over any one. And what men of aedilitian rank! and of tribunitian rank! and of quaestorian rank! Why need I make a long story of it, so great was the dignity of the senators of our party, so great too were their numbers, that those men have need of some very valid excuse who did not join that camp. Now listen to the rest of the letter.

XV. "You have the defeated Cicero for your general."

I am the more glad to hear that word "general," because he certainly uses it against his will, for as for his saying "defeated," I do not mind that, for it is my fate that I can neither be victorious nor defeated without the republic being so at the same time.

"You are fortifying Macedonia with armies".

Yes, indeed, and we have wrested one from your brother, who does not in the least degenerate from you.

"You have entrusted Africa to Varus, who has been twice taken prisoner".

Here he thinks that he is making out a case against his own brother Lucius.

"You have sent Capius into Syria".

Do you not see then, O Antonius, that the whole world is open to our party, but that you have no spot out of your own fortifications, where you can set your foot?

"You have allowed Casca to discharge the office of tribune".

What then? Were we to remove a man, as if he had been Marullus, or Caesetius, to whom we own it, that this and many other things like this can never happen for the future?

"You have taken away from the Luperci the revenues which Julius Caesar assigned to them."

Does he dare to make mention of the Luperci? Does he not shudder at the recollection of that day on which, smelling of wine, reeking with perfumes, and naked, he dared to exhort the indignant Roman people to embrace slavery?

"You, by a resolution of the senate, have removed the colonies of the veterans which had been legally settled".

Have we removed them, or have we rather ratified a law which was passed in the comitia centunata? See, rather, whether it is not you who have ruined these veterans (those at least who are ruined,) and settled them in a place from which they themselves now feel that they shall never be able to make their escape.

"You are promising to restore to the people of Marseilles what has been taken from them by the laws of war."

I am not going to discuss the laws of war. It is a discussion far more easy to begin than necessary. But take notice of this, O conscript fathers, what a born enemy to the republic Antonius is, who is so violent in his hatred of that city which he knows to have been at all times most firmly attached to this republic.

XVI. " that no one of the party of Pompeius, who is still alive, can, by the Hirtian law, possess any rank?"

What, I should like to know, is the object of now making mention of the Hirtian law?—a law of which I believe the framer himself repents no less than those against whom it was passed. According to my opinion, it is utterly wrong to call it a law at all; and, even if it be a law, we ought not to think it a law of Hirtius.

"You have furnished Brutus with money belonging to Apuleius."

Well? Suppose the republic had furnished that excellent man with all its treasures and resources, what good man would have disapproved of it? For without money he could not have supported an army, nor without an army could he have taken your brother prisoner.

"You have praised the execution of Paetus and Menedemus, men who had been presented with the freedom of the city, and who were united by ties of hospitality to Caesar."

We do not praise what we have never even heard of; we were very likely, in such a state of confusion, and such a critical period of the republic, to busy our minds about two worthless Greeklings!

"You took no notice of Theopompus having been stripped, and driven out by Trebonius, and compelled to flee to Alexandria."

The senate has indeed been very guilty! We have taken no notice of that great man Theopompus! Why, who on earth knows or cares where he is, or what he is doing; or, indeed, whether he is alive or dead? "You endure the sight of Sergius Galba in your camp, armed with the same dagger with which he slew Caesar."

I shall make you no reply at all about Galba; a most gallant and courageous citizen. He will meet you face to face; and he being present, and that dagger which you reproach him with, shall give you your answer.

"You have enlisted my soldiers, and many veterans, under the pretence of intending the destruction of those men who slew Caesar; and then, when they expected no such step, you have led them on to attack their quaestor, their general, and their former comrades!"

No doubt we deceived them; we humbugged them completely! no doubt the Martial legion, the fourth legion, and the veterans had no idea what was going on! They were not following the authority of the senate, or the liberty of the Roman people.—They were anxious to avenge the death of Caesar, which they all regarded as an act of destiny! No doubt you were the person whom they were anxious to see safe, and happy, and flourishing!

XVII. Oh miserable man, not only in fact, but also in the circumstance of not perceiving yourself how miserable you are! But listen to the most serious charge of all.

"In fact, what have you not sanctioned,—what have you not done? what would be done if he were to come to life again, by?—"

By whom? For I suppose he means to bring forward some instance of a very wicked man.

"Cnaeus Pompeius himself?"

Oh how base must we be, if indeed we have been imitating Cnaeus Pompeius!

"Or his son, if he could be at home?"

He soon will be at home, believe me; for in a very few days he will enter on his home, and on his father's villas.

"Lastly, you declare that peace cannot be made unless I either allow Brutus to quit Mutina, or supply him with corn."

It is others who say that: I say, that even if you were to do so, there never could be peace between this city and you.

"What? is this the opinion of those veteran soldiers, to whom as yet either course is open?"

I do not see that there is any course so open to them, as now to begin and attack that general whom they previously were so zealous and unanimous in defending.

"Since you yourselves have sold yourselves for flatteries and poisoned gifts".

Are those men depraved and corrupted, who have been persuaded to pursue a most detestable enemy with most righteous war?

"But you say, you are bringing assistance to troops who are hemmed in. I have no objection to their being saved, and departing wherever you wish, if they only allow that man to be put to death who has deserved it."

How very kind of him! The soldiers availing themselves of the liberality of Antonius have deserted their general, and have fled in alarm to his enemy, and if it had not been for them, Dolabella, in offering the sacrifice which he did to the shade of his general, would not have been beforehand with Antonius in propitiating the spirit of his colleague by a similar offering.

"You write me word that there has been mention of peace made in the senate, and that five ambassadors of consular rank have been appointed. It is hard to believe that those men, who drove me in haste from the city, when I offered the fairest conditions, and when I was even thinking of relaxing somewhat of them, should now think of acting with moderation or humanity. And it is hardly probable, that those men who have pronounced Dolabella a public enemy for a most righteous action, should bring themselves to spare us who are influenced by the same sentiments as he".

Does it appear a trifling matter, that he confesses himself a partner with Dolabella in all his atrocities? Do you not see that all these crimes flow from one source? He himself confesses, shrewdly and correctly enough, that those who have pronounced Dolabella a public enemy for a most righteous action (for so it appears to Antonius), cannot possibly spare him who agrees with Dolabella in opinion.

XVIII. What can you do with a man who puts on paper and records the fact, that his agreement with Dolabella is so complete, that he would kill Trebonius, and, if he could, Brutus and Cassius too, with every circumstance of torture; and inflict the same punishment on us also? Certainly, a man who makes so pious and fair a treaty is a citizen to be taken care of! He, also, complains that the conditions which he offered, those reasonable and modest conditions, were rejected; namely, that he was to have the further Gaul,—the province the most suitable of all for renewing and carrying on the war; that the legionaries of the Alauda should be judges in the third decury; that is to say, that there shall be an asylum for all crimes, to the indelible disgrace of the republic; that his own acts should be ratified, his,—when not one trace of his consulship has been allowed to remain! He showed his regard also for the interests of Lucius Antonius, who had been a most equitable surveyor of private and public domains, with Nucula and Lento for his colleagues.

"Consider then, both of you, whether it is more becoming and more advantageous for your party, for you to seek to avenge the death of Trebonius, or that of Caesar; and whether it is more reasonable for you and me to meet in battle, in order that the cause of the Pompeians, which has so frequently had its throat cut, may the more easily revive; or to agree together, so as not to be a laughing-stock to our enemies."

If its throat had been cut, it never could revive. "Which," says he, "is more becoming." In this war he talks of what is becoming! "And more advantageous for your party."—"Parties," you senseless man, is a suitable expression for the forum, or the senate house. You have declared a wicked war against your country; you are attacking Mutina; you are besieging the consul elect; two consuls are carrying on war against you; and with them, Caesar, the propraetor; all Italy is armed against you; and then do you call yours "a party," instead of a revolt from the republic? "To seek to avenge the death of Trebonius, or that of Caesar." We have avenged Trebonius sufficiently by pronouncing Dolabella a public enemy. The death of Caesar is best defended by oblivion and silence. But take notice what his object is.—When he thinks that the death of Caesar ought to be revenged, he is threatening with death, not those only who perpetrated that action, but those also who were not indignant at it.

XIX. "Men who will count the destruction of either you or me gain to them. A spectacle which as yet Fortune herself has taken care to avoid, unwilling to see two armies which belong to one body fighting, with Cicero acting as master of the show; a fellow who is so far happy that he has cajoled you both with the same compliments as those with which he boasted that he had deceived Caesar."

He proceeds in his abuse of me, as if he had been very fortunate in all his former reproaches of me; but I will brand him with the most thoroughly deserved marks of infamy, and pillory him for the everlasting recollection of posterity. I a "master of the show of gladiators!" indeed he is not wholly wrong, for I do wish to see the worst party slain, and the best victorious. He writes that "whichever of them are destroyed we shall count as so much gain." Admirable gain, when, if you, O Antonius, are victorious, (may the gods avert such a disaster!) the death of those men who depart from life untortured will be accounted happy! He says that Hirtius and Caesar "have been cajoled by me by the same compliments." I should like to know what compliment has been as yet paid to Hirtius by me; for still more and greater ones than have been paid him already are due to Caesar. But do you, O Antonius, dare to say that Caesar, the father, was deceived by me? You, it was you, I say, who really slew him at the Lupercal games. Why, O most ungrateful of men, have you abandoned your office of priest to him? But remark now the admirable wisdom and consistency of this great and illustrious man.

"I am quite resolved to brook no insult either to myself or to my friends; nor to desert that party which Pompeius hated, nor to allow the veterans to be removed from their abodes; nor to allow individuals to be dragged out to torture, nor to violate the faith which I pledged to Dolabella."

I say nothing of the rest of this sentence, "the faith pledged to Dolabella," to that most holy man, this pious gentleman will by no means violate. What faith? Was it a pledge to murder every virtuous citizen, to partition the city and Italy, to distribute the provinces among, and to hand them over to be plundered by, their followers? For what else was there which could have been ratified by treaty and mutual pledges between Antonius and Dolabella, those foul and parricidal traitors?

"Nor to violate my treaty of alliance with Lepidus, the most conscientious of men."

You have any alliance with Lepidus or with any (I will not say virtuous citizen, as he is, but with any) man in his senses! Your object is to make Lepidus appear either an impious man, or a madman. But you are doing no good, (although it is a hard matter to speak positively of another,) especially with a man like Lepidus, whom I will never fear, but I shall hope good things of him unless I am prevented from doing so. Lepidus wished to recal you from your frenzy, not to be the assistant of your insanity. But you seek your friends not only among conscientious men, but among most conscientious men. And you actually, so godlike is your piety, invent a new word to express it which has no existence in the Latin language.

"Nor to betray Plancus, the partner of my counsels."

Plancus, the partner of your counsels? He, whose ever memorable and divine virtue brings a light to the republic: (unless, mayhap, you think that it is as a reinforcement to you that he has come with those most gallant legions, and with a numerous Gallic force of both cavalry and infantry); and who, if before his arrival you have not by your punishment made atonement to the republic for your wickedness, will be chief leader in this war. For although the first succours that arrive are more useful to the republic, yet the last are the more acceptable.

XX. However, at last he recollects himself and begins to philosophize.

"If the immortal gods assist me, as I trust that they will, going on my way with proper feelings, I shall live happily; but if another fate awaits me, I have already a foretaste of joy in the certainty of your punishment. For if the Pompeians when defeated are so insolent, you will be sure to experience what they will be when victorious."

You are very welcome to your foretaste of joy. For you are at war not only with the Pompeians, but with the entire republic. Every one, gods and men, the highest rank, the middle class, the lowest dregs of the people, citizens and foreigners, men and women, free men and slaves, all hate you. We saw this the other day on some false news that came; but we shall soon see it from the way in which true news is received. And if you ponder these things with yourself a little, you will die with more equanimity, and greater comfort.

"Lastly, this is the sum of my opinion and determination; I will bear with the insults offered me by my friends, if they themselves are willing to forget that they have offered them; or if they are prepared to unite with me in avenging Caesar's death."

Now that they know this resolution of Antonius, do you think that Aulus Hirtius and Caius Pansa, the consuls, can hesitate to pass over to Antonius? to besiege Brutus? to be eager to attack Mutina? Why do

I say Hirtius and Pansa? Will Caesar, that young man of singular piety, be able to restrain himself from seeking to avenge the injuries of his father in the blood of Decimus Brutus? Therefore, as soon as they had read this letter, the course which they adopted was to approach nearer to the fortifications. And on this account we ought to consider Caesar a still more admirable young man; and that a still greater kindness of the immortal gods which gave him to the republic, as he has never been misled by the specious use of his father's name; nor by any false idea of piety and affection. He sees clearly that the greatest piety consists in the salvation of one's country. But if it were a contest between parties, the name of which is utterly extinct, then would Antonius and Ventidius be the proper persons to uphold the party of Caesar, rather than in the first place, Caesar, a young man full of the greatest piety and the most affectionate recollection of his parent? and next to him Pansa and Hirtius, who held, (if I may use such an expression,) the two horns of Caesar, at the time when that deserved to be called a party. But what parties are these, when the one proposes to itself to uphold the authority of the senate, the liberty of the Roman people, and the safety of the republic, while the other fixes its eyes on the slaughter of all good men, and on the partition of the city and of Italy.

XXI. Let us come at last to the end.

"I do not believe that ambassadors are coming—".

He knows me well.

"To a place where war exists."

Especially with the example of Dolabella before our eyes. Ambassadors, I should think, will have privileges more respected than two consuls against whom he is bearing arms; or than Caesar, whose father's priest he is; or than the consul elect, whom he is attacking; or than Mutina, which he is besieging; or than his country, which he is threatening with fire and sword.

"When they do come I shall see what they demand."

Plagues and tortures seize you! Will any one come to you, unless he be a man like Ventidius? We sent men of the very highest character to extinguish the rising conflagration; you rejected them. Shall we now send men when the fire has become so large and has risen to such a height, and when you have left yourself no possible room, not only for peace, but not even for a surrender?

I have read you this letter, O conscript fathers, not because I thought it worth reading, but in order to let you see all his parricidal treasons revealed by his own confessions. Would Marcus Lepidus, that man so richly endowed with all the gifts of virtue and fortune, if he saw this letter, either wish for peace with this man, or even think it possible that peace should be made? "Sooner shall fire and water mingle" as some poet or other says; sooner shall anything in the world happen than either the republic become reconciled to the Antonii, or the Antonii to the republic. Those men are monsters, prodigies, portentous pests of the republic. It would be better for this city to be uplifted from its foundations and transported, if such a thing were possible, into other regions, where it should never hear of the actions or the name of the Antonii, than for it to see those men, driven out by the valour of Caesar, and hemmed in by the courage of Brutus, inside these walls. The most desirable thing is victory; the next best thing is to think no disaster too great to bear in defence of the dignity and freedom of one's country. The remaining alternative, I will not call it the third, but the lowest of all, is to undergo the greatest disgrace from a desire of life.

Since, then, this is the case, as to the letters and messages of Marcus Lepidus, that most illustrious man, I agree with Servilius. And I further give my vote, that Magnus Pompeius, the Son of Cnaeus, has acted as might have been expected from the affection and zeal of his father and forefathers towards the republic, and from his own previous virtue and industry and loyal principles in promising to the senate and people of Rome his own assistance, and that of those men whom he had with him; and that that conduct of his is grateful and acceptable to the senate and people of Rome, and that it shall tend to his own honour and dignity. This may either be added to the resolution of the senate which is before us, or it may be separated from it and drawn up by itself, so as to let Pompeius be seen to be extolled in a distinct resolution of the senate.

THE FOURTEENTH PHILIPPIC

THE ARGUMENT

After the last speech was delivered, Brutus gained great advantages in Macedonia over Caius Antonius, and took him prisoner. He treated him with great lenity, so much so as to displease Cicero, who remonstrated with him strongly on his design of setting him at liberty. He was also under some apprehension as to the steadiness of Plancus's loyalty to the senate; but on his writing to that body to assure them of his obedience, Cicero procured a vote of some extraordinary honours to him.

Cassius also about the same time was very successful in Syria, of which he wrote Cicero a full account. Meantime reports were being spread in the city by the partizans of Antonius, of his success before Mutina; and even of his having gained over the consuls. Cicero too was personally much annoyed at a report which they spread of his having formed the design of making himself master of the city and assuming the title of Dictator; but when Apuleius, one of his friends, and a tribune of the people, proceeded to make a speech to the people in Cicero's justification, the people all cried out that he had never done anything which was not for the advantage of the republic. About the same time news arrived of a victory gained over Antonius at Mutina.

Pansa was now on the point of joining Hirtius with four new legions, and Antonius endeavoured to surprise him on the road before he could effect that junction. A severe battle ensued, in which Hirtius came to Pansa's aid, and Antonius was defeated with great loss. On the receipt of the news the populace assembled about Cicero's house, and carried him in triumph to the Capitol. The next day Marcus Cornutus, the praetor, summoned the senate to deliberate on the letters received from the consuls and Octavius, giving an account of the victory. Servilius declared his opinion that the citizens should relinquish the sagum, or robe of war; and that a supplication should be decreed in honour of the consuls and Octavius. Cicero rose next and delivered the following speech, objecting to the relinquishment of the robe of war, and blaming Servilius for not calling Antonius an enemy.

The measures which he himself proposed were carried.

I. IF, O conscript fathers, while I learnt from the letters which have been read that the army of our most wicked enemies had been defeated and routed, I had also learnt what we all wish for above all things, and which we do suppose has resulted from that victory which has been achieved,—namely, that Decimus Brutus had already quitted Mutina,—then I should without any hesitation give my vote for our returning to our usual dress out of joy at the safety of that citizen on account of whose danger it was that we adopted the robe of war. But before any news of that event which the city looks for with the greatest eagerness arrives, we have sufficient reason indeed for joy at this most important and most illustrious battle; but reserve, I beg you, your return to your usual dress for the time of complete victory. But the completion of this war is the safety of Decimus Brutus.

But what is the meaning of this proposal that our dress shall be changed just for to-day, and that to-morrow we should again come forth in the garb of war? Rather when we have once returned to that dress which we wish and desire to assume, let us strive to retain it for ever; for this is not only discreditable, but it is displeasing also to the immortal gods, to leave their altars, which we have approached in the attire of peace, for the purpose of assuming the garb of war. And I notice, O conscript fathers, that there are some who favour this proposal: whose intention and design is, as they see that that will be a most glorious day for Decimus Brutus on which we return to our usual dress out of joy for his safety, to deprive him of this great reward, so that it may not be handed down to the recollection of posterity that the Roman people had recourse to the garb of war on account of the danger of one single citizen, and then returned to then gowns of peace on account of his safety. Take away this reason, and you will find no other for so absurd a proposal. But do you, O conscript fathers, preserve your authority, adhere to your own opinions, preserve in your recollection, what you have often declared, that the whole result of this entire war depends on the life of one most brave and excellent man.

II. For the purpose of effecting the liberation of Decimus Brutus, the chief men of the state were sent as ambassadors, to give notice to that enemy and parricidal traitor to retire from Mutina; for the sake of preserving that same Decimus Brutus, Aulus Hirtius, the consul, went by lot to conduct the war, a man the weakness of whose bodily health was made up for by the strength of his courage, and encouraged by the hope of victory. Caesar, too, after he, with an army levied by his own resources and on his own authority, had delivered the republic from the first dangers that assailed it, in order to prevent any subsequent wicked attempts from being originated, departed to assist in the deliverance of the same Brutus, and subdued some family vexation which he may have felt by his attachment to his country. What other object had Caius Pansa in holding the levies which he did, and in collecting money, and in carrying the most severe resolutions of the senate against Antonius, and in exhorting us, and in inviting the Roman people to embrace the cause of liberty, except to ensure the deliverance of Decimus Brutus? For the Roman people in crowds demanded at his hands the safety of Decimus Brutus with such unanimous outcries, that he was compelled to prefer it not only to any consideration of his own personal advantage, but even to his own necessities. And that end we now, O conscript fathers, are entitled to hope is either at the point of being achieved, or is actually gained, but it is right for the reward of our hopes to be reserved for the issue and event of the business, lest we should appear either to have anticipated the kindness of the gods by our over precipitation, or to have despised the bounty of fortune through our own folly.

But since the manner of your behaviour shows plainly enough what you think of this matter, I will come to the letters which have arrived from the consuls and the propraetor, after I have said a few words relating to the letters themselves.

III. The swords, O conscript fathers, of our legions and armies have been stained with, or rather, I should say, dipped deep in blood in two battles which have taken place under the consuls, and a third, which has been fought under the command of Caesar. If it was the blood of enemies, then great is the piety of the soldiers; but it is nefarious wickedness if it was the blood of citizens. How long, then, is that man, who has surpassed all enemies in wickedness, to be spared the name of enemy? unless you wish to see the very swords of our soldiers trembling in their hands while they doubt whether they are piercing a citizen or an enemy. You vote a supplication; you do not call Antonius an enemy. Very pleasing indeed to the immortal gods will our thanksgivings be, very pleasing too the victims, after a multitude of our citizens has been slain! "For the victory," says the proposer of the supplication, "over wicked and audacious men." For that is what this most illustrious man calls them; expressions of blame suited to lawsuits carried on in the city, not denunciations of searing infamy such as deserved by internecine war. I suppose they are forging wills, or trespassing on their neighbours, or cheating some young men; for it is men implicated in these and similar practices that we are in the habit of terming wicked and audacious. One man, the foulest of all banditti, is waging an irreconcileable war against four consuls. He is at the same time carrying on war against the senate and people of Rome. He is (although he is himself hastening to destruction, through the disasters which he has met with) threatening all of us with destruction, and devastation, and torments, and tortures. He declares that that inhuman and savage act of Dolabella's, which no nation of barbarians would have owned, was done by his advice; and what he himself would do in this city, if this very Jupiter, who now looks down upon us assembled in his temple, had not repelled him from this temple and from these walls, he showed, in the miseries of those inhabitants of Parma, whom, virtuous and honourable men as they were, and most intimately connected with the authority of this order, and with the dignity of the Roman people, that villain and monster, Lucius Antonius, that object of the extraordinary detestation of all men, and (if the gods hate those whom they ought) of all the gods also, murdered with every circumstance of cruelty. My mind shudders at the recollection, O conscript fathers, and shrinks from relating the cruelties which Lucius Antonius perpetrated on the children and wives of the citizens of Parma. For whatever infamy the Antonii have willingly undergone in their own persons to their own infamy, they triumph in the fact of having inflicted on others by violence. But it is a miserable violence which they offered to them; most unholy lust, such as the whole life of the Antonii is polluted with.

IV. Is there then any one who is afraid to call those men enemies, whose wickedness he admits to have surpassed even the inhumanity of the Carthaginians? For in what city, when taken by storm, did Hannibal even behave with such ferocity as Antonius did in Parma, which he filched by surprise? Unless, mayhap, Antonius is not to be considered the enemy of this colony, and of the others towards which he is animated with the same feelings. But if he is beyond all question the enemy of the colonies and municipal towns, then what do you consider him with respect to this city which he is so eager for, to satiate the indigence of his band of robbers? which that skilful and experienced surveyor of his, Saxa, has already marked out with his rule. Recollect, I entreat you, in the name of the immortal gods, O conscript fathers, what we have been fearing for the last two days, in consequence of infamous rumours carefully disseminated by enemies within the walls. Who has been able to look upon his children or upon his wife without weeping? who has been able to bear the sight of his home, of his house, and his household gods? Already all of us were expecting a most ignominious death, or meditating a miserable flight. And shall we hesitate to call the men at whose hands we feared all these things enemies? If any one should propose a more severe designation I will willingly agree to it; I am hardly content with this ordinary one, and will certainly not employ a more moderate one.

Therefore, as we are bound to vote, and as Servilius has already proposed a most just supplication for those letters which have been read to you; I will propose altogether to increase the number of the days which it is to last, especially as it is to be decreed in honour of three generals conjointly. But first of all I will insist on styling those men imperator by whose valour, and wisdom, and good fortune we have been released from the most imminent danger of slavery and death. Indeed, who is there within the last twenty years who has had a supplication decreed to him without being himself styled imperator, though he may have performed the most insignificant exploits, or even almost none at all. Wherefore, the senator who spoke before me ought either not to have moved for a supplication at all, or he ought to have paid the usual and established compliment to those men to whom even new and extraordinary honours are justly due.

V. Shall the senate, according to this custom which has now obtained, style a man imperator if he has slain a thousand or two of Spaniards, or Gauls, or Thracians; and now that so many legions have been routed, now that such a multitude of enemies has been slain,—aye, enemies, I say, although our enemies within the city do not fancy this expression,—shall we pay to our most illustrious generals the honour of a supplication, and refuse them the name of imperator? For with what great honour, and joy, and exultation ought the deliverers of this city themselves to enter into this temple, when yesterday, on account of the exploits which they have performed, the Roman people carried me in an ovation, almost in a triumph from my house to the Capitol, and back again from the Capitol to my own house? That is indeed in my opinion a just and genuine triumph, when men who have deserved well of the republic receive public testimony to their merits from the unanimous consent of the senate. For if, at a time of general rejoicing on the part of the Roman people, they addressed their congratulations to one individual, that is a great proof of their opinion of him; if they gave him thanks, that is a greater still; if they did both, then nothing more honourable to him can be possibly imagined.

Are you saying all this of yourself? some one will ask. It is indeed against my will that I do so; but my indignation at injustice makes me boastful, contrary to my usual habit. Is it not sufficient that thanks should not be given to men who have well earned them, by men who are ignorant of the very nature of virtue? And shall accusations and odium be attempted to be excited against those men who devote all their thoughts to ensuring the safety of the republic? For you well know that there has been a common report for the last few days, that the day before the wine feast, that is to say, on this very day, I was intending to come forth with the fasces as dictator. One would think that this story was invented against some gladiator, or robber, or Catiline, and not against a man who had prevented any such step from ever being taken in the republic. Was I, who defeated and overthrew and crushed Catiline, when he was attempting such wickedness, a likely man myself all on a sudden to turn out Catiline? Under what auspices could I, an augur, take those fasces? How long should I have been likely to keep them? to whom was I to deliver them as my successor? The idea of any one having been so wicked as to invent such a tale! or so mad as to believe it! In what could such a suspicion, or rather such gossip, have originated?

VI. When, as you know, during the last three or four days a report of bad news from Mutina has been creeping abroad, the disloyal part of the citizens, inflated with exultation and insolence, began to collect in one place, at that senate-house which has been more fatal to their party than to the republic. There, while they were forming a plan to massacre us, and were distributing the different duties among one another, and settling who was to seize on the Capitol, who on the rostra, who on the gates of the city, they thought that all the citizens would flock to me. And in order to bring me into unpopularity, and even into danger of my life, they spread abroad this report about the fasces. They themselves had some idea of bringing the fasces to my house; and then, on pretence of that having been done by my wish, they had prepared a band of hired ruffians to make an attack on me as on a tyrant, and a massacre of all of you was intended to follow. The fact is already notorious, O conscript fathers, but the origin of all this wickedness will be revealed in its fitting time.

Therefore Publius Apuleius, a tribune of the people, who ever since my consulship has been the witness and partaker of, and my assistant in all my designs and all my dangers could not endure the grief of witnessing my indignation. He convened a numerous assembly, as the whole Roman people were animated with one feeling on the subject. And when in the harangue which he then made, he, as was natural from our great intimacy and friendship, was going to exculpate me from all suspicion in the matter of the fasces, the whole assembly cried out with one voice, that I had never had any intentions with regard to the republic which were not excellent. After this assembly was over, within two or three hours, these most welcome messengers and letters arrived; so that the same day not only delivered me from a most unjust odium, but increased my credit by that most extraordinary act with which the Roman people distinguished me.

I have made this digression, O conscript fathers, not so much for the sake of speaking of myself, (for I should be in a sorry plight if I were not sufficiently acquitted in your eyes without the necessity of making a formal defence,) as with the view of warning some men of too grovelling and narrow minds, to adopt the line of conduct which I myself have always pursued, and to think the virtue of excellent citizens worthy of imitation, not of envy. There is a great field in the republic, as Crassus used very wisely to say; the road to glory is open to many.

VII. Would that those great men were still alive, who, after my consulship, when I myself was willing to yield to them, were themselves desirous to see me in the post of leader. But at the present moment, when there is such a dearth of wise and fearless men of consular rank, how great do you not suppose must be my grief and indignation, when I see some men absolutely disaffected to the republic, others wholly indifferent to everything, others incapable of persevering with any firmness in the cause which they have espoused; and regulating their opinions not always by the advantage of the republic, but sometimes by hope, and sometimes by fear. But if any one is anxious and inclined to struggle for the leadership—though struggle there ought to be none—he acts very foolishly, if he proposes to combat virtue with vices. For as speed is only outstripped by speed, so among brave men virtue is only surpassed by virtue. Will you, if I am full of excellent sentiments with respect to the republic, adopt the worst possible sentiments yourself for the purpose of excelling me? Or if you see a race taking place for the acquisition of honours, will you summon all the wicked men you can find to your banner? I should be sorry for you to do so; first of all, for the sake of the republic, and secondly, for that of your own dignity. But if the leadership of the state were at stake, which I have never coveted, what could be more desirable for me than such conduct on your part? For it is impossible that I should be defeated by wicked sentiments and measures,—by good ones perhaps I might be, and I willingly would be.

Some people are vexed that the Roman people should see, and take notice of, and form their opinion on these matters. Was it possible for men not to form their opinion of each individual as he deserved? For as the Roman people forms a most correct judgment of the entire senate, thinking that at no period in the history of the republic was this order ever more firm or more courageous; so also they all inquire diligently concerning every individual among us; and especially in the case of those among us who deliver our sentiments at length in this place, they are anxious to know what those sentiments are; and in that way they judge of each one of us, as they think that he deserves. They recollect that on the nineteenth of December I was the main cause of recovering our freedom; that from the first of January to this hour I have never ceased watching over the republic; that day and night my house and my ears have been open to the instruction and admonition of every one; that it has been by my letters, and my messengers, and my exhortations, that all men in every part of the empire have been roused to the protection of our country; that it is owing to the open declaration of my opinion ever since the first of January, that no ambassadors have been ever sent to Antonius; that I have always called him a public enemy, and this a war; so that I, who on every occasion have been the adviser of genuine peace have been a determined enemy to this pretence of fatal peace.

Have not I also at all times pronounced Ventidius an enemy, when others wished to call him a tribune of the people? If the consuls had chosen to divide the senate on my opinion, their arms would long since have been wrested from the hands of all those robbers by the positive authority of the senate.

VIII. But what could not be done then, O conscript fathers, at present not only can be, but even must be done. I mean, those men who are in reality enemies must be branded in plain language, must be declared enemies by our formal resolution. Formerly, when I used the words War or Enemy, men more than once objected to record my proposition among the other propositions. But that cannot be done on the present occasion. For in consequence of the letters of Caius Pansa and Aulus Hirtius, the consuls, and of Caius Caesar, propraetor, we have all voted that honours be paid to the immortal gods. The very man who lately proposed and carried a vote for a supplication, without intending it pronounced those men enemies; for a supplication has never been decreed for success in civil war. Decreed, do I say? It has never even been asked for in the letters of the conqueror. Sylla as consul carried on a civil war; he led his legions into the city and expelled whomsoever he chose; he slew those whom he had in his power: there was no mention made of any supplication. The violent war with Octavius followed. Cinna the conqueror had no supplication voted to him. Sylla as imperator revenged the victory of Cinna, still no supplication was decreed by the senate. I ask you yourself, O Publius Servilius, did your colleague send you any letters concerning that most lamentable battle of Pharsalia? Did he wish you to make any motion about a supplication? Certainly not. But he did afterwards when he took Alexandria; when he defeated Pharnaces; but for the battle of Pharsalia he did not even celebrate a triumph. For that battle had destroyed those citizens whose, I will not say lives, but even whose victory might have been quite compatible with the safety and prosperity of the state. And the same thing had happened in the previous civil wars. For though a supplication was decreed in my honour when I was consul, though no arms had been had recourse to at all, still that was voted by a new and wholly unprecedented kind of decree, not for the slaughter of enemies, but for the preservation of the citizens. Wherefore, a supplication on account of the affairs of the republic having been successfully conducted must, O conscript fathers, be refused by you even though your generals demand it; a stigma which has never been affixed on any one except Gabinius; or else, by the mere fact of decreeing a supplication, it is quite inevitable that you must pronounce those men, for whose defeat you do decree it, enemies of the state.

IX. What then Servilius did in effect, I do in express terms, when I style those men imperators. By using this name, I pronounce those who have been already defeated, and those who still remain, enemies in calling their conquerors imperators. For what title can I more suitably bestow on Pansa? Though he has, indeed, the title of the highest honour in the republic. What, too, shall I call Hirtius? He, indeed, is consul; but this latter title is indicative of the kindness of the Roman people; the other of valour and victory. What? Shall I hesitate to call Caesar imperator, a man born for the republic by the express kindness of the gods? He who was the first man who turned aside the savage and disgraceful cruelty of Antonius, not only from our throats, but from our limbs and bowels? What numerous and what important virtues, O ye immortal gods, were displayed on that single day. For Pansa was the leader of all in engaging in battle and in combating with Antonius; O general worthy of the martial legion, legion worthy of its general! Indeed, if he had been able to restrain its irresistible impetuosity, the whole war would have been terminated by that one battle. But as the legion, eager for liberty, had rushed with too much precipitation against the enemy's line of battle, and as Pansa himself was fighting in the front ranks, he received two dangerous wounds, and was borne out of the battle, to preserve his life for the republic. But I pronounce him not only imperator, but a most illustrious imperator; who, as he had pledged himself to discharge his duty to the republic either by death or by victory, has fulfilled one half of his promise; may the immortal gods prevent the fulfilment of the other half!

X. Why need I speak of Hirtius? who, the moment he heard of what was going on, with incredible promptness and courage led forth two legions out of the camp; that noble fourth legion, which, having deserted Antonius, formerly united itself to the martial legion; and the seventh, which, consisting wholly of veterans, gave proof in that battle that the name of the senate and people of Rome was dear to those soldiers who preserved the recollection of the kindness of Caesar. With these twenty cohorts, with no cavalry, while Hirtius himself was bearing the eagle of the fourth legion,—and we never heard of a more noble office being assumed by any general,—he fought with the three legions of Antonius and with his cavalry, and overthrew, and routed, and put to the sword those impious men who were the real enemies to this temple of the all-good and all-powerful Jupiter, and to the rest of the temples of the immortal gods, and the houses of the city, and the freedom of the Roman people, and our lives and actual existence; so that that chief and leader of robbers fled away with a very few followers, concealed by the darkness of night, and frightened out of all his senses.

Oh what a most blessed day was that, which, while the carcases of those parricidal traitors were strewed about everywhere, beheld Antonius flying with a few followers, before he reached his place of concealment.

But will any one hesitate to call Caesar imperator? Most certainly his age will not deter any one from agreeing to this proposition, since he has gone beyond his age in virtue. And to me, indeed, the services of Caius Caesar have always appeared the more thankworthy, in proportion as they were less to have been expected from a man of his age. For when we conferred military command on him, we were in fact encouraging the hope with which his name inspired us; and now that he has fulfilled those hopes, he has sanctioned the authority of our decree by his exploits. This young man of great mind, as Hirtius most truly calls him in his letters, with a few cohorts defended the camp of many legions, and fought a successful battle. And in this manner the republic has on one day been preserved in many places by the valour, and wisdom, and good fortune of three imperators of the Roman people.

XI. I therefore propose supplications of fifty days in the joint names of the three. The reasons I will embrace in the words of the resolution, using the most honourable language that I can devise.

But it becomes our good faith and our piety to show plainly to our most gallant soldiers how mindful of their services and how grateful for them we are; and accordingly I give my vote that our promises, and those pledges too which we promised to bestow on the legions when the war was finished, be repeated in the resolution which we are going to pass this day. For it is quite fair that the honour of the soldiers, especially of such soldiers as those, should be united with that of their commanders. And I wish, O conscript fathers, that it was lawful for us to dispense rewards to all the citizens; although we will give those which we have promised with the most careful usury. But that remains, as I well hope, to the conquerors, to whom the faith of the senate is pledged; and, as they have adhered to it at a most critical period of the republic, we are bound to take care that they never have cause to repent of their conduct. But it is easy for us to deal fairly by those men whose very services, though mute, appear to demand our liberality. This is a much more praiseworthy and more important duty, to pay a proper tribute of grateful recollection to the valour of those men who have shed their blood in the cause of their country. And I wish more suggestions could occur to me in the way of doing honour to those men. The two ideas which principally do occur to me, I will at all events not pass over; the one of which has reference to the everlasting glory of those bravest of men; the other may tend to mitigate the sorrow and mourning of their relations.

XII. I therefore give my vote, O conscript fathers, that the most honourable monument possible be erected to the soldiers of the martial legion, and to those soldiers also who died fighting by their side. Great and incredible are the services done by this legion to the republic. This was the first legion to tear itself from the piratical band of Antonius; this was the legion which encamped at Alba; this was the legion that went over to Caesar; and it was in imitation of the conduct of this legion that the fourth legion has earned almost equal glory for its virtue. The fourth is victorious without having lost a man; some of the martial legion fell in the very moment of victory. Oh happy death, which, due to nature, has been paid in the cause of one's country! But I consider you men born for your country; you whose very name is derived from Mars, so that the same god who begot this city for the advantage of the nations, appears to have begotten you for the advantage of this city. Death in flight is infamous; in victory glorious. In truth, Mars himself seems to select all the bravest men from the battle array. Those impious men whom you slew, shall even in the shades below pay the penalty of their parricidal treason. But you, who have poured forth your latest breath in victory, have earned an abode and place among the pious. A brief life has been allotted to us by nature; but the memory of a well-spent life is imperishable. And if that memory were no longer than this life, who would be so senseless as to strive to attain even the highest praise and glory by the most enormous labours and dangers?

You then have fared most admirably, being the bravest of soldiers while you lived, and now the most holy of warriors, because it will be impossible for your virtue to be buried, either through the forgetfulness of the men of the present age, or the silence of posterity, since the senate and Roman people will have raised to you an imperishable monument, I may almost say with their own hands. Many armies at various times have been great and illustrious in the Punic, and Gallic, and Italian wars; but to none of them have honours been paid of the description which are now conferred on you. And I wish that we could pay you even greater honours, since we have received from you the greatest possible services. You it was who turned aside the furious Antonius from this city; you it was who repelled him when endeavouring to return. There shall therefore be a vast monument erected with the most sumptuous work, and an inscription engraved upon it, as the everlasting witness of your god-like virtue. And never shall the most grateful language of all who either see or hear of your monument cease to be heard. And in this manner you, in exchange for your mortal condition of life, have attained immortality.

XIII. But since, O conscript fathers, the gift of glory is conferred on these most excellent and gallant citizens by the honour of a monument, let us comfort their relations, to whom this indeed is the best consolation. The greatest comfort for their parents is the reflection that they have produced sons who have been such bulwarks of the republic; for their children, that they will have such examples of virtue in their family; for their wives, that the husbands whom they have lost are men whom it is a credit to praise, and to have a right to mourn for; and for their brothers, that they may trust that, as they resemble them in their persons, so they do also in their virtues.

Would that we were able by the expression of our sentiments and by our votes to wipe away the tears of all these persons; or that any such oration as this could be publicly addressed to them, to cause them to lay aside their grief and mourning, and to rejoice rather, that, while many various kinds of death impend over men, the most honourable kind of all has fallen to the lot of their friends; and that they are not unburied, nor deserted; though even that fate, when incurred for one's country, is not accounted miserable; nor burnt with equable obsequies in scattered graves, but entombed in honourable sepulchres, and honoured with public offerings; and with a building which will be an altar of their valour to ensure the recollection of eternal ages.

Wherefore it will be the greatest possible comfort to their relations, that by the same monument are clearly displayed the valour of their kinsmen, and also their piety, and the good faith of the senate, and the memory of this most inhuman war, in which, if the valour of the soldiers had been less conspicuous, the very name of the Roman people would have perished by the parricidal treason of Marcus Antonius. And I think also, O conscript fathers, that those rewards which we promised to bestow on the soldiers when we had recovered the republic, we should give with abundant usury to those who are alive and victorious when the time comes; and that in the case of the men to whom those rewards were promised, but who have died in the defence of their country, I think those same rewards should be given to their parents or children, or wives or brothers.

XIV. But that I may reduce my sentiments into a formal motion, I give my vote that:

"As Caius Pansa, consul, imperator, set the example of fighting with the enemy in a battle in which the martial legion defended the freedom of the Roman people with admirable and incredible valour, and the legions of the recruits behaved equally well; and as Caius Pansa, consul, imperator, while engaged in the middle of the ranks of the enemy received wounds; and as Aulus Hirtius, consul, imperator, the moment that he heard of the battle, and knew what was going on, with a most gallant and loyal soul, led his army out of his camp and attacked Marcus Antonius and his army, and put his troops to the sword, with so little injury to his own army that he did not lose one single man; and as Caius Caesar, propraetor, imperator, with great prudence and energy defended the camp successfully, and routed and put to the sword the forces of the enemy which had come near the camp:

"On these accounts the senate thinks and declares that the Roman people has been released from the most disgraceful and cruel slavery by the valour, and military skill, and prudence, and firmness, and perseverance, and greatness of mind and good fortune of these their generals. And decrees that, as they have preserved the republic, the city, the temples of the immortal gods, the property and fortunes and families of all the citizens, by their own exertions in battle, and at the risk of their own lives; on account of these virtuous and gallant and successful achievements, Caius Pansa and Aulus Hirtius, the consuls, imperators, one or both of them, or, in their absence, Marcus Cornutus, the city praetor, shall appoint a supplication at all the altars for fifty days.

And as the valour of the legions has shown itself worthy of their most illustrious generals, the senate will with great eagerness, now that the republic is recovered, bestow on our legions and armies all the rewards which it formerly promised them. And as the martial legion was the first to engage with the enemy, and fought in such a manner against superior numbers as to slay many and take some prisoners; and as they shed their blood for their country without any shrinking; and as the soldiers of the other legions encountered death with similar valour in defence of the safety and freedom of the Roman people;—the senate does decree that Caius Pansa and Aulus Hirtius, the consuls, imperators, one or both of them if it seems good to them, shall see to the issuing of a contract for, and to the erecting, the most honourable possible monument to those men who shed their blood for the lives and liberties and fortunes of the Roman people, and for the city and temples of the immortal gods; that for that purpose they shall order the city quaestors to furnish and pay money, in order that it may be a witness for the everlasting recollection of posterity of the wickedness of our most cruel enemies, and the god-like valour of our soldiers. And that the rewards which the senate previously appointed for the soldiers, be paid to the parents or children, or wives or brothers of those men who in this war have fallen in defence of their country; and that all honours be bestowed on them which should have been bestowed on the soldiers themselves if those men had lived who gained the victory by their death."

Made in the USA
Middletown, DE
08 August 2023